DATE DUE

Nov 2			

GAYLORD   PRINTED IN U.S.A.

SOUTHEAST ASIA
A Critical Bibliography

SOUTHEAST ASIA
A Critical Bibliography

KENNEDY G. TREGONNING

THE UNIVERSITY OF ARIZONA PRESS
TUCSON, ARIZONA

ABOUT THE AUTHOR

KENNEDY G. TREGONNING, before joining the Hale School in Western Australia as headmaster, was Raffles Professor of History at the University of Singapore and editor of the *Journal of Southeastern Asian History,* as well as secretary of the Center for Southwest Asian Studies. A R.A.A.F. pilot in World War II, he was graduated from Adelaide and Oxford universities, and worked in Singapore for 14 years. In 1961 he convened the first International Conference of Southeast Asian Historians in Singapore. In 1963 he was awarded a Carnegie fellowship to visit centers of Southeast Asian studies in the U.S.A. He is the author of some eight works, including *A History of Modern Sabah* (Oxford University Press, 1965); *The British in Malaya: The First Forty Years* (Association for Asian Studies Monograph No. XVIII, The University of Arizona Press, 1965); *North Borneo* (HMSO, 1966); and *Home Port Singapore* (Oxford University Press, 1967), as well as numerous journal articles and reviews on Southeast Asian affairs.

Published in Asia east of Burma,
in Australia and New Zealand by
UNIVERSITY OF MALAYA PRESS

Sole Distributors in these areas

Oxford University Press, Ely House, London, W.l.
Glasgow, New York, Toronto, Melbourne, Wellington,
Cape Town, Salisbury, Ibadan, Nairobi, Lusaka, Addis Ababa,
Bombay, Calcutta, Madras, Karachi, Lahore, Dacca,
Kuala Lumpur, Hong Kong, Tokyo

Bangunan Loke Yew, Kuala Lumpur

THE UNIVERSITY OF ARIZONA PRESS

FOREWORD

Southeast Asia: A Critical Bibliography is one result of a continuing effort by the Oriental Studies Committee of the University of Arizona to produce a series of reference guides to facilitate the study of Asia in American colleges. Three guides in the series are already well known to teachers and students — Charles O. Hucker's CHINA; Bernard S. Silberman's JAPAN AND KOREA, and J. Michael Mahar's INDIA.

This bibliography follows the pattern established by the others in the series. It is a selected, graded, annotated list of works, mainly in English, that contribute to the academic study of traditional and modern Southeast Asia.

Entries appear in the order in which they are recommended to an introductory college student. They proceed in general from items that are most authoritative to those that are less so, from those of a general scope to those of narrow range, and from those readily available to those that are more difficult to obtain. Southeast Asian English-language scholarship has been developed so recently that it has been possible, in most of the countries treated here, to make a virtue of necessity by confining the bibliography almost exclusively to items published after 1945.

It will be clear from this limitation and from comparison of this bibliography with the other three in the series, that there is indeed a contrast between Southeast Asia and the great cultures that flourish on its flanks. Southeast Asia is not a great culture, but a collection of small states, not one of which can lay claim to a long-lasting civilization comparable to that of Japan, China or India. In addition, English-language scholarship of the region, since this scholarship is not long established, is uneven in emphasis, and indigenous historiography is scanty. The generations of work devoted by many scholars to various aspects of other regions of Asia, and their vast legacies of a great past flowing into the present, do not exist for much of Southeast Asia. For these reasons, then, there are lacking the detailed works and the depth of knowledge available for other Asiatic areas.

The modern generation of scholars in many lands, however, finds in these gaps not a deterrent but a challenge. These scholars are turning to the task of filling the gaps with a thoroughness and a vividness of written expression that make Southeast Asia one of the more stimulating areas of Asian studies today.

The assistance of Mrs. Jenny Chan in preparation of this bibliography is acknowledged with gratitude as is the cooperation of the University of Arizona Committee on Oriental Studies and the University of Arizona Press in making the book a tangible reality.

KENNEDY G. TREGONNING

Wembley Downs, Western Australia

CONTENTS

SOUTHEAST ASIA

BURMA

THAILAND

CONTENTS

CAMBODIA

LAOS

VIETNAM

NORTH VIETNAM

MALAYSIA

CONTENTS

CONTENTS

THE PHILIPPINES

SOUTHEAST ASIA
A Critical Bibliography

SOUTHEAST ASIA

There are ten political units grouped in the tropical southeast corner of Asia, consisting of Burma, Thailand, Cambodia, Laos, South Vietnam and North Vietnam, Indonesia, Malaysia, Singapore and the Philippines. Two isolated colonial pockets still survive in an antediluvian way, in Brunei and Timor. Sharing a roughly similar climate, these states each participate, to some extent, in the culture and history of their immediate neighbors. There are, however, many differences. Some of Asia's great cultural and political divides run through the region, separating the countries more successfully than common experiences encourage cooperation. Diverse cultures and peoples make for interesting study while the contemporary challenges of world powers in the area provide stimulus. Many difficulties face the scholar, however, not least in the attempt at any regional assessment.

GENERAL

Bibliographies

Bibliographies relating to specified countries are incorporated in their national listings.

1

Nunn, G. Raymond. *South and Southeast Asia. A bibliography of bibliographies.* Honolulu: Occasional Paper 4, East-West Center Library, University of Hawaii, 1966. An extremely useful listing, principally by country, with further sub-arrangement by date of materials covered, of 350 bibliographies relating to South or Southeast Asia.

2

Wilson, Patrick. "Bibliographical Article: a Survey of Bibliographies on Southern Asia." *Journal of Asian Studies* 18 (1959) 365-376. Includes annotated sections entitled: Indonesia; Philippine Islands; Mainland Southeast Asia; Archaeology, History, Geography; Humanities; and Periodicals and Newspapers; all of relevance to Southeast Asia.

3

"Bibliography of Asian Studies." *Journal of Asian Studies.* Ann Arbor, Michigan. This annual issue of the Journal of Asian Studies, the 5th each year, provides an unannotated, comprehensive listing of works published that year, in subject headings, country by country; of great value.

4

Hobbs, Cecil. *Southeast Asia. An Annotated Bibliography of Selected Reference Sources in Western Languages.* Washington: Library of Congress, 1964. Some 500 entries, fully described; recent works of each country grouped under: general background; history, politics and government; economics; social conditions; cultural life.

5

Pelzer, Karl J. *Selected Bibliography on the Geography of Southeast Asia.* 3 vols. New Haven: Human Relations Area Files, 1949-1956. Vol. 3, Malaya, is expanded beyond the scope of the earlier two, which deal with the physical, cultural, economic and political geography of Southeast Asia in general, and the Philippines, to devote greater attention to anthropology.

6

Embree, John F. and Lillian Ota Dotson. *Bibliography of the Peoples and Cultures of Mainland Southeast Asia.* New Haven: Southeast Asia Studies, Yale University, 1950. A major work of over 800 pages, with the great majority of the 12,000 unannotated items culled from journals; ethnology, religion, language, literature, history and the humanities well covered.

7

Hay, Stephen N. and Margaret H. Case. *Southeast Asian History. A Bibliographic Guide.* New York: Praeger, 1962. A small but useful guide, giving reviewers' opinions to a selection of important books and articles recently published.

8

Echols, John M. (ed.), with others. "Southeast Asia," in *The American Historical Association's Guide to Historical Literature.* New York: MacMillan, 1961. 319-334. Concentrates on the history; 270 annotated items contributed by a group of specialists.

9

Hart, Donn V. "Southeast Asia: An Introduction to the Literature." *Social Education* 27 (1964) 461-469. A brief survey, of particular use to the high school or college establishing a preliminary study program.

10

Stucki, Curtis W. *American Doctoral Dissertations on Asia, 1933–1958.* Ithaca: Southeast Asia Program, Cornell University, 1959. A guide to otherwise almost inaccessible material which collectively is of great value.

11

Neff, Kenneth L. *Selected Bibliography on Education in Southeast Asia.* Washington: U. S. Department of Health, Education, and Welfare, 1963. Materials, fully annotated, are listed under individual countries; most items are in English.

12

Gosling, Peter L. A. *Maps, Atlases and Gazetteers for Asian Studies. A Critical Guide.* New York: University of the State of New York, 1965. Being Occasional Paper 2 of the Foreign Area Materials Center, this is a most useful guide for maps, atlases, and gazetteers dealing with Southeast Asia.

13

Wainwright, M.D. and N. Mathews. *A Guide to Western Manuscripts and Documents in the British Isles Relating to South and Southeast Asia.* London: Oxford University Press, 1965. The vast collection of primary materials in London in particular, acquired throughout a long imperial past, are here listed, although in sequence of repositories, and not area or country wise; a detailed index compensates for this.

14

Hall, D. G. E. (ed.). *Historians of South-East Asia.* London: Oxford University Press 1961. Papers submitted by an international group of scholars contain considerable bibliographical and historiographical material on the area.

Journals

15

Journal of Asian Studies. Ann Arbor: Association of Asian Studies, 1956– . Known as the *Far Eastern Quarterly* prior to 1956. Articles on Southeast Asia by scholars of many disciplines are published here, and occupy, by and large, perhaps a third of the journal; the range of subjects and periods is wide and represents some of the best efforts of scholars concerned with Southeast Asia.

16

Asian Survey. Berkeley: Institute of International Studies, University of California, 1961– . A fortnightly review of contemporary Asian affairs, with Southeast Asia figuring prominently throughout the year. Successor to the *Far Eastern Survey* published from 1932–1961 by the Institute of Pacific Relations, which also is cited frequently in this bibliography.

17

Pacific Affairs. Vancouver Institute of Pacific Relations, 1928– . The contemporary problems and major developments in Southeast Asia have come to assume considerably more importance in this journal in post-war years, while the quality and depth of its articles have remained of significant value.

18

Journal, Southeast Asian History. Singapore. University of Singapore, 1960– . Of wide range and interests, reflecting the personal preoccupation of its founder-editor 1960–66, in utilizing the findings of many disciplines to throw light on the past and present.

19

Far Eastern Economic Review. Hong Kong. An informed weekly, which carries articles on contemporary economic and political developments throughout East and Southeast Asia.

20

Bulletin of the Institute of Ethnology, Academia Sinica. Taiwan. Contains articles in English (or Chinese with English summary) on prehistory, ethnology of East and Southeast Asia.

21

Asian Perspectives. Hong Kong University 1957– . The Bulletin of the Far Eastern Prehistory Association, edited in the U.S.A., carries articles on the prehistory of Southeast Asia.

22

Pacific Viewpoint. Wellington, 1960– . A geographical journal which devotes considerable space to scholarly articles on the Southeast Asian region.

23

Journal, Malaysian Branch Royal Asiatic Society. Kuala Lumpur 1963– . Formerly the Malayan Branch, and before that from 1877 the Straits Branch, R.A.S. a quarterly with wide range of scholarly articles on the Malaysian region and its neighbors.

24

Asian Survey. Manila, 1961– . Historical and sociological articles mainly on Southeast Asia.

25

France-Asia. Paris and Tokyo. Concentrates on the former French possessions of Southeast Asia.

26

Bijdragen Tot De Taal-, Land- Eu Volkenkunde. 'S-Gravenhage. Nijhoff. 1852– . A scholarly journal since 1946, published in Dutch and English; concentrates on Indonesia, and occasionally its near neighbors.

27

Economic Bulletin for Asia and The Far East. United Nations, 1949– . A quarterly which considers trends and patterns of trade, agriculture, industry, and gives details of statistics and official activities and economic plans of relevance to the region.

28

Economic Survey of Asia and the Far East. United Nations, 1946– . An annual report by ECAFE, covering the economic development of the region.

29

Artibus Asiae. Ascona, Switzerland, 1925– . History of art and archaeological articles on Asia with an editorial bias toward Southeast Asia.

30

The Geographical Review. New York. Contains a permanent section on Asia which frequently includes an article on Southeast Asia.

31

Specialized journals such as the following also upon occasion carry articles pertaining to Southeast Asia: *American Anthropologist, American Political Science Review, Annals, American Academy of Political and Social Science, Comparative Studies in Society and History, Current History, China Quarterly, Economic Development and Cultural Change, Foreign Affairs, History Today, International Affairs, Journal of Political Economy, Man, Southwestern Journal of Anthropology, Western Political Quarterly, World Today; World Politics; Journal, Royal Asiatic Society* (London), *Australian Journal of Politics and History* (Brisbane), *Australian Quarterly* (Sydney), *Minerva* (London), *The Mariners Mirror* (Cambridge).

Land, People, and Language

PHYSICAL AND CULTURAL GEOGRAPHY

32

Dobby, E. H. G. *Southeast Asia.* 7th ed. London: University of London Press, 1960. A standard geography text, prepared by the former professor of geography at the University of Singapore, covering the natural landscape, the land usage and the human geography of Southeast Asia, a major work with numerous maps, diagrams, and charts.

33

Fisher, C. A. *Southeast Asia; a Social, Economic and Political Geography.* New York: E. P. Dutton, 1964. A quarter of this 800-page work deals with Southeast Asia as an entity, defining the personality of the area, the physical environment, indigenous peoples, the political geography of the pre-European period, and finally the impact of the West. The remainder deals with the economic, social and political problems of each country, with particular attention to Indonesia.

34

Spencer, Joseph E. *Asia East by South: a Cultural Geography.* New York: John Wiley, 1954. A stimulating survey of Southeast Asia by a cultural geographer, with less detail than the two previous sources but with some provocative ideas.

35

Cressy, G. B. *Asia's Lands and Peoples, a geography of one-third the earth and two-thirds its people.* 3rd rev. ed. New York: McGraw-Hill, 1963. In 45 chapters and 650 pages; Southeast Asian geography is considered in 9 chapters, 257-372. Land use, population patterns, physical geography, and other aspects of each country in turn; well illustrated.

36

McGee, T. G. *The Southeast Asian City: A Study of the Primate Cities of Southeast Asia.* London: G. Bell & Sons, 1967. A detailed study of the geographical, historical and economic factors that have produced the capitals and great ocean ports of Southeast Asia.

37

Murphey, Rhoads. "New Capitals of Asia." *Economic Development and Cultural Change* 5 (1956–57) 216-243. The new capitals of Southeast Asia are largely ocean port cities, formed by foreigners; their growth and nature is here examined in a stimulating piece of analysis.

38

Murphey, Rhoads. "The City in the Swamp: Aspects of the Site and Early Growth of Calcutta." *The Geographical Journal* 130, 2 (1964) 241-256. As one of the Western-founded port cities in Asia, this is the prototype of Rangoon, Singapore, Hong Kong, and others in Southeast Asia.

39

Ginsberg, Norton S. "The Great City in Southeast Asia." *American Journal of Sociology* 60 (1955) 455-462. Outlines features of the young, foreign-created, metropolitan but not nationally oriented ocean ports of Southeast Asia.

40

Pelzer, Karl J. *Pioneer Settlement in the Asiatic Tropics Studies in Land Utilization and Agricultural Colonization in Southeastern Asia.* New York: Institute of Pacific Relations, 1945. Although part 2 deals specifically with Indonesia and the Philippines, part 1 is a broad survey of the region as a whole, dealing with various systems of agricultural land use in Southeast Asia.

41

Ginsberg, Norton, John E. Brush, and others. *The Pattern of Asia.* Englewood: Prentice-Hall, 1959. A college geography text, clear and straightforward.

42

Dobby, E. H. G. *Monsoon Asia.* London: University of London Press, 1961. A simple geographical outline, establishing the major features of the region.

43

Stamp, Lawrence Dudley. *Asia, A Regional and Economic Geography*. 10th rev. ed. London: Methuen, 1959. Several chapters are devoted to Southeast Asia in this major and effective geographical survey.

44

East, William Gordon, and Spate, O. H. K. (eds.). *The Changing Map of Asia; A Political Geography*. New York: E. P. Dutton, 1950. Southeast Asia is outlined in Section 3, by C. A. Fisher.

45

Karnow, Stanley and the Editors of Life. *Southeast Asia*. Netherlands: Time-Life International, 1964. A book of excellent photographs, taking a topic approach to the region.

46

Buell, Hal. *Main Streets of Southeast Asia*. New York: Dodd, Mead, 1962. A collection of brilliantly evocative photographs, dealing with the various Southeast Asian countries.

47

Withington, William A. and Margaret Fisher. *Southeast Asia*. Grand Rapids, Mich: Fideler, 1963. A simple text for high schools and beginners.

48

Grist, D. H. *Rice*. 3rd ed. London: Longmans, Green, 1959. Frequent references to areas in Southeast Asia in an examination of all aspects of planting and cultivating this crop.

PEOPLES

49

Lebar, Frank M., Gerald C. Hickey and John K. Musgrave. *Ethnic Groups of Mainland Southeast Asia*. New Haven: Human Relations Area Files Press, 1964. In four main groupings, the characteristics of each of the many hill and valley peoples of mainland Southeast Asia are given, one by one; a major work of ethnography, complete with comprehensive bibliographies.

50

Sopher, David E. *The Sea Nomads. A Study based on the Literature of the Maritime Boat People of Southeast Asia*. Memoir of the National Museum No. 5. Singapore: Government Printer, 1965. A survey of the distribution, range, nomenclature, physical and culture characteristics, and history of the nomadic boat dwellers throughout Southeast Asia by one who never met them.

51

Kunstadter, Peter (ed.). *Southeast Asian Tribes, Minorities, and Nations*. 2 vols. Princeton: Princeton University Press, 1967. A collection of papers by twenty specialists, based on field work in Burma, China, India, Laos, Malaysia, Thailand, and Vietnam. 896 pages.

52

Cole, Fay-Cooper. *The Peoples of Malaysia*. New York: Van Nostrand, 1945.

MAPS

53

Hall, D. G. E. (ed.). *Atlas of Southeast Asia*. New York: St. Martins Press, 1964. The best atlas on the region, with 84 pages of maps on agriculture, communications, climate, populations, on towns and cities, and much else pertaining to Southeast Asia.

54

Sellman, Roger Raymond. *An Outline Atlas of Eastern History*. London: Arnold, 1954. Fifty-three maps, many of relevance to Southeast Asia.

55

Roolvink, R. *Historical Atlas of the Muslim Peoples*. Cambridge: Harvard University Press, 1957. Of some relevance to Southeast Asia, particularly to the Moslem lands of Indonesia and Malaysia.

56

The Times Atlas of the World. Vol. 1. London: The Times Publishing Company, 1958. Has double page maps of Eastern Indonesia and Australia, Malaya, Sumatra, Java and Borneo, Celebes and the Philippines.

57

Denoyer-Geppert Map Co. *East and Southeast Asia,* Westermann map, 72″ x 80″, 64 miles to inch. Physical-political. Catalogue No. GWe80rp.

58

_____. *Southeast Asia,* 96″ x 90″, 32 miles to inch. German text. Physical-political. Catalogue No. HP381.

59

_____. *Southeast Asia.* 44″ x 36″, 80 miles to inch. Political. Catalogue No. P381.

60

_____. *Malaya.* 36″ x 47″, 9 miles to inch. Physical-Communications. Catalogue No. P318r.

61

_____. *Philippines.* 52″ x 60″, 16 miles to inch. Physical-Administrative. Catalogue No. PG188.

62

_____. *Philippines.* 36″ x 49″, 24 miles to inch. Physical. Catalogue No. 188rp.

63

_____. *Indochina.* 40″ x 48″, 26 miles to inch. Land use. French text. HF55e.

64

_____. *Indochina.* 41″ x 49″, 26 miles to inch. Physical-Political, French text. DE 55irp.

65

Nystrom, A. J. & Co. *Southeast Asia and Australia.* 44″ x 60″, 170 miles to inch. Physical-Political. Catalogue No. PR83.

66

_____. *Southeast Asia and Australia.* 44″ x 44″, 170 miles to inch. Political. Catalogue No. AG83.

67

_____. *Southeast Asia.* Haack German-text map. 95″ x 88″. Physical-Political. Catalogue No. HG83.

HISTORY

Although nothing comparable to the records of China or India is available, nor the legacy of accumulated scholarship that is their glory, the broad regional pattern of Southeast Asian history is known to us. Southeast Asia emerges into history some 2000 years ago, as, gradually, small units of settled communities appear. Throughout the first millennium these states become greater, and the major faiths of the world begin to make an impact. It is not until the second millennium, however, that it is possible to consider any continuous history, and not until European records, from the 16th century onwards, is it possible to give detail. During these centuries there are many changes, culminating in the shared colonial experience of the 19th and 20th centuries, and the new independence of the contemporary scene.

68

Hall, D. G. E. *A History of Southeast Asia*. 2nd ed. New York: St. Martins Press, 1964. A basic and substantial reference work, which reviews Southeast Asian history from earliest times. Four main periods are discussed: To the beginning of the 16th century; Southeast Asia during the earlier phase of European expansion; The period of

Hall, D. G. E. (continued)
European territorial expansion; Nationalism and the challenge to European domination. A select 30-page bibliography accompanies the 900-page text.

69

Cady, John F. *Southeast Asia: Its Historical Development.* New York: McGraw-Hill, 1964. A comprehensive history of the region, of equal quality to Hall. Six major sections are presented: The Setting; Early Empires; Transition to Modern Times; European Commercial Dominance; Intensive Economic Development; and Political Reform and Nationalist Revival. One senses that Cady is interested in the later rather than the earlier periods, and that Hall reverses the interest.

70

Harrison, B. *South-East Asia. A Short History.* 3rd ed. New York: St. Martins Press, 1966. A stimulating outline, throwing out many interesting theories and generalizations, and providing a useful introductory assessment.

71

Pearn, B. R. *An Introduction to the History of South-East Asia.* London: Longmans, 1963.

72

Fitzgerald, C. P. *A Concise History of East Asia.* London: Heinemann, 1966. Southeast Asia is considered in one of the three main sections; a survey from earliest times.

Historiography

A fundamental weakness of a large number of the earlier works on Southeast Asia has been that they have described the European in Asia and not Asia. Another weakness, in contrast to, say, Chinese historiography, has been the primitive and pioneer periodization attempts. The whole conceptual framework is still being discussed and defined by the scholars of today.

73

Benda, H. "The Structure of Southeast Asian History: Some Preliminary Observations." *Journal, Southeast Asian History* 3 (1962) 106-138. Demonstrates a structural or generic approach to Southeast Asian history, with need for a genuine Southeast Asian periodization.

74

Hall, D. G. E. "On the Study of Southeast Asian History." *Pacific Affairs* 33 (1960) 268-281. A stimulating survey on periodization, on work already done by many disciplines, and on the need for a new concentration upon historical research in a free atmosphere.

75

Smail, John. "On the Possibility of an Autonomous History of Modern Southeast Asia." *Journal, Southeast Asian History* 2, 2(July 1961) 72-102. The concepts of Europocentric and Asia-centric histories of Southeast Asia are discarded in favor of a balanced stand inside Southeast Asia, with the Southeast Asian society itself being the basic factor of consideration.

76

Trager, F. N. "Recent Southeast Asian Historiography." *Pacific Affairs* 30 (1957) 358-366. A brief survey of changing approaches and recently published works.

77

Coedes, George. "Some Problems in the Ancient History of the Hinduized States of South-East Asia." *Journal, Southeast Asian History* 5, 2 (1964) 1-14. Raises unsolved problems of periodization and historiography affecting the first 15 hundred years A.D.

Prehistory

Southeast Asia was more of an entity at the time of man's pre-historic beginnings than it is today. It was a period of time when basic cultural changes were made. The transformation of life was more dramatic in its results, and the area more profoundly affected than anything which followed.

78

Chang, Kwang-chih. "Major Problems in the Culture History of Southeast Asia." *Bulletin of the Institute of Ethnology, Academia Sinica* 13 (1962) 1-26. A stimulating re-consideration of the food-gathering, early agricultural and irrigation beginnings, together with migratory origins; an excellent survey of a period vital for its cultural changes.

79

Sharp, Lauriston. "Cultural continuities and discontinuities in Southeast Asia." *Journal of Asian Studies* 22 (1962) 3-11. Looks in vain for any major cultural stream flowing steadily out of a distant past, discusses in particular the importance of the agricultural late neolithic period in Southeast Asia.

80

Barth, F. "The Southern Mongoloid Migrations." *Man* 52 (1952) 5-8. Outlines the pressures behind the migrations into Southeast Asia of Indonesians, Mon-Khmers and Thai, and their displacement of indigenous peoples; attributes their success to a knowledge of wet rice cultivation.

81

Chang Kwang-chih. "Prehistoric and Early Historic Culture Horizons and Traditions in South China." *Current Anthropology* 5 (1964) 359, 368-75. Outlines the culture of South China from the appearance of agriculture to the Han civilization, which merges in part with the prehistoric traditions of Southeast Asia.

82

Chang Kwang-chih. "A Working Hypothesis for the Early Cultural History of South China." *Bulletin of the Institute of Ethnology, Academia Sinica* 6 (1958) 67-78. Original nomadic settlements gradually were replaced by settled fishing and agricultural villages, and the social pattern changed with them.

83

Chang Kwang-chih. "Chinese Prehistory in Pacific Perspective: Some Hypotheses and Problems." *Harvard Journal of Asiatic Studies* 22 (1959).

84

Movins, H. L. "Palaeolithic Archaeology in Southern and Eastern Asia, exclusive of India." *Journal of World History* 11 (1954) 257-282, 520-553. With a comprehensive 15-page bibliography, this is a detailed survey of work done in this field.

85

Solheim, Wilhelm G. "Pottery and the Malayo-Polynesians." *Current Anthropology* 5 (1964) 360, 376-384. Prehistoric pottery distribution sheds light on cultural and racial relationships and movements in Southeast Asia.

86

Pearson, Richard. "Dongso'n and its Origins." *Bulletin of the Institute of Ethnology, Academia Sinica* 13 (1962) 27-50. The prehistoric bronze culture is examined at two major sites, and is fitted into a larger picture of Southeast Asian prehistory; a 4-page bibliography.

87

Christie, Anthony. "The Sea-Locked Lands. The diverse traditions of South East Asia," in Stuart Piggot (ed.) *The Dawn of Civilization.* London: Thames and Hudson, 1961. 277-300. A vividly illustrated outline of the prehistoric period and the early centuries A.D. with particular emphasis on the Dong-so'n bronze culture of Southeast Asia.

88

Clark, Graham. *World Prehistory: An Outline.* Cambridge: Cambridge University Press, 1961. 201-205. The origins of rice cultivation, and the Hoabinhian culture, together with the bronzes of mainland Southeast Asia, Indonesia and the Philippines, are sketched in, as part of a world survey.

89

Weins, Harold J. *China's March Towards the Tropics*. Hamden, Conn.: The Shoe String Press, 1954. A discussion of the southward penetration of China's culture, peoples, and political control in relation to the non-Chinese peoples of South China.

Period Surveys

90

Coedes, G. *The Making of South East Asia*. London: Routledge & Kegan Paul, 1966. Mainland Southeast Asia, from the time of man's first settlement up to the climax of the 13th century; an assessment of those centuries when the area was profoundly influenced by an Indianized culture, and when Angkor dominated a wide region.

91

Coedes, G. *Les états hindouises d'Indochine et d'Indonesie*. Paris: E. de Boccard, 1948. Long acclaimed as a classic survey of Indonesian and Indochinese history in the centuries before the European appeared, this work is now being translated by East-West Press, Hawaii.

92

Pannikkar, K. M. *Asia and Western Dominance. A Survey of the Vasco da Gama Epoch of Asian History 1498–1945*. London: Allen & Unwin, 1953. An eminent Asian author attempts, not unsuccessfully, to lay the blame for nearly everything during these 400 years, on the European; singles out Christian missions for a near 100-page treatment, and presents a work with a sting in it.

93

Purcell, Victor. *The Chinese in Southeast Asia*. 2nd ed. London: Oxford University Press, 1965. An historical study from the earliest times of the role of the Chinese in Southeast Asia, but giving particular emphasis to the 19th and 20th centuries, when their settlements increased to sizeable proportions and their place warranted major attention.

94

Williams, Lea. *The Future of the Overseas Chinese in Southeast Asia*. New York: McGraw-Hill, 1966. Demonstrates that the Chinese are moving towards greater political integration within their countries of residence, and to the establishment of firmer roots in their new homes. A survey of the entire region, but with emphasis on Malaysia-Singapore in the Post War period.

95

Purcell, Victor. *The Revolution in Southeast Asia*. London: Thames & Hudson, 1962. The revolution here is the political revolution, the anti-colonial movement of the last 100 years that led to the independent countries of today; a good survey of the 20th century.

96

Romein, J. and W. F. Wertheim. *A World On The Move*. A History of Colonialism and Nationalism in Asia and North Africa from the Turn of the Century to the Bandung Conference. Amsterdam: Djambatan, 1956. A vivid picture album, with searing text, on national and anti-colonial movements.

97

Brimmell, J. H. *Communism in South-East Asia*. London: Oxford University Press, 1959. A penetrating and detailed historical study of communism in each country of the region, together with an analysis of the ideology itself.

98

Rose, Saul. *Britain and South-East Asia*. Baltimore: Johns Hopkins Press, 1962. An essay outlining the expansion of Britain into Southeast Asia, the political, strategical and economic interests that developed between the world wars and the cash nexus now existing; together with comments on the withdrawal of the British, and the future.

99

Benda, H. and John A. Larkin. (eds.). *The World of Southeast Asia: Selected Historical Readings*. New York: Harper & Row, 1967.

100

Elsbree, Willard H. *Japan's Role in Southeast Asian Nationalist Movements, 1940–1945*. Cambridge: Harvard University Press, 1953. A survey of a crucial period in modern Southeast Asian history.

101

Buss, C. A. *The Arc of Crisis*. Garden City: Doubleday, 1961. The arc stretches from India to Japan, and the crisis is poverty; a crisis that is a danger and an opportunity for all who are interested. A survey of a contemporary Southeast Asia, and American participation there.

102

Harlow, V. T. *The Founding of the Second British Empire 1763–1793*. Vol. 1. *History and Revolution*. London: Longmans, 1952. European activities over a wide area of Southeast Asia at this time are in chapters 3 and 4, 62-145.

103

Buss, Claude A. *Southeast Asia and the World Today*. New York: van Nostrand, 1958. A general statement of historical developments of the pre-war and post-war scene, with one-half of the work devoted to readings from basic documents.

104

Sansom, G. B. *The Western World and Japan*. London: Cresset, 1950. Southeast Asia figures prominently in the early selections of this work, which has the Portuguese and others moving towards Japan.

105

Purcell, V. *South and East Asia since 1800*. Cambridge: Cambridge University Press, 1965. A general historical survey, with Southeast Asia included.

106

Tregonning, K. G. *World History for Malaysians from earliest times to 1511* A.D. 2 ed. London: University of London Press, 1967. Contains a succinct survey of Southeast Asian history prior to the arrival of the Portuguese.

Specialized Studies

107

Lamb, Alastair. "A Visit to Siraf, an ancient port on the Persian Gulf." *Journal, Malayan Branch, Royal Asiatic Society* 37 (1964) 1-19. Interesting comments on possible 8th-10th century Southeast Asian trade with the Middle East.

108

Jack-Hinton, C. "Marco Polo in South-East Asia. A preliminary essay in reconstruction." *Journal, Southeast Asian History* 5, 2 (1964) 43-103. Detailed examination of the evidence leads to identification of the 12 Southeast Asian localities visited by the celebrated traveler at the end of the 12th century.

109

Tregonning, K. G. "Kublai Khan and South-east Asia." *History Today* 7 (1957) 163-170. The Mongol military adventures in Burma, Indo-China and Java in the late 13th century.

110

Duyvendak, J. J. "The True Dates of the Chinese Maritime Expeditions in the Early Fifteenth Century." *T'oung Pao* 34 (1939) 341-412. A brilliant and sustained study of the voyages of Cheng Ho into and beyond Southeast Asia in the 15th century.

111

Hall, D. G. E. "From Mergui to Singapore 1686–1819. A Neglected Chapter in the Naval History of the Indian Ocean." *Journal, Siam Society* 41 (1953) 1-18; outlines the long felt need by the British for a naval base on the eastern side of the Indian Ocean, and traces the search for one from 1686 to 1819.

112

Benda, Harry J. "Peasant Movements in Colonial Southeast Asia." *Asian Studies* 3 (1965) 420-434. Peasant revolts in Java, Burma, Vietnam, and the Philippines during the 20th century are examined, and the general significance of peasants on the move, as distinct from city mobs, is estimated.

113

Benda, Harry J. "Political Ethics in Colonial Southeast Asia: An Historical Analysis." *Comparative Studies in Society and History* 7 (1965) 233-251. Another penetrating survey by a leading historian.

POLITICAL PATTERNS

The political patterns of Southeast Asia are more interesting, perhaps, to the scholar than to the statesman. There is fascination for the academic in the diversity of the region, whereas the statesman fears the continuing weakness of each individual political framework, and the lack of regional cohesion. The modern colonial background, itself varied and different for each state, super-imposed on a region lacking any cultural homogeneity, and itself creating the boundaries of a modern state, produced independent, multi-racial countries ill prepared to govern themselves. They emerged with little interest in any economic or political cooperation, and with their patterns of administration distinct and different from their neighbor. This diversity of government has continued, and although some scholars can point to one broad similarity, namely an authoritarian regime in every country, the political pattern ranges widely, from a democratic system patterned on the American model in the Philippines, to a one party rule by the army in Burma and the communists in North Vietnam. The region, politically, is in a revolutionary stage. Over the last decade the pattern of nearly every state has been broken by a coup, an internal revolution, or disguised infiltration and organized attempts at overthrow from outside. This has resulted in a general, regional wide weakness in political stability. Only the minimal attempts at political cooperation have been made; virtually all of these have ended in failure.

General Works

114

Kahin, G. McT. (ed.). *Government and Politics of Southeast Asia.* 2 ed. Ithaca: Cornell University Press, 1964. Major coverage on every country in Southeast Asia is provided by a political scientist recently in the region; each writer contributes under four headings: the historical background; the contemporary setting; the political process; major problems. A useful reading list is supplied for each country. Students of Southeast Asian affairs are indebted to the major contributions made by Cornell; this work, indispensible for all interested in the area, is not the least of its achievements.

115

Vandenbosch, Amry, and Richard Butwell. *The Changing Face of Southeast Asia.* Lexington: University of Kentucky Press, 1966. A concise account of recent developments in Indonesia, Malaysia, Philippines, Vietnam, Laos, Cambodia, Burma, and Thailand; the international relations of the area, and American policy is considered.

116

Bone, Robert C. *Contemporary Southeast Asia.* New York: Random House, 1962. An excellent brief survey, sketching in the rapid post Pacific War events with clarity and understanding.

117

Durdin, Tillman. *Southeast Asia.* New York: Atheneum, 1966. A slim essay by the London *Times* correspondent, which outlines both the diversity of the region, and its instability, and the forces making for integration.

118

Trager, Frank N. (ed.). *Marxism in Southeast Asia.* Stanford: Stanford University Press, 1960. A number of excellent essays on the contemporary position of the communist elements inside each Southeast Asian state, with some outline of their origins.

119

Brecher, M. *The New States of Asia. A political analysis.* London: Oxford University Press, 1964. A collection of essays on contemporary Asia, including "neutralism — an analysis" which clarifies Southeast Asian attitudes.

120

Butwell, Richards A. *Southeast Asia Today — and Tomorrow. A Political Analysis.* rev. ed. New York: Praeger, 1964. A successful contemporary survey of the rapidly changing political developments within the region, by an experienced political scientist.

121

Emerson, Rupert. *Representative Government in Southeast Asia.* Cambridge: Harvard University Press, 1955. Although the details of government here no longer prevail, the astute and informed comments of the author are still topical and relevant and make this a useful reference for broad issues.

122

Crozier, Brian. *Southeast Asia in Turmoil.* Harmondsworth: Penguin Books, 1965. Emphasis on the contemporary scene, particularly in Vietnam and Indonesia.

123

Romein, J. *The Asian Century. A history of modern nationalism in Asia.* Berkeley: University of California Press, 1962. A broad survey, in which the efforts of the countries of Southeast Asia to secure and maintain their independence are sympathetically outlined.

124

Rose, Saul. *Socialism in Southern Asia.* London: Oxford University Press, 1959. An account of the Asian socialist conference at Rangoon in 1953; discusses democratic socialist developments in the region, and reviews the dismal story of the Asian Socialist non-communist movement.

125

Thayer, P. W. and W. T. Philips (eds.). *Nationalism and Progress in Free Asia.* Baltimore: Johns Hopkins, 1956. An excellent series of papers and comments by an international group of scholars on the political and economic motivations of contemporary Southeast Asia.

126

Hanna, Willard A. *Eight Nation Makers: Southeast Asia's Charismatic Statesmen.* New York: St. Martins Press, 1964. Essays written after personal interviews and detailed study in the field on the background of the contemporary political leaders of Southeast Asia; more vivid and penetrating than John Gunther.

127

Gordon, Bernard K. *The Dimensions of Conflict in Southeast Asia.* Englewood Cliffs: Prentice-Hall, 1966. A survey of the 1965 scene, and an assessment of regional cooperation.

128

Holland, W. L. (ed.). *Asian Nationalism and the West.* New York: MacMillan, 1953. Published for the Institute of Pacific Relations, which has done invaluable pioneer work in promoting scholarly work in this region, this contains three major sections, on the immediate post-war developments in: Indonesia; Malaya; Vietnam.

129

Emerson, Rupert (ed.). *Government and Nationalism in Southeast Asia.* New York: Institute of Pacific Relations, 1942. With Lennox Mills and Virginia Thompson, a survey of the governments and nationalist movements in pre-war Southeast Asia.

130
Thompson, Virginia and Richard Adloff. *Minority Problems in Southeast Asia.* Stanford: Stanford University Press, 1955. A survey, country by country, of minorities and their political activities and aspirations.

131
Thompson, Virginia and R. Adloff. *The Left Wing in Southeast Asia.* New York: Sloane, 1950. A pioneer but still useful survey of the newly activated political groups in an area struggling for independence, and where political loyalties were suspect.

132
Mende, Tibor. *South-East Asia between Two Worlds.* London: Turnstile Press, 1955. Published originally in France, a survey of the political and economic problems of Indonesia, Burma and Pakistan, between the worlds of modernity and traditionalism.

133
Gordon, Bernard K. "Problems of Regional Co-operation in Southeast Asia." *World Politics* 16 (1964) 222-253. Ancient and modern grievances and disputes make regional grouping difficult; the attempts already tried have failed.

134
Von Der Mehden, *Religion and Nationalism in Southeast Asia.* Wisconsin: Wisconsin University Press, 1963. Religion as a motivating force in the nationalism of Burma, Indonesia and the Philippines.

135
Bellah, Robert N. *Religion and Progress in Modern Asia.* New York: The Free Press, 1965. Conference papers discuss the retarding influence of traditional attitudes, reinforced by a traditional faith, on political and economic modernization; a stimulating and searching memorandum on this theme by Soedjatmoko of Indonesia highlights the work.

136
Thayer, Philip W. (ed.). *Southeast Asia in the Coming World.* Baltimore: J. Hopkins Press, 1953. Papers contributed to a School of Advanced International Studies Seminar, on the political scene of Southeast Asia, associated topics.

137
Mills, L. A. (ed.). *The New World of Southeast Asia.* Minneapolis: University of Minnesota Press, 1949. A post-war survey undertaken by a pioneer group of American political scientists with interests in Southeast Asia, writing very largely for an uninformed public.

138
Lasker, Bruno (ed.). *New Forces in Asia.* New York: Wilson, 1950. Contains useful articles on Vietnam and other countries.

139
Ward, Robert E. and Roy C. Macridis. *Modern Political Systems: Asia.* Englewood Cliffs: Prentice-Hall, 1963. A survey, country by country, of the politics and governments of Asia, including Southeast Asia.

140
Talbot, P. *South Asia in the World Today.* Chicago: Chicago University Press, 1951.

International Relations

The countries of Southeast Asia have reappeared as independent states only within the last 25 years. Few regional studies of the international relations of this group have been made. Individual countries have received attention, but for the most part it has been the impact of the U.S.A. on the area that has attracted interest.

141
Fifield, Russell H. *The Diplomacy of Southeast Asia 1945–1958.* New York: Harper, 1958. A broad descriptive survey, country by country, of the initial international relations of the newly independent countries of Southeast Asia, at a period of grave implications.

142
Fifield, Russell H. *Southeast Asia in United States Policy.* New York: Praeger, 1963. American interest in Southeast Asia steadily increased in the last decade, despite a weakening of economic ties; author examines this in the light of international communism.

143
Jordan, Amos. *Foreign Aid and the Defense of Southeast Asia.* New York: Praeger, 1962. U. S. government financial and other assistance to the various countries of Southeast Asia are examined here as part of the Cold War.

144
Montgomery, John D. *The Politics of Foreign Aid: American Experience in Southeast Asia.* New York: Praeger, 1962. South Vietnam, Burma, Thailand and Taiwan have all received U. S. aid; the contrasts in response and reaction are so great as to make any generalization difficult, apart from a broad conclusion that the whole exercise is unsatisfactory.

145
Martin, Lawrence W. (ed.). *Neutralism and Non Alignment: The New States in World Affairs.* New York: Praeger, 1962. Although not dealing specifically with Southeast Asia, nevertheless useful in understanding the underlying feeling of the region towards international relations.

146
Staley, Eugene. *The Future of Underdeveloped Countries. Political Implications of Economic Development.* New York: Harper, 1961. Sponsored by the Council on Foreign Relations, international development is seen here as a basic element in U. S. foreign policy; in that light the transformation sweeping the underdeveloped countries, including Southeast Asia, is examined, the communist and non-communist paths to development reviewed, and a world approach to the problem advocated.

147
McLane, Charles B. *Soviet Strategies in Southeast Asia.* Princeton: Princeton University Press, 1966.

148
Modelski, G. A. (ed.). *SEATO: Six Studies.* Melbourne: Cheshire, 1963. Six research papers from the Australian National University, on various aspects of the formation and functioning of the South East Asia Treaty Organization.

149
Tregonning, K. G. "Australia's Imperialist Image in South-East Asia." *Australian Quarterly* 33, 3 (1961) 43-51. A critical survey of Australia's attitude and policies in Southeast Asia, including West Irian and Seato.

150
Isaacs, Harold R. (ed.). *New Cycle in Asia: Selected Documents on Major International Developments in the Far East, 1943–1947.* New York: MacMillan, 1947. Documents on Burma, Indo-China, Indonesia and the Philippines are included.

151
Braibanti, Ralph. "The Southeast Asia Collective Defense Treaty." *Pacific Affairs* 30 (1957) 321-341. An analysis of the treaty and an appraisal of its mechanism for achieving international objectives.

Development

Southeast Asia as a region today shares common characteristics with other parts of the "underdeveloped" or "developing" world. Some valuable surveys have been made and comparisons and assessments drawn, and although the works listed are not directly based on Southeast Asia, nevertheless they are useful to any appreciation of it.

152

Shils, Edward. *Political Development in the New States.* London: Mouton, 1962. A general essay, which while not concerned specifically with Southeast Asia, has relevance to any understanding of the region.

153

Kautsky, John H. (ed.). *Political Change in Underdeveloped Countries: nationalism and communism.* New York: J. Wiley & Sons, 1962. A collection of scholarly articles by Harry Benda, Merle Kling, Richard Lowenthal and others, together with a 100-page survey of the attractions of nationalism, communism and totalitarianism in the underdeveloped world.

154

Almond, Gabriel A. and James S. Coleman. *The Politics of the Developing Areas.* 2nd imp. Princeton: Princeton University Press, 1961. In this major and influential work, students of comparative politics are provided with a theoretical framework, together with the politics of five developing areas, including the politics of Southeast Asia by Lucian W. Pye, for study.

155

Braibanti, Ralph and Joseph J. Spengler (eds.). *Tradition, Values and Socio-Economic Development.* Durham: Duke University Press, 1961. A collection of stimulating papers on the effect of traditions and values on modernization; of relevance to Southeast Asia.

156

Huq, Muhammad Shamsul. *Education and Development Strategy in South and Southeast Asia.* Honolulu: East-West Press, 1965. The basic role in development of education is analyzed here in reference to two Southeast and two South Asian countries.

157

Shils, Edward. "The Intellectuals in the political development of the new States." *World Politics* 12 (1960) 329-368. Although not concerned specifically with Southeast Asia, nevertheless a stimulating and influential article.

158

Sigmund, Paul C. (ed.). *The Ideologies of the Developing Nations.* New York: Praeger, 1963. The theories of government and state are taken from the speeches of the leaders of the developing nations; includes Sukarno and U Nu.

Administration

159

Riggs, Fred. *Administration in Developing Countries; the theory of prismatic society.* Boston: H. Mifflin, 1964. Based on experience in the Philippines, in Thailand and elsewhere, a theoretical approach to public administration.

160

Riggs, Fred. *The Ecology of Public Administration.* Bombay and New York: Asia Publishing House, 1961.

ECONOMIC PATTERNS

The economic patterns of Southeast Asia have received far more attention within a national framework than within a regional one. By far the most substantial and detailed works on these patterns are to be found listed with each separate country. Yet there are many overall factors of similarity. For most of its historic past Southeast Asia had one discernible pattern which applied to the whole region. It was an area existing essentially on a subsistence economy. There was a regional self-sufficiency, but a sufficiency which was maintained only because wants for nearly all were confined to basic foods and other necessities of life. This regional unity was replaced by another, when European imperialists imposed a colonial type economy over the whole region. Crops varied, no doubt, rubber was grown here and coffee there, but by and large a colonial type of economy ushered the region into the modern world. The region also was united in what it lacked; no industry was discernible, no central bank, no indigenous entrepreneurial class. And then when independence came to Southeast Asia, again the economic pattern was broadly similar, with countries facing similar problems and attempting to develop by similar stratagems. Yet this has been looked at, very largely, through national eyes, and the regional pattern has not been investigated, as yet, in a sustained manner.

General Works

161

Economic Survey of Asia and the Far East. New York: UN, 1965. Annually. This survey of economic conditions in Southeast Asia includes data submitted to the U. S., by all the countries concerned.

162

The United Nations and Asia. A collection of Basic Information on the Economic and Social Activities of the United Nations and Related Agencies in Asia. New York: UN, 1962. A survey of the regional projects which such bodies as ECAFE, WHO, UNESCO, FAO, and ILO are operating in Asia, together with a background account of the conditions that have warranted UN activity.

163

Onslow, C. (ed.). *Asian Economic Development. The economic problems of India, Pakistan, Ceylon, Thailand, Burma, and Malaya.* London: Weidenfeld and Nicholson, 1965. In this country by country survey, the actual achievements of these Southeast Asian states are outlined by national experts.

164

Bauer, P. T. *Economic Analysis and Policy in Underdeveloped Countries.* Durham: Duke University Press, 1957. An examination of the shortcomings in economic thinking and policies by Southeast Asian countries, and alternative suggestions for growth offered.

165

Geertz, Clifford (ed.). *Old Societies and New States: the quest for modernity in Asia and Africa.* New York: Free Press, 1963. Articles by eminent scholars of various disciplines, who examine the economic, social and political factors that are retarding or encouraging growth in Southeast Asia and elsewhere.

166

Zinkin, Maurice. *Asia and the West.* London: Chatto & Windus, 1957. A survey of the economic and social patterns among independent Asia, with specific chapters on Burma, Java and Malaya, Philippines and Thailand, with in each case a socio-historical survey of its 20th century.

167

Mills, L. A. *Southeast Asia. Illusion and Reality in Politics and Economics.* Minneapolis: University of Minnesota Press, 1964. Considers the authoritarian regimes in power, and examines the economic problems of their states; deals at length with the issue of overseas aid, and the unlimited population growth.

168

Thompson, Warren S. *Population and Progress in the Far East.* Chicago: University of Chicago Press, 1959. A basic, common problem over all of Southeast Asia is the population growth of the 20th century; here considered in 2 chapters.

169

Louka, Kathryn. *The Role of Population in the Development of Southeast Asia.* Washington: George Washington University, 1960. Outlines the demography of Southeast Asia, excluding the Philippines.

170

Taeuber, Irene B. "Population: Dilemma of Modernization in Southeast Asia." *Asia: A Selection of Papers Delivered Before the Asia Society.* Vol. 1. New York: The Asia Society, 1964. An account of the exploding populations in Southeast Asia by a recognized authority.

171

Robequain, Charles. *Malaya, Indonesia, Borneo and the Philippines: A Geographical, Economic, and Political description of Malaya, the East Indies and the Philippines.* 2nd ed. London: Longmans Green, 1959. A comprehensive survey, with the impact of the West particularly evident in the detailed account of the economic systems of the states involved.

172

Paauw, Douglas. "Economic Progress in Southeast Asia." *Journal of Asian Studies* 22 (1963) 69-92. A study of various indicators of post-war growth, or lack thereof, demonstrating a marked difference between the Philippines and Thailand on the one hand, and Burma and Indonesia on the other.

Specialized Studies

173

Wightman, D. *Towards Economic Co-operation in Asia. The United Nations Economic Commission for Asia and the Far East.* New Haven: Yale University Press, 1963. A study of the formation and work of ECAFE, and the various problems it has encountered in its effort to secure support from Asians and Europeans in the Southeast Asian region, and to promote economic development through international co-operation.

174

Shils, Edward. "The Concentration and Dispersion of Charisma: Their Bearing on Economic Policy in Underdeveloped Countries." *World Politics* 11 (1958) 1-19. An assessment of the intellectual political leader, in Southeast Asia and elsewhere, and his part in the economic development of his backward region.

175

Matossian, Mary. "Ideologies of Delayed Industrialization: Some Tensions and Ambiguities." *Economic Development and Cultural Change* 6 (1958) 217-228. Patterns of ideas that are accepted by those on the defensive, wanting no longer to be behind in modernization; these when accepted then produce tensions as the economic and social lag continues.

176

Cowan, C. D. (ed.). *Economic Development of South-East Asia. Studies in Economic History and Political Economy.* London: Allen and Unwin, 1964. Eight papers on various aspects of the modern economic history of some of the countries of Southeast Asia.

177

Wightman, D. "The Struggle for Economic Co-operation in Asia and the Far East: The Experience of Ecafe." *The World Today.* 18 (1962) 30-42. Asian moves were blocked by European powers and retarded by world markets and their own narrow attitudes.

178

Jacoby, Erich H. *Agrarian Unrest in Southeast Asia.* Bombay: Asia Publishing House, 1961. The causes of unrest are remarkably similar in all the countries surveyed; rural indebtedness, low levels of health, economic avarice by middlemen, widespread tenancy, and landless peasants.

179

Thompson, Virginia. *Labor Problems in Southeast Asia.* New Haven: Yale University Press, 1947. Labor conditions in the immediate pre-war period.

180

Bauer, P. T., and B. S. Yamey. *The Economics of Underdeveloped Countries.* 4 imp. London: J. Nisbet, 1960. A stimulating text on an aspect of economics, considering human resources, capital and growth, government and economic development, and necessary policy measures, all applicable to Southeast Asia.

181

Meyer, F. V. *Britain's Colonies in World Trade.* London: Oxford University Press, 1948. Relates in particular to Britain's trade with Malaya and Hong Kong, and Malaya's regional trade in Southeast Asia, which receives considerable attention.

182

Mitchell, Kate L. *Industrialization of the Western Pacific.* New York: Institute of Pacific Relations, 1942. A survey of the pre-war economic patterns of the Southeast Asian colonies is given on 151-240.

183

Mills, L. A. *Southeast Asia. Illusion and Reality in Politics and Economics.* Minneapolis: University of Minnesota Press, 1964. As many other works listed under Political Patterns, this survey considers the economic problems and prospects of the area; gives particular attention to overseas aid and the population explosion.

184

Pelzer, Karl J. *An Economic Survey of the Pacific Area. Part 1. Population and Land Utilization.* New York: Institute of Pacific Relations, 1941. A 200 page outline, with the population patterns, land use, and tenure systems receiving the main consideration.

185

Wickizer, U. D. and M. K. Bennett. *The Rice Economy of Monsoon Asia.* Stanford: Stanford University Press, 1941. A survey of pre-war conditions of all aspects of this agrarian economy.

Banks and Shipping

186

Collis, Maurice. *Wayfoong; the Hongkong and Shanghai Banking Corporation. A Study of East Asia's transportation, political, financial and economic.* London: Faber and Faber, 1965. A profusely illustrated outline history of one of the major banks in Eastern Asia; its branches in Southeast Asia are mentioned throughout.

187

MacKenzie, Compton. *Realms of Silver; one hundred years of banking in the East.* London: Routledge and Kegan Paul, 1954. A history of The Chartered Bank, one of the two main British banks in Southeast Asia, with branches throughout the region.

188

Chiang Hai Ding. "Silver Dollars in Southeast Asia." *Asian Studies* 3 (1965) 459-469). The abandonment in the early 20th century of the silver dollar throughout Southeast Asia brought on by the decline in its value in gold.

189

Hyde, Francis E. *Blue Funnel. A History of Alfred Holt & Co. of Liverpool from 1865 to 1914.* Liverpool: Liverpool University Press, 1957. A detailed and scholarly account of a distinctive shipping company with its fortune and future in Southeast and East Asia.

190

Blake, G. *B. I. Centenary, 1856–1956.* London: Collins, 1956. The British-India line played an important role in the modernization of Burma in particular.

191

Tregonning, K. G. *Home Port Singapore. A History of Straits Steamship Company 1890–1965.* Kuala Lumpur: Oxford University Press, 1967. A coastal shipping company operating out of Singapore which participated in the trade of the entire region.

SOCIAL AND CULTURAL PATTERNS

The social patterns in any one country of Southeast Asia are diverse enough to call for a considerable number of detailed studies, while an attempt to outline the pattern of a region so complex can rarely end other than in failure. This accounts, possibly, for the paucity of works which cover all of Southeast Asia, for even if one were to oversimplify, and say that the family is the focus or basis of social patterns, this has little meaning. Southeast Asia is still largely agrarian, and the social pattern there is a rural one; and here again there is perhaps room for a broad generalization. Another basis of culture, however, is in religion, and here there is considerable diversity. Islam is the accepted belief of Indonesia and of parts of Malaysia and the Philippines. Even within the one faith, however, there are markedly different social patterns, with the matrilineal people of the Minangkabau in contrast to the more orthodox Moslems elsewhere. In addition to Islam, however, Buddhism is the dominant social force in Burma, Thailand, Cambodia and Vietnam; but in each country the social pattern varies — and has been studied in varying degrees; in Vietnam, as yet, scarcely at all. Among the minority groups, Indians and Chinese in particular, there are other faiths and other social patterns. The various aborigine groups again live in a social pattern distinct from the more modern communities who possess political authority over their territory. These different patterns were imposed, more often than not, millennia ago, and the factors that influenced the culture, and shaped the way of life of Southeast Asianers is treated in the earlier prehistorical section, as well as here.

General Works

192

Burling, Robbins. *Hill Farms and Padi Fields. Life in Mainland Southeast Asia.* Englewood Cliffs: Prentice-Hall, 1966. Explains the various cultural changes and historical developments that over the last 2 millenia have affected the way of life in the villages of mainland Southeast Asia.

193

Wales, H. G. Quaritch. *The Making of Greater India.* A Study in Southeast culture change. 2nd ed. London: B. Quaritch, 1961. A survey of early Southeast Asia, concentrating particularly on the art and culture change of the Javanese, Chams and Khmers, and their response to the cultural expansion of India.

194

Wales, H. G. Quaritch. "Culture Change in Greater India." *Journal, Royal Asiatics Society* (1948) 2-32. A provocative essay illustrating the main waves of Indianized cultural impact on Southeast Asia, and the evolution of a Southeast Asian culture, in the 1st millennium A.D.

195

Le May, Reginald. *The Culture of South-East Asia.* London: Allen & Unwin, 1954. Main attention is given to the Indian inspired art of Cambodia, Burma and Thailand, of A.D. 500–1500, and the culture thus produced.

196

Bellah, Robert N. (ed.). *Religion and Progress in Modern Asia.* New York: The Free Press, 1965. Religion as an important element in the cultural patterns of Southeast Asia is examined to see what to what extent it retards economic development and modernization of traditional areas. Wide-ranging bibliography.

197

Wales, H. G. Quaritch. *The Mountain of God. A Study in early religion and kingship.* London: B. Quaritch, 1953. The worship of holy forces concentrated on a sacred mountain or pyramid-shrine is examined in Bali, Java, and Cambodia, as well as India, Mesopotamia, and China.

198

Benz, Ernst. *Buddhism or Communism: Which Holds the Future of Asia?* Garden City: Doubleday, 1965. A professor of church history believes Buddhism as a cultural and political force in Ceylon, Burma and Thailand is more effective, on the intellectual in particular, than communism.

199

Du Bois, Cora. *Social Forces in Southeast Asia.* 3rd printing. Cambridge: Harvard University Press, 1962. Published originally in 1949, these three lectures on social factors and their potentialities in Southeast Asia are still pertinent to the area.

200

Murdock, George Peter (ed.). *Social Structure in Southeast Asia.* Viking Fund Publications in Anthropology, 29. Chicago: Quadrangle Books, 1960. Essays on the social patterns of people in the Philippines, Borneo, Java and Ceylon.

201

Lasker, Bruno. *Human Bondage in Southeast Asia.* Chapel Hill: University of North Carolina, 1950. The lack of personal freedom as a major social characteristic is treated historically, with the many aspects of this as evidenced throughout Southeast Asia outlined.

202

Landon, Kenneth P. *Southeast Asia: Crossroads of Religions.* Chicago: University of Chicago Press, 1949. Outlines the ways in which cultural patterns in Southeast Asia were affected by the arrival and influence of the Buddhist, Islamic and Confucionist faiths; useful bibliography.

203

Wales, H. G. Quaritch. *Prehistory and Religion in Southeast Asia.* London: B. Quaritch, 1957. Indicates the strong influence of the prehistoric cultural changes on the development of religion in Southeast Asia; gives particular attention to the palaeolithic, neolithic and bronze ages.

204

Bowers, Faubion. *Theatre in the East: A Survey of Asian Dance and Drama.* New York: Nelson and Sons, 1956. Includes material on classical and modern drama, dance, puppetry and associated topics in chapters on Southeast Asia; a broad survey of an important element in the area's diverse culture.

205

Frederic, Louis. *The Temples and Sculpture of Southeast Asia.* London: Thames and Hudson, 1965. A beautiful book for the coffee table, but with much information accompanying its magnificent illustrations.

206

Latourette, Kenneth Scott. *A History of the Expansion of Christianity.* Vol. 6. *The Great Century in northern Africa and Asia AD 1800–1914.* New York: Harper & Brothers, 1944. Missionary activities and successes in Burma, Malaya, Siam and Indo-China are described on 215-252.

207

Neuman, Stephanie (ed.). "Social Research in Southeast Asia." *The American Behavioral Scientist* 5, 10 (1962). A special issue devoted exclusively to aspects of the social patterns of the area.

208
Geertz, Clifford (ed.). *Old Societies and New States; the quest for modernity in Asia and Africa.* New York: Free Press, 1963. Contains articles by Edward Shils, Clifford Geertz and others, on the forces at work changing the cultural patterns of Southeast Asia.

Specialized Studies
209
Loeb, Edwin M. and Jan O. M. Broek. "Social Organization and the Long House in Southeast Asia." *American Anthropologist* 49 (1947) 414-425. Distinguishes 2 types of Long House, and outlines the correlation between them and their society; covers 70 tribal areas throughout Southeast Asia; map.

210
Conklin, Harold C. "The Study of Shifting Cultivation." *Current Anthropology* 2 (1961) 27-61. A brief discussion of the problems involved in this, followed by an extensive geographically arranged bibliography of world literature, in which Southeast Asia figures prominently.

211
Eggan, Fred. "Cultural Drift and Social Change." *Current Anthropology* 4 (1963) 347-355. Takes the concept of Herskovits, that cultural drift represents the cumulative effect of small variations whose day to day effect is scarcely noticeable, but whose continuation results in long-range changes in social patterns, and applies this to one small segment of Southeast Asia, a village in the Philippines.

212
Hauser, P. M. "Cultural and Personal Obstacles to Economic Development in the Less Developed Areas." *Human Organization* 18 (1959) 78-84. Considers these cultural obstacles in Southeast Asia to be of two kinds; aspects of the colonial heritage and elements of the indigenous cultures.

213
Van der Kroef, Justus M. "Southeast Asia — Some Anthropological Aspects." *Human Organization* 10 (1951) 5-15. The impact of Western technology on the Southeast Asian mind.

Education
214
Huq, Muhammad Shamsul. *Education and Development Strategy in South and Southeast Asia.* Honolulu: East-West Press, 1965. A major and detailed work, in which the economic value of education, and its role in change of cultural values, are studied in Indonesia, Philippines, India and Pakistan.

215
Silcock, T. H. *Southeast Asian University: A Comparative Account of Some Developmental Problems.* Durham: Duke University Press, 1964. A former dean of University of Singapore surveys in a general manner the difficulties, shortages and successes of Southeast Asian universities, and their role in the community.

216
Hayden, Howard. *Higher Education and Development in South-East Asia.* Paris: Unesco, 1965. A report on an inquiry into the role of institutions of higher learning in the development of their Southeast Asian countries begun in 1961, and surveying the present position and estimating the future responsibilities of higher education in the region.

217
Fischer, Joseph. "The University Student in South and South-East Asia." *Minerva* 2 (1963) 39-53. Their widespread involvement in politics, and the causes of student unrest.

218
Hla Myint, U. "The Universities of Southeast Asia and Economic Development." *Pacific Affairs* 35 (1962) 116-127. The relationship of higher education to government, and other issues, are treated here.

219
Neff, Kenneth. *Selected Bibliography on Education in Southeast Asia.* Washington: Government Printers, 1963. Produced by the then Department of Health, Education, and Welfare, this annotated list surveys recent publications of each country in turn.

BURMA

GENERAL

Burma is a Buddhist land, with an inward-looking tradition that today is very much alive. Ringed by mountains and jungle where independent-minded peoples wander, a central plain that in antiquity produced several states now supports a rice-growing population. The few decades of new independence, after one hundred years of British administration and uncomfortable association with India, have been insufficient as yet to produce stability and progress. The former appears possible; the later not yet acknowledged by all as an acceptable dogma justifying existence.

Several generations of scholars have labored over the relics of the ancient past and the more utilitarian records of the contemporary scene. Burma's society, its history and languages, have received attention, particularly from British and Burmese scholars, and, more recently, by Americans. Nevertheless this scholarship has but scratched the surface, and as with other countries of Southeast Asia, the gaps in our knowledge of this state and its people are wide.

Bibliographies
220
Trager, Frank N. (ed.). *Annotated Bibliography of Burma.* New Haven: Human Relations Area Files, 1956. An easily available and useful 230 page bibliography covering books and articles in English on the social and human sciences.

221
Trager, Frank N. *Furnivall of Burma: an annotated bibliography of the works of John S. Furnivall.* New Haven: Yale University, 1963. A useful list.

222
Tin Ohn. "Modern Historical Writing in Burmese 1724–1942," in D. G. E. Hall (ed.). *Historians of South East Asia.* London: Oxford University Press, 1961. 85-93. A bibliographical essay dealing with non-European writings on Burmese history.

223
Shorto, H. L. and others. *Bibliographies of Mon-Khmer and Tai Linguistics.* London: Oxford University Press, 1963. Eight sections are devoted to the Mon-Khmer area, covering Mon, Mon-Khmer, Khasi, Malay Peninsula (non Malay) Cham and Nicobarese languages.

224
Yi Yi, Ma. "Burmese Sources for the History of the Konbaung Period 1752–1885." *Journal, Southeast Asian History* 6 (1965) 48-66. Inscriptions, chronicles, literature and Burmese official records are described.

Journals

225

Journal, Burma Research Society, Rangoon: University of Rangoon. Established in 1911, publishes articles on Burmese history and social sciences.

Land, People, and Language

PHYSICAL AND CULTURAL GEOGRAPHY

226

Dobby, E. H. G. *Southeast Asia.* London: University of London Press, 8th ed. 1964. Chapters 9, 10 and 11 are on Burma, covering in depth physical, climatic, political and social aspects of geography.

227

Stamp, Lawrence Dudley. *India, Pakistan, Ceylon and Burma.* London: Methuen, 1957. Burma is treated in this reprint of the relevant sections of the 9th edition of his *Asia: A Regional and Economic Geography* (where Burma is chapter 4) on 381-406. A description, with maps, of its physical and climatic geography and contemporary land use.

228

Spencer, Joseph E. *Asia East by South: a Cultural Geography.* New York: John Wiley, 1954. A brief but excellent study of Burmese historical geography in chapter 16, "The Irrawaddy Valley Becomes Burma."

229

Dunlop, Richard. *Burma.* New York: Doubleday, 1959. A simple outline prepared with the co-operation of the American Geographical Society.

230

Spate, O. H. K. and Trueblood, L. W. *"Rangoon: A study in Urban Geography." The Geographical Review* 32 (1942) 56-73. Nine maps of Rangoon add strength to notes on the site of the city, demography, port activity, and functional topography.

231

Fisher, Charles A. *Southeast Asia.* 2nd ed. New York: E. P. Dutton, 1964. Burma receives attention in this major geographical work on pp. 430-483, as well as in the section on the "Mainland States — Physical Introduction," on pp. 407-429. Useful bibliography.

232

Fisher, Charles A. "Burma," in W. Gordon East and O. H. K. Spate (eds.). *The Changing Map of Asia, a Political Geography.* New York: E. P. Dutton, 1950. 179-246. Concentrates on political geography, although the physical and cultural geography of Burma also is reviewed.

233

Stamp, L. Dudley. *A New Geography of India, Burma and Ceylon.* Bombay: Orient Longmans, 1948.

234

Khin Ma Lay. "Urban Study of the Sittang Valley." *Journal, Burma Research Society* 45 (1962) 163-180. Compares settlement patterns and land use in and near four major agricultural towns.

235

Chibber, H. L. "Geography of South Tenasserium and the Mergui Archipelago." *Journal, Burma Research Society* 17 (1927) 127-156. Covers in particular economic geography, such as tin, rubber, fisheries, and population, as of 1926.

236

Stamp, L. D. "The Irrawaddy River." *Geographical Journal* 95 (1940) 329-359.

237

Taylor, Carl. *Getting to Know Burma.* New York: Coward-McCann, 1962. A simple survey of the country and its people.

PEOPLES

238

Scott, Sir J. G. *The Burman: His Life and Notions,* by Shway Yoe (pseud.). Introduction by John K. Musgrave. Norton, 1963. A reissue of a two-volume classic published originally in 1882, describing Burmese life and customs; per-haps still the best single source of information on Burmese culture. A mine of information.

239

Koop, John Clement. *The Eurasian Population in Burma.* New Haven: Cultural Report 6, Southeast Asia Studies, Yale University, 1960. Two brief studies, previously published, here brought together by Dr. Richard Coughlin. One survey in 1948 is on social and economic conditions, the other a demographic survey.

240

Lehman, F. K. *The Structure of a Chin Society. A tribal people of Burma adapted to a non-western civilization.* Illinois Studies in Anthropology 3. Urbana: University of Illinois, 1964. A detailed study of one of the minority races of Burma.

241

Theodorson, G. A. "Minority Peoples in Burma." *Journal, Southeast Asian History* 5 (1964) 1-16. Historical and demographic data on the Karens, Shans, Indians, Chinese, Mons, Arakanese, Kachins, Chins and others.

242

Lowis, Cecil Champain. *The Tribes of Burma.* Rangoon: Government Printing, 1949. First published in 1910, as Vol. 4 of *The Ethnographical Survey of Burma,* this has still useful bibliographic notes on the various peoples of Burma.

243

Stevenson, H. N. C. *The Hill Peoples of Burma.* London: Longmans, Green, 1944. A brief but excellent 50-page description.

244

Thet, Kyaw. "Cultural Minorities in Burma." In H. Passim (ed.). *Cultural Freedom in Asia.* Rutland: C. E. Tuttle, 1956.

245

Yegar, Moshe. "The Panthay (Chinese Muslims) of Burma and Yunnan." *Journal, Southeast Asian History* 7 (1966) 73-85. A group who revolted in Yunnan, China in 1856 and were crushed by 1875; many fled to Burma and still exist as a small community.

246

Leach, Edmund R. *Political Systems of Highland Burma, A Study of Kachin Social Structure.* London: G. Bell, 1954. A sociological study which concentrates on the social structure of the Kachins, referring also to religion and folk tales; much theory interwoven with field research.

247

Marshall, Harry. *The Karen Peoples of Burma: A Study in Anthropology & Ethnology.* Columbus: Ohio State University, 1922. Perhaps still the best study, of the few attempted, of this distinctive minority group in Burma.

248

McCall, Anthony Gilchist. *Lushai Chrysalis.* London: Luzac, 1949. A sympathetic study of the Chin people in India near the Burma border, by an I.C.S. officer who lived among them in the Lushai Hills.

249

Collis, Maurice S. *Lords of the Sunset, a Tour of the Shan States.* London: Faber & Faber, 1938. The Shan princes and their courts, and the Shan area generally.

250

White, Walter Grainge. *The Sea Gypsies of Malaya.* London: Seeley, Service, 1922. Despite its title, an account of the nomads of the Mergui Archipelago, their customs and way of life.

LANGUAGE

251

Judson, Adoniram. *Judson's English and Burmese Dictionary.* Unabridged 9 ed. As revised and enlarged by E. O. Stevens, Fr. Mason and F. H. Eveleth. Rangoon: Baptist Board of Publications, 1956. The most comprehensive dictionary available.

252

Halliday, R. *A Mon-English Dictionary.* Bangkok: Siam Society, 1922. A 500-page compilation by a missionary who worked largely among the Mons, not of Burma, but Thailand.

HISTORY

The history of Burma has been well summarized by John Cady, who distinguishes Old Burma, British Colonial Rule and Independent Burma. We have few accounts of "Old Burma," the period of over 1,000 years, when successive Burmese States, based on Prome, Thaton, Pagan and Pegu had their hour and died. Even the last of these, the Burma of Ava, is only a little better known, and it is only the Kongbaung dynasty, with its fatal clash with the British in Bengal, that has been narrated in any detail.

The colonial period of Burma, the 19th and 20th century, is better known. A transformation occurred; whether temporary or not, superficial or profound, has yet to be seen, but the outside world crashed into Burma and influenced it for 100 years. This has been studied to some extent, as has the new independence; difficulties hindering research and study in Burma today suggest, however, it may be as difficult to analyze the current scene as to investigate the history of early Pegu.

General Works

253

Cady, John. *A History of Modern Burma.* Ithaca: Cornell University Press, 1958. A substantial and stimulating work. In four sections: Old Burma and its Disappearance; British Colonial Rule; The Renaissance of Burmese Nationalism; Re-emergence of Independent Burma; with a supplement covering the years after 1956, entitled: The Swing of the Pendulum. Substantial bibliography. The pivot for modern historical studies of Burma.

254

Silverstein, Josef. "Burma," in George McT. Kahin (ed.). *Governments and Politics of Southeast Asia.* 2nd ed. Ithaca: Cornell University Press, 1964. As with the other sections of this work, this is an able and extremely useful survey in four parts: The Historical Background; The Contemporary Setting; The Political Process; Major Problems; together with useful reading list.

255

Furnivall, John J. *Colonial Policy and Practice; a Comparative Study of Burma and Netherlands India.* New York: New York University Press, 1956. A thorough, original and temperate critique of the colonial policies of Burma and the Netherland Indies (Indonesia).

256

Trager, Frank N. *Burma — From Kingdom to Republic. A Historical and Political Analysis.* New York: Praeger, 1966. A comprehensive survey, which after a brief outline of 19th and 20th century Burmese history under the British gives an analysis of the complex factors that produced post-war Burma; together with an evaluation of its present neutral attitude in foreign affairs.

257

Woodman, Dorothy. *The Making of Burma.* London: The Cresset Press, 1962. A general history and study of Burma today, based for the most part on secondary sources, but with original contributions in interpretation.

258

Hall, D. G. E. *Burma,* London: Hutchinsons, 3rd ed. 1960. A compact history which gives a clear and reliable summary of events.

259

Desai, Walter Sadgun. *India and Burma.* Calcutta: Orient Longmans, 1954. Sponsored by the Indian Council on World Affairs, this is a survey of Indian-Burmese relations from antiquity to post-war times and the Burmese re-expression of its national desires and feelings.

260

Hall, D. G. E. *Europe and Burma.* London: Oxford University Press, 1945. A succinct account in 18 brief chapters, of British, Portuguese, Dutch and French contacts with Burma from the 16th century to the annexation of Thibaw's Kingdom in 1886.

261

Harvey, G. E. *British Rule in Burma 1824–1942.* London: Faber & Faber, 1946. A critical look at the destructive aspects of British administration and the lawlessness that followed the elimination of traditional authority.

262

Pearn, B. R. *History of Rangoon.* Rangoon: American Baptist Press, 1939. One of the few studies of the great ports of Southeast Asia, a scholarly study of Rangoon's 19th and 20th century role by a former lecturer at the University who later became historical adviser to the British foreign office.

263

Htin Aung, Maung. *The Stricken Peacock: Anglo-Burmese Relations 1752–1948.* The Hague: N. Nijhoff, 1965.

264

Ray, Nihar-Ranjen. *An Introduction to the Study of Theravada Buddhism in Burma.* Calcutta: Calcutta University Press, 1946. An historical study, based upon temple inscriptions and Burmese language materials, of the arrival and dissemination of Buddhist thought, up to the early 19th century.

265

Burma Research Society Journal. Fiftieth Anniversary Publications. 2 vols. Rangoon. Sarpay Beikman Press, 1960, 1961. Papers published at its 50th anniversary conference providing a comprehensive survey of Burmese history; articles by John Cady, W. S. Desai, F. N. Trager, Maung Maung Hla, L. D. Stamp, B. R. Pearn, and others.

Pagan, Ava, and the Toungoo Dynasty

266

Hall, D. G. E. *A History of South-East Asia.* London: MacMillan, 1964. A straightforward account of the empires of Pagan and Ava is given in chapters 6 and 19.

267

Wales, H. G. Quaritch. *Ancient South-East Asian Warfare.* London: Bernard Quaritch, 1952. Burma's indebtedness to India in this aspect of its culture is stressed, in two chapters, pp. 115-90.

268

Luce, G. H. "Notes on the Peoples of Burma in the 12th and 13th Century A.D." *Journal, Burma Research Society* 42 (1959) 52-74. Information on peoples, places and history culled from the 300-odd inscriptions of the Pagan dynasty.

269

_____. "Burma's debt to Pagan." *Journal, Burma Research Society* 22 (1932). The leading scholar of this period writes on the A.D. 1044-1287 empire.

270

_____. "Fu-kan-tu-lu." *Journal, Burma Research Society* 14 (1924) 91-99. Among other Southeast Asian references, Chinese sources of the Han dynasty describe parts of Burma.

271

_____. "Old Kyaukse and the coming of the Burmans." *Journal, Burma Research Society* 42 (1959) 75-112. Demonstrates that Kyaukse was the first home of Burmans in the plains, and uses Chinese, Pali and other sources of the 863–1174 period to fill in an obscure part of Burmese history.

272

Harvey, G. E. *History of Burma from the Earliest Times to 10 March 1824, the Beginning of the English Conquest.* London: Longmans Green, 1925. A pioneer work with detailed notes, tables and maps that subsequent generations of scholars still find provocative and valuable; based on Dutch, English, Chinese and Portuguese sources as well as inscriptions and other material in Burma.

273

Collis, Maurice. *She Was A Queen*. rev. ed. London: Faber & Faber, 1951. Based on a Burmese chronicle, a re-creation of the fall of the Pagan dynasty in the 13th century.

274

Damrong, Rajanubhah Prince. "Our Wars with the Burmese." *Journal, Burma Research Society* 38 (1955) 121-196; 40 (1957) 135-240, 241-347. Translated from the Siamese by U. Aung Thein, the wars between Burma and Siam from 1537 up to the 19th century are treated by an eminent Thai scholar.

275

Than Tun. "Religion in Burma: A.D. 1000–1300." *Journal, Burma Research Society* 42 (1959) 47-70. Old Burmese Buddhism: The heirarchy, followers, the way of life of the monks and then specifically the most famous of them.

276

_____. "History of Burma: A.D. 1300–1400." *Journal, Burma Research Society* 42 (1959) 119-133. A scholarly paper which with the following one, 135-150, "History of Burma: A.D. 1400–1500," by Tin Hla Thaw, contributes to our understanding of this period.

277

Pe Maung Tin, U and G H. Luce (trs.). *The Glass Palace Chronicle of the Kings of Burma*. London: Oxford University Press, 1923. A translation of part of a Royal Chronicle, giving an official account of Burmese history to the fall of Pagan, 1287; with a useful sketch of Burmese historiography in the introduction.

278

Furnivall, John S. "The History of Syrian." *Journal, Burma Research Society* 5 (1915) 1-8, 49-57, 129-151. A Pali text, found in a monastery in Syrian, together with English translation; information from A.D. 573 on administration and other aspects of history.

279

Le May, Reginald. *The Culture of South-East Asia*. London: Allen & Unwin, 1954. Burma from the 5th century onwards, at Old Prome, Thaton, Pagan and Pegu, is dealt with on pp. 44-60; with many illustrations.

Early European Contacts

280

Hall, D. G. E. *English Intercourse with Burma 1587–1743*. London: Longmans Green, 1928. The first book on Burma by the eminent British historian, who at this stage was professor of history at Rangoon; deals with East India Company interest, early contacts and unsuccessful settlement. This elaborates his "English Relations with Burma 1587–1686." *Journal, Burma Research Society* 17 (1927) 1-79.

281

Collis, Maurice. *The Grand Peregrination being the life and adventures of Fernao Mendes Pinto*. London: Faber & Faber, 1959. A biography of a Portuguese adventurer in 16th century Asia; Burma in 1539–40 is described on pp. 166-200, 207-229.

282

_____. *Siamese White*. London: Faber & Faber, 1941. A well-written account based on primary material of the adventurer who was at Mergui from 1683 to 1687.

283

Hall, D. G. E. "Studies in Dutch Relations with Arakan." *Journal, Burma Research Society*. 26 (1936) 1-31.

284

Ba, Vivian. "One Centenary Recalls Another." *Journal, Burma Research Society* 46 (1963) 65-79. Draws attention to the great stock of first-hand information on Burma left by the early Catholic missionaries and available in various parts of Italy; and gives extracts from *Storia del Cristianesimo nell' Impero Barmano Preceduta dalle notizie del Paese* by Luigi Gallo, published in 1862, it being the first account of the Catholic Church in Burma from the 16th century.

285

Furnivall, John S. "Europeans in Burma: the Early Portuguese." *Journal, Burma Research Society* 31 (1941) 35-40. A brief note of interest.

286

MacGregor, A. (trs.). "A Brief Account of the Kingdom of Pegu." *Journal, Burma Research Society* 16 (1926) 99-138. A translation, together with an historical introduction by D. G. E. Hall, of a contemporary Portuguese account of its fort at Pegu, 1600–1602, and a picture of lower Burma, 1599–1605.

The Konbaung Dynasty

During this period Burmese indigenous rule collapsed. A misguided attempt to invade India brought British retribution and the first Anglo-Burmese War of 1824. Britain acquired the coastline. During the remainder of the dynasty two other wars were fought, with King Mindon and Thibaw. In 1885 Britain acquired all of Burma and the last ruler was deposed after a brief resistance.

THE EARLY PERIOD

287

Hall, D. G. E. (ed.). *Michael Symes. Journal of His Second Embassy to the Court of Ava in 1802*. London: Allen & Unwin, 1955. The editor's 80-page historical introduction is a valuable addition to this diary of the dramatic events observed by Symes on his way to Ava. Twenty-four well-edited documents are included.

288

Pearn, B. R. "The Burmese Embassy to Vietnam, 1823–24." *Journal, Burma Research Society* 47 (1964) 149-172. Seeking support against the Thai, an unsuccessful mission to Hue.

289

Hall, D. G. E. "From Mergui to Singapore 1686–1819. A Neglected Chapter in the Naval History of the Indian Ocean." *Journal, Siam Society* 41 (1953) 1-18. Outlines the long-felt need by the British for a naval base on the eastern side of the Indian Ocean, and traces the search for it.

290

Pearn, B. R. "Araken and the First Anglo-Burmese War 1824–25." *Far Eastern Quarterly* 4 (1944) 27-40. Conflicting claims by the Burmese and the British over this border province led to war, the detailed troop movements of which are described.

291

Hall, D. G. E. "R. B. Pemberton's Journey from Munipoor to Ava and from thence across the Yooma Mountains to Arracan. (14 July–October 1830)." *Journal, Burma Research Society* 43 (1960) 1-96. A keen-eyed observer gives a picture of Burma unobtainable elsewhere.

292

_____. "Burney's Comments on the Court of Ava, 1832." *Bulletin, School of Oriental and African Studies, University of London*. 20 (1957) 305-314. Notes by the British emissary, with annotations.

293

Desai, Walter Sadgun. *History of the British Residency in Burma, 1826–1840*. Rangoon: University of Rangoon, 1939. A large work that deals in detail with 14 momentous years, involving the efforts of the British in India to keep out of hostilities, the Anglo-Burmese War of 1824–25 and the early years of King Tharrawaddy.

294

_____. "Events at the Court and Capital of Ava During the First Anglo-Burmese War." *Journal, Burma Research Society* 27 (1937) 1-14. Burmese ignorance and pride accompanied the disastrous and confused events as the British proved irresistible.

295

Furnivall, J. S. "As it was in the beginning." *Journal, Burma Research Society* 18 (1928) 51-61, and "The Early Revenue History of Tenasserim: Land Revenue," 83-93. Two scholarly articles involving A. D. Maingy, the first British Officer in Mergui and Tavoy in the 1820's, when this southern area was controlled by Penang.

296

Sarkar, S. C. "The Negrais Settlement and After." *Journal, Burma Research Society* 22 (1932) 47-67. Thirty pages of records dealing with the 1752-1759 British settlement on the island, and subsequent developments after its capture by Alaungpaya.

297

Hall, D. G. E. "The Tragedy of Negrais." *Journal, Burma Research Society* 21 (1931) 59-133. A detailed account of the East India Company's settlement on the island and the massacre of its inhabitants in 1759.

298

Luce, G. H. "Chinese Invasions of Burma in the 18th Century." *Journal, Burma Research Society* 15 (1925) 115-128. Based on Burmese and Chinese sources; Alaungpaya is surprised by a 1766 Chinese invasion or "invasion?" and bitter fighting in 1766 and 1767 resulted.

299

Low, James. "History of Tenasserim." *Journal, Royal Asiatic Society* 2 (1835) 248-275, 3 (1836) 25-54, 287-336, 4 (1837) 42-108, 304-332, 5 (1839) 141-164, 216-263. A history in the grand manner of long ago, with demography, ethnology, religion, laws, language (Mon), revenue, geology, geography, trade and music, sharing chapters with history. Burmese history is Irrawaddy valley-centered: this is not.

300

Crawford, John. *Journal of an Embassy from the Governor-General of India to the Court of Ava in the year 1827.* 2 vols. London: Henry Colburn, 1934. A clear and intelligent account by a British diplomat-scholar, supplemented by information from various sources; an invaluable contemporary record.

THE LATER PERIOD

301

Saimong Mangrai, Sao. *The Shan States and the British Annexation.* Ithaca: Data Paper 57, Southeast Asia Program, Cornell University, 1965. The British occupation of this mountainous area after the deposition of King Thibaw in 1885, together with an account of the people and the area itself, with copious quotations from contemporary sources.

302

Harvey, G. E. "The Conquest of Upper Burma," in H. H. Dodwell (ed.) *The Cambridge History of the British Empire. 5. The Indian Empire.* Cambridge: Cambridge University Press, 1932. 432-447. A concise account covering the period 1852-1918, dealing with annexation and administration.

303

Furnivall, J. S. "Safety First — A Study in the Economic History of Burma." *Journal, Burma Research Society* 40 (1957) 24-39. Gives a number of examples illustrating the impact of the Suez Canal opened in 1869 on Burma's economic development; draws a clear contrast between 1861 and 1885.

304

Ma Kyan. "King Mindon's Councillors." *Journal, Burma Research Society* 44 (1961) 43-60. Describes the 5 courts which administered the civil, military, and judicial branches of government, and names the ministers who controlled power in Mindon's time.

305

Thaung. "Burmese Kingship in Theory and in Practice During the Reign of Mindon." *Journal, Burma Research Society* 42 (1959) 171-185

306

Christian, John L. "Thebaw: Last King of Burma." *Far Eastern Quarterly* 3 (1944) 309-312. A brief note on his life in exile after his deposition in 1885.

307

Langham-Carter, R. R. "The Burmese Army." *Journal, Burma Research Society* 27 (1937) 254-276. Describes the partly western-influenced army of the late 19th century.

308

Anderson, Courtney. *To The Golden Shore; the Life of Adoniram Judson.* Toronto: Little Brown, 1956. A large work, describing the career of the first Protestant missionary in Burma 1813-1850, who absorbed himself in educational work and became a much loved and influential figure; comparable to Bliss of Beirut.

309

Trager, Helen G. *Burma Through Alien Eyes. Missionary Views of the Burmese in the Nineteenth Century.* New York: Praeger, 1966. Well-chosen excerpts from the writings of 19th century Christian missionaries on Burmese people, politics, religion and culture.

310

Kaung, U. "A Survey of the History of Education in Burma Before the British Conquest and After." *Journal, Burma Research Society* 47 (1963) 1-124. A London thesis, on the monastic and lay schools of the early 19th century, the Christian mission schools, developments after 1824 and government controlled teaching from 1867.

311

Htin Aung, M. (coll. & trs.). *Burmese Monk's Tales.* New York: Columbia University Press, 1966. A collection of tales told by the chief monk under King Mindon, as a way of commenting on current conditions and problems, which portray the Burmese way of life on the eve of Burma's final annexation by the British.

The Colonial Period

GOVERNMENT

312

Ba, U. *My Burma: The Autobiography of a President.* New York: Taplinger, 1958. Author was a lawyer and former president, and writes here a personal narrative of Burmese politics and relations with the British and Japanese in the 1930's and 1940's.

313

Thompson, John Seabury. "Marxism in Burma," in Frank N. Trager (ed.) *Marxism in Southeast Asia, a Study of Four Countries.* Stanford: Stanford University Press, 1959. 14-57. The pre-war Marxist influence of the 1930's among the young nationalists, and their activities then and in the forties, is described in detail.

314

Donnison, F. S. V. *Public Administration in Burma: a Study of Development During the British Connection.* London: Royal Institute of International Affairs, 1953. A brief outline of the constitutional and administrative steps taken in the development of government in British Burma.

315

Thompson, Virginia and R. Adloff. *The Left Wing in Southeast Asia.* New York: William Sloan Associates, 1950. The pre-war Thakins and other nationalists are in chapter 4; a useful study based on interviews and contemporary sources.

316

Collis, Maurice. *Trials in Burma.* London: Faber & Faber, 1938 (New York: Penguin, 1945). An eye-witness account of the Saya San rebellion, anti-Indian riots and other disturbances of 1930-31.

317

_____. *The Journey Outward: An Autobiography.* London: Faber & Faber, 1952; and *Into Hidden Burma: An Autobiography.* London: Faber & Faber, 1953. A two volume account by a staunch supporter of the Burmese of his experiences as an officer in Burma from 1912 as well as general political developments, to 1934.

318

Sens, Nirmal C. *A Peep into Burma Politics 1917–1932*. Allahabad; Kitabistan, 1945. A book of memoirs written by an exile during the war, who recalls his early acquaintanceship with the nationalist pioneers.

319

Mya Sein, Daw. *Administration of Burma: Sir Charles Crosthwaite and the Consolidation of Burma*. Rangoon: Zabu Meitswe Pitaka Press, 1938. Burmese and British sources are used to explain administrative developments after 1885 at the village and district level.

320

White, Sir Herbert Thirkell. *A Civil Servant in Burma*. London: Arnold, 1913. Author served for over 30 years, rose to be Lt. Governor; gives here a clear account of British administration between 1878 and 1910. Subsequently wrote one of the provincial geographies of India, entitled *Burma*. Cambridge: Cambridge University Press, 1923.

321

Crosthwaite, Sir Charles Hawkes Todd. *The Pacification of Burma*. London: Arnold, 1912. Author was involved in British Burma administration after 1885, and was primarily responsible for the abolition of the indigenous village administration system.

322

Ireland, Alleyne. *The Province of Burma, a Report Prepared on Behalf of the University of Chicago*. 2 vols. Boston: Houghton, Mifflin, 1907. A wide survey of the state, with appendices containing considerable official material.

323

Nisbet, John. *Burma under British Rule — and Before*. 2 vols. London: Constable, 1901. A useful picture of Burma in the late 19th century, with chapters on administration, agriculture, the people, history.

324

Aung, Maung Tha and Maung Mya Din. "The Pacification of Upper Burma, A vernacular history." *Journal, Burma Research Society* 31 (1941) 80-136.

325

Great Britain. *Government of India Act. 1935. Government of Burma Act 1935*. London: His Majesty's Stationery Office, 1936. Cmd. 5181. The great Acts which separated the two countries and set them clearly on the way to self-rule and independence.

326

————. *Report on the Rebellion in Burma Up to May 3 1931, and Communique Issued by the Governor of Burma May 19, 1931*. London: His Majesty's Stationery Office, 1931. Cmd. 3900. The detailed result of the official inquiry into the Saya San Rebellion.

327

Great Britain, India Office. *Report on Indian Constitutional Reforms*. London: His Majesty's Stationery Office, 1918. Cmd. 9109. Known as the Montague-Chelmsford Report, this policy recommendation has relevance to Burma, as one of the provinces of India.

ECONOMICS

328

Christian, John Leroy. *Modern Burma, A Survey of Political and Economic Development*. Berkeley: University of California Press, 1942. A wide survey of pre-war Burma, and although weak on nationalist movements, reliable and impartial; with useful statistics and a bibliography of now hard to secure materials.

329

Tun Wai, U. *Economic Development of Burma from 1800 to 1940*. Rangoon: University of Rangoon, 1961. A Burmese presents his Yale M.A. thesis.

330

Zinkin, Maurice. *Asia and the West*. London: Chatto and Windus, 1951. A survey of Burma's Socio-Economic problems of the 20th century, pp. 93-110.

331

Andrus, James Russell. *Burmese Economic Life*. Stanford: Stanford University Press, 1948. A good description of the economy of pre-war Burma, surveying agriculture, timber, oil and other primary industries, with particular emphasis on the decade after 1937. The economic consequences of the Japanese occupation are made clear; well documented and with extensive use of basic statistics.

332

Furnivall, J. S. *An Introduction to the Political Economy of Burma*. Rangoon: Burma Book Club, 1931. Author takes a decidedly anti-colonial stand in considering the economic developments of Burma, most of which were of little benefit to the Burmese.

333

Aye Hlaing. "Trends of Economic Growth and Income Distribution, 1870–1940." *Journal, Burma Research Society* 47 (1964) 89-148. A subsistence economy is replaced by the development of rice, forestry, petroleum and other export products, calling for labor and investment imports.

334

Binns, Sir Bernard Ottwell. *Agricultural Economy in Burma*. Rangoon: Government Printing & Stationery, 1948. An official report written in India in 1943 by an agricultural specialist. This is a detailed survey of agriculture before 1941.

335

Cheng, Siok Hwa. "The Development of the Burmese Rice Industry in the Late Nineteenth Century." *Journal, Southeast Asian History* 6 (1965) 67-80. Describes the rapid growth of the rice industry after the Irrawaddy delta plain came under British rule in 1852.

336

————. "Land Tenure Problems in Burma, 1852 to 1940." *Journal, Malaysian Branch, Royal Asiatic Society* 38 (1965) 106-134. Land alienation, unsatisfactory tenancy conditions, unhappy peasants, and the legislative measures taken to ameliorate this.

337

Baxter, James. *Report on Indian Immigration*. Rangoon: Government Printing and Stationery, 1941. A detailed official study, the Baxter Report underlines the economic and social problems presented to the Burmese by the Indians as well as their dependence for many basic services upon them.

338

Andrew, E. J. L. *Indian Labor in Rangoon*. London: Oxford University Press, 1934. A substantial study of the mass movement that brought Indian labor in the early 20th century to work in the docks and elsewhere in Rangoon, and the problems that then arose.

339

Silverstein, Josef. "Politics and Railroads in Burma and India." *Journal, Southeast Asian History* 5 (1964) 17-28. The government of India introduced the railroad to Burma in 1887. The railroad was managed and developed by the government, with little relevance to Burmese conditions.

340

Maung Shein. "State Investment in Burma Railways 1874–1914." *Journal, Burma Research Society* 44 (1961) 165-182. Outlines how 215 million rupees were invested on 1600 miles of railroad, and estimates their impact on the economy.

341

Callis, Helmut G. *Foreign Capital in Southeast Asia*. New York: Institute of Pacific Relations, 1942. A brief study in which chapter eight, pp. 88-96 touches on Burma, outlining European but not Indian investment.

342

Crozier, Ralph. "Antecedents of the Burma Road in Nineteenth Century." *Journal, Southeast Asian History* 3 (1962) 1-18. The long discussions, plans, projects, and expeditions to build a railway to Yunnan in the late 19th century.

The Japanese Occupation

343

Elsbree, Willard H., *Japan's Role in Southeast Asian Nationalist Movements, 1940 to 1945*. Cambridge: Harvard University Press, 1953. The war-time political measures of the Japanese in Burma, and the role of Aung San and other Burmese leaders are set out clearly.

344

Nu, Thakin. *Burma Under the Japanese*. New York: St. Martins Press, 1954. An account of the war years by U Nu, later to become prime minister of an independent post-war Burma, which focuses narrowly on the collaborating government and Japanese-Burmese relations in Rangoon.

345

Khin, U. *U Hla Pe's Narrative of the Japanese Occupation of Burma*. Ithaca: Data Paper 41, Southeast Asia Program, Cornell University, 1961. A narrative recorded by the author, giving a vivid eye-witness account of the 1942–1945 period.

346

Slim, Sir William. *Defeat into Victory*. London: Cassell, 1956. A classic study of the war. The commanding general of the British 14th Army narrates the retreat to India and the victorious return, 1942–45.

347

Kirby, S. Woodburn. *The War Against Japan*. Vol. II, *India's Most Dangerous Hour*. London: Her Majesty's Stationery Office, 1958; Vol. III. *The Decisive Battles*. HMSO, 1962; and Vol. IV. *The Reconquest of Burma*. HMSO, 1965. The official British war history; detailed and accurate.

348

Mountbatten of Burma, Vice-Admiral The Earl. *Report to the Combined Chiefs of Staff by the Supreme Commander, South East Asia 1943–1945*. London: His Majesty's Stationery Office, 1951. A valuable survey of the Burmese campaign; of interest also for the political developments of the immediate Burmese post-war scene, in which the liberal earl played some part.

349

Donnison, F. S. V. *British Military Administration in the Far East, 1943–46*. London: Her Majesty's Stationery Office, 1956. Burma receives major treatment here, with British and Burmese developments considered in an impartial manner.

350

Collis, Maurice S. *Last and First in Burma*. London: Faber & Faber, 1956. Based on the official and personal papers of the last governor of colonial Burma, explains the conquest and the controversial immediate post-war years.

351

Guyot, Dorothy. "The Burma Independence Army: A Political Movement in Military Garb," in Josef Silverstein (ed.). *Southeast Asia in World War II: Four Essays*. New Haven: Monograph Series 7, Southeast Asia Studies, Yale University, 1966. 55-66. How the pre-war aims of the Thakins were maintained by Aung San during the war, and the integrated army which resulted.

352

Masters, John. *The Road Past Mandalay*. London: Michael Josef, 1961. A well-written biography of a British Gurkha officer who participated in the jungle war.

353

Morrison, Ian. *Grandfather Long Legs*. London: Faber & Faber, 1947. Wartime life in Burma with the Karens, who were attacked both by the Japanese and the Burmese.

354

Romanus, Charles F. and Riley Sunderland. *Stilwell's Mission to China*. K. R. Greenfield (ed.). *The United States Army in World War II. China-Burma-Indian Theatre*. Washington: Office of the Chief of the Military History, Department of the Army, 1953. The controversial role of General Stilwell in the Burma campaign receives official recognition.

355

Silverstein, Josef. "Transportation in Burma During the Japanese Occupation." *Journal, Burma Research Society* 39 (1956) 1-17. Outlines water, rail and road transport operated by the Japanese, and discusses the attitude of the Burmese.

356

Sykes, Christopher. *Orde Wingate: A Biography*. Cleveland & New York: The World Publishing Co., 1959. The leader of the Chindits.

357

Ogburn, Charton. *The Marauders*. New York: Harper & Brothers, 1959. American participation outlined.

358

Yuji, Aida, *Prisoner of the British. A Japanese Soldier's Experiences in Burma*. London: Cresset Press, 1966.

POLITICAL PATTERNS

The political patterns of independent Burma present an interesting study. Here we can see the fairly rapid decline and discrediting of the parliamentary democracy with which the new state had begun its life. A leader, U. Nu, made little effort to have it accepted and the efforts of many others rendered it more and more ineffective. During the last few years, a military regime has been groping, as were the civilians before it, for a type of government more attune to indigenous attitudes and way of life; a system which would enable them to achieve their desired goals in a way that all could accept as Burmese. Such a search by the mid-1960's produced neither internal peace nor progress, but there seemed little interest in returning to the rejected parliamentary pattern of the 1940's.

Burma remains, somewhat reluctantly it would appear, as a member of the family of nations. It is not, as it was for many centuries, entire unto itself, and it has to have some awareness and relationship with other powers. Its chief interest in foreign relations has been with China.

General Works

359

Tinker, Hugh. *The Union of Burma: a Study of the First Years of Independence*. 3rd ed. London: Oxford University Press, 1961. An authoritative and absorbing study by a political scientist, which deals in detail with the country's government and administration, culture and religion, education and social services, land, trade, communications, politics, defense and foreign relations.

360

Maung Maung. *Burma's Constitution*. The Hague: M. Nijhoff, 1961. An historical and legal account, illuminating difficulties with candor, of independent Burma's constitution; includes the texts of numerous documents.

361

Pye, Lucian W. *Politics, Personality and Nation Building: Burma's Search for Identity*. New Haven: Yale University Press, 1962. An examination of the way in which Burma is dealing with the processes of change and acculturation, with the problems of shortages of capital, training and other facilities, and with the forces of nationalism; doubts eventual success in its efforts to build a nation.

362

Silverstein, Josef. "Burma," in George McT. Kahin (ed.). *Governments and Politics of Southeast Asia*. 2nd ed. Ithaca: Cornell University Press, 1965. 75-179. Excellent for any study of the political patterns of contemporary Burma.

363

Trager, Frank N. *Building a Welfare State in Burma 1948–1956*. New York: Institute of Pacific Relations, 1958. A sound study of the difficult years immediately following independence, when an inexperienced leadership grappled with a war-torn land, a chaotic and insurrectionary state and devastated economy.

364

———— and associates. *Burma*. 3 vols. New Haven: Human Relations Area Files, 1956. A most comprehensive survey of virtually all aspects of contemporary Burma; uneven in quality, but nevertheless of great utility.

365

Thomas, Samuel Bernard. "Burma," in Lawrence K. Rosinger & Associates. *The State of Asia. A Contemporary Survey*. New York: A. A. Knopf, 1951. A useful account of the 1948–1950 period.

366

Cady, John, and others. *The Development of Self-Rule and Independence in Burma, Malaya and the Philippines*. New York: Institute of Pacific Relations, 1948. Most useful for the immediate post-war years.

367

Von Der Mehden, Fred R. *Religion and Nationalism in Southeast Asia*. Madison: University of Wisconsin, 1963. Buddhism as an animating force for Burmese nationalists figures prominently here, both on the pre-war scene and in the politics of independent Burma.

368

Smith, D. E. *Religion and Politics in Burma*. Princeton: Princeton University Press, 1965. A major work which surveys the relationship of Buddhism to politics, which has varied since pre-British days; fully half the book discusses the interaction of organized religion with politics in the contemporary period.

369

Nash, Manning. "Party Building in Upper Burma." *Asian Survey* 3 (1963) 197-202. Burmese ideas about personal power provide the key to understanding political organization in the villages of Upper Burma.

370

Isaacs, Harold R. (ed.). *New Cycle in Asia. Selected Documents on Major International Developments in the Far East 1942–1947*. New York: MacMillan, 1947. Sponsored by the IPR, this selection contains the British Government's Command Paper 7029 of 1947, being the independence agreement between Prime Minister Attlee and Aung San.

371

Furnivall, J. S. *The Governance of Modern Burma*. New York: Institute of Pacific Relations, 1958. A brief study of post-war Burma by one who participated in the administration devised.

Aung San and U Nu

372

Maung Maung (ed.). *Aung San of Burma*. The Hague: M. Nijhoff, 1962. Ably introduced by Harry Benda, this is an unorthodox biography, in 5 parts, of Burma's radical nationalist leader, a charismatic figure whose assassination precipitated a national crisis.

373

————. *A Trial in Burma; the Assassination of Aung San*. The Hague: M. Nijhoff, 1962. The Trial of U. Saw and others who killed Burma's great leader in 1947.

374

Thompson, John Seabury. "Marxism in Burma," in Frank N. Trager (ed.) *Marxism in Southeast Asia, a Study of Four Countries*. Stanford: Stanford University Press, 1959. 14-57. Aung San and his radical political movement is well described here, as are Burmese politics, 1946–56.

375

Butwell, R. *U Nu of Burma*. Stanford: Stanford University Press, 1963. A major biographical study of a charismatic personality and a truly great man in many respects, which throws light on the nationalist movement from the 1920's, as well as making clear the failure of parliamentary democracy in the post-war period.

376

Tinker, Hugh. "Nu, the Serene Statesman." *Pacific Affairs* 30 (1957). His career from university days to political activity; and, in detail, post-war leadership of his country.

377

Silverstein, Josef. "Politics, Parties and the National Elections in Burma." *Far Eastern Survey* 25 (1956) 177-184. The 1955–56 election campaign and the April 1956 election.

Army Rule

378

Trager, Frank N. "The Failure of U Nu and the Return of the Armed Forces in Burma." *The Review of Politics* 25 (1963) 309-328. Describes the background to the coup staged on March 2, 1962 by general Ne Win, and his replacement of an incompetent civilian parliamentary government with military rule.

379

Silverstein, Josef. "Burma: Ne Wins Revolution Reconsidered." *Asian Survey* 6 (1966) 95-102. A survey of developments since the army rule began in 1962, but particularly in 1965.

380

Pye, Lucian W. "The Army in Burmese Politics," in John J. Johnson (ed.) *The Role of the Military in Underdeveloped Countries*. Princeton: Princeton University Press, 1962. 231-251. A penetrating study not merely of the 1958 movement, but which, taken with his other article in the same book, "Armies in the process of political modernization," pp. 69-90, gives an appreciation of the general role of the army in underdeveloped countries.

381

Dupuy, Trevor N. "Burma and its Army: A Contrast in Motivations and Characteristics." *Antioch Review* 20 (1960-61) 428-440. A study of the role of the army in the 1958 coup.

382

Badgley, John H. "Burma's Military Government: A Political Analysis." *Asian Survey* 11 (1962) 24-31. An eye-witness account of the Burmese Revolutionary Council following the military take-over.

383

Burma, Revolutionary Council. *The Burmese Way to Socialism: The Policy Declaration of the Revolutionary Council*. Rangoon: Ministry of Information, 1962. The official reasons why the army in command has decided to pursue a Buddhist-Socialist path.

384

Badgley, John H. "The Communist Parties of Burma," in Robert Scalopino (ed.) *The Communist Revolution in Asia*. New Jersey: Prentice-Hall, 1965. 290-309. Describes the splintered communist movement in Burma with its four rival groups and outlines the chaotic history of communism in Burma from the 1930's.

385

Von Der Mehden, Fred. "Burma's Religious Campaign against Communism." *Pacific Affairs* 33 (1960) 290-300. Outlines the way in which the army in power used Buddhism in a systematic attempt to combat communism.

386

Furnivall, J. S. "Communism and Nationalism in Burma." *Far Eastern Survey* 18 (1949) 193-197. Little danger Burma will go communist, great danger it will go to pieces.

387

Butwell, Richard and Fred Von Der Mehden. "The 1960 Election in Burma." *Pacific Affairs* 33 (1960) 144-157. A thoughtful study of the 18-month caretaker government of General Ne Win, the faction rivalry that developed and the elections of February 1960 when the Clean AFPFL won an overwhelming victory.

388

Cady, John F. "Religion and Politics in Modern Burma." *Far Eastern Quarterly* 12 (1953) 149-163. An excellent survey of the differing role played by the Buddhist religious leaders in the political life of old Burma, in colonial Burma and in the immediate post-war period, followed by a discussion of three important religious Acts of 1950, and the new importance being given to old values.

389

Josey, A. "The Political Significance of the Burma Workers Party." *Pacific Affairs* 31 (1958) 372-379. Socialists and left-wingers generally receive sympathetic treatment.

390

Trager, Frank N. "The Political Split in Burma." *Far Eastern Survey* 27 (1958) 145-155. Reviews the 1955-57 background to the internal dissensions inside the ruling Anti-Fascist Peoples Freedom League, and the army take-over in September 1958.

Minority Problems

391

Silverstein, Josef. "Politics in the Shan State: The Question of Secession from the Union of Burma." *Journal of Asian Studies* 18 (1958) 43-58. The Shan State had the constitutional right to secede from January 4, 1958; discusses its grievances, political movements and possibilities, and the role of the army.

392

_____. "The Federal Dilemma in Burma." *Far Eastern Survey* 28 (1959) 97-105. Outlines the political problems caused by the multi-racial composition of the one state.

393

Fairbairn, Geoffrey. "Some Minority Problems in Burma." *Pacific Affairs* 30 (1957) 299-311. The Shan State and Arakan are considered.

394

Thet, Kyaw. "Burma: the Political Integration of Linguistic and Religious Minorities," in P. Thayer (ed.) *Nationalism and Progress in Free Asia*. Baltimore: Johns Hopkins, 1956. 156-168. A brief survey of the difficulties involved in creating an integrated state out of the numerous groups with different languages and cultural backgrounds.

395

Mahajani, Usha. *The Role of Indian Minorities in Burma and Malaya*. Bombay: Vora & Co., 1960.

Foreign Relations

396

Johnstone, William C. *Burma's Foreign Policy*. Cambridge: Harvard University Press, 1963. Burma's attempt to maintain itself as a nonaligned nation, neutral in everything, is examined in the light of its proximity to China, and in comparison with other small nations. A useful bibliography of published data papers on specific foreign policy episodes, and other material.

397

Maung Maung. *Burma in the Family of Nations*. Amsterdam: Djambatan, 1957. The relations of the Burmese State with the outside world during the 19th and 20th centuries, as seen by a lawyer-diplomat; with nearly 80 pages of diplomatic and political documents.

398

Trager, Frank. "Burma and China." *Journal, Southeast Asian History* 5 (1964) 29-61. Sino-Burmese relations traced from the Pagan dynasty of the 13th century; major attention given to the border problems of independent Burma.

399

Whittam, Daphne E. "The Sino-Burmese Boundary Treaty." *Pacific Affairs* 34 (1961) 174-181.

400

Hinton, Harold C. *China's Relations with Burma and Vietnam*. New York: Institute of Pacific Relations, 1958.

401

Leach, E. "The Frontiers of 'Burma'." *Comparative Studies in Society and History* 3, (1960) 49-68. The idea that states should have a definite boundary corresponding with a clear difference of culture and language is considered as a European myth; then looks at "Burma," the imprecisely defined frontier region, and the position of hill people and valley people.

402

Thomson, John S. "Burmese Neutralism," *Political Science Quarterly* 72 (1957) 261-283. Burma's attitude during Chinese border penetration in 1956, the Suez crisis, the Hungary revolt, as well as Korea in 1950, is justified, although misunderstood, by the U. S. A.

403

Kozicki, Richard J. "The Sino-Burmese Frontier Problem." *Far Eastern Survey* 26 (1957) 33-38. The problem of precisely demarcating a boundary along a mountainous, sparsely inhabited region that had belonged at various times to various people.

404

Tinker, Hugh. "Burma's Northeast Borderland Problems." *Pacific Affairs* 29 (1956) 324-346. The geographical, historical and human factors that complicate the establishment in 1956 of a satisfactory border with China.

405

Thomson, John S. "Burma: A Neutral in China's Shadow." *Review of Politics* 19 (1957) 330-350. Deals with U Nu's attitude to China, Burma's determination, through fear of China, to give no pretext for Chinese interference.

406

Trager, Frank N. "Burma's Foreign Policy, 1948-1956. Neutralism, Third Force and Rice." *Journal of Asian Studies* 16 (1956) 89-102. An analysis of Burma's non-aligned, socialist foreign policy, as practiced from 1948 by U Nu and the Anti Facist Peoples Freedom League.

407

Kozicki, Richard J. "Burma and Israel: A Study in Friendly Asian Relations." *Middle East Affairs* 10 (1959) 109-116. Israel, attempting to secure friends behind the Moslem lands that ring her, has won the tacit support of Burma.

408

Kaznacheev, Alex U. *Inside a Soviet Embassy: Experiences of a Russian Diplomat in Burma*. Philadelphia: Lippincott, 1962. A diplomat who defected gives an interesting account of how Russian efforts were made in Rangoon, for the most part unavailing and badly managed, to influence the Burmese by propaganda and espionage.

Miscellaneous Works

409

Lewis, Norman. *Golden Earth, Travels in Burma*. New York: Scribner's, 1952. A keen-eyed observer describes post-war Burma with insight; excellent photographs.

410

Mannin, Ethel. *Land of the Crested Lion. A Journey through Modern Burma*. London: Jarrods, 1955. A sympathetic yet penetrating description of modern Burma by an author who was the guest of the Buddha Sasana Council in a 1954 tour of Burma.

411

Seagrave, G. S. *Burma Surgeon*. New York: W. W. Norton, 1944. An American missionary doctor describes in this and subsequent books, *Burma Surgeon Returns* (1946) and *My Hospital in the Hills* (1955), his work in the Shan State he loved so well.

412

Kyaw Yin. "The Problem of Crime and the Criminal, and its solution in Socialist Burma." *Journal, Burma Research Society* 47 (1964) 205-224. Surveys colonial law and its inadequacies in a Buddhist society, and outlines the new institutional measures of the revolutionary government.

413

Nyi Nyi. "The Development of University Education in Burma." *Journal, Burma Research Society* 47 (1964) 11-76. Outlines the history of the University of Rangoon from 1920, when it had its first political-student strike; with details of post-war political-university matters.

ECONOMIC PATTERNS

Like the other countries of Southeast Asia, the economic pattern of Burma is essentially agrarian. Rice is the major crop, with other primary products also prominent. It has few industries but, due partly to the ineffective administration of the independent government, partly to a wealth of other reasons, it has numerous economic problems. These have been little studied and rarely solved.

414

Walinsky, Louis J. *Economic Development in Burma, 1951–1960*. New York: Twentieth Century Fund, 1962. A fully documented analysis and appraisal of Burma's eight-year development plan by the former chief economic advisor to the government of Burma, who is not uncritical of U. S. aid efforts nor of Burmese policy.

415

Tun Wai, U. *Burma's Currency and Credit*. Bombay: Orient Longmans, 1962. The country's banking, currency, its various credit facilities and other aspects of Burma's economics; the role of the post-war government in central banking and in state-owned institutions receives considerable attention.

416

Hauser, Philip M. *Development of Statistics in Burma 1951–52*. New York: UN Technical Assistance Program, 1954. A brief 30-page summary of modern Burmese statistical organizations by the man who initiated them.

417

Thompson, Warren S. *Population and Progress in the Far East*. Chicago: University of Chicago Press, 1959. The unprecedented population growth of modern times presents much of the world with a major problem; Burma is discussed on pp. 302-12.

418

Myo Htun Lynn. *Labour and the Labour Movement in Burma*. Rangoon: University of Rangoon Press, 1961. A study of the labor movement from 1948, undertaken in rather difficult conditions.

419

Hagen, Everett E. *On the Theory of Social Change. How Economic Growth Begins*. Homewood, Illinois: The Dorsey Press, 1962. Chapter 18 (432-470). Examines colonial rule in Burma and the Burmese character, in order to help explain the failure of post-independent Burma to achieve economic growth.

420

Thet Tun. "Organization of Planning Machinery: Lessons from Burmese Experience." *Journal, Burma Research Society* 46 (1963) 27-34. A brief outline of Burmese planning organization, first established by the constitution of independent Burma.

421

Madi, K. S. "Public Expenditures and Inflationary Impact in Burma 1951–59." *Journal, Burma Research Society* 45 (1962) 49-78. Government operations, as the single most important factor in the economy, are critically examined.

422

Tin Htoo. "An Overall View of the Rubber Industry of Burma." *Journal, Burma Research Society* 45 (1962) 91-108. Rubber exports, acreage, production, ownership; with maps, tables and charts. See also his "A District by District Account of the Rubber Industry of Burma," on pp. 181-192, same issue; again with excellent maps.

423

Allen, Robert L. "Burma Clearing Accounts Agreements." *Pacific Affairs* 31 (1958) 147-164.

424

Ady, Peter. "Economic Bases of Unrest in Burma." *Foreign Affairs* 29 (1951) 475-481. Outlines the numerous problems inherited from the past and those of the first two years of independence.

425

Jacoby, Erich H. *Agrarian Unrest in Southeast Asia*. New York: Columbia University Press, 1949. Burma is considered in chapter three, pp. 70-100. Population pressure, agricultural indebtedness, unsatisfactory tenancy occupation, labor inadequacies, lack of capital, rebellions and riots; a sad story.

426

Thompson, Virginia. *Labour Problems in Southeast Asia*. New Haven: Yale University Press, 1947. Burma's problems are on pp. 17-61.

SOCIAL AND CULTURAL PATTERNS

Burma is essentially a Buddhist land. This is its major social characteristic. The adjustment of this ancient faith to the sometimes conflicting challenges of modernity provide part of the fascinating pattern observable in Burma. The various minority races, with different ways of life, provide another. The pre-Buddhist elements still flourishing, the village adjustments to the independent state, the individual in the city and his reaction to politics, all these facets help to shape a social pattern of some perplexity.

427

Nash, Manning. *The Golden Road to Modernity; Village Life in Contemporary Burma*. New York: Wiley, 1965. A traditional society on the eve of modernity is studied, in all its socio-cultural aspects, by an anthropologist in complete command of his materials.

428

Brant, Charles S. *Tadagale. A Burmese Village in 1950*. Ithaca: Data Paper 13, Southeast Asia Program, Cornell University, 1954. A forty-page study.

429

Sarkisyanz, E. *Buddhist Backgrounds of the Burmese Revolution*. The Hague: M. Nijhoff 1965. Endeavors to show that a modernistic re-interpretation of Buddhism is the major social factor promoting national union.

430

Brohm, John F. "Buddhism and Animism in a Burmese Village." *Journal of Asian Studies* 22 (1963) 155-167. The persistent life of pre-Buddhist elements is noted, as well as aspects of the more sophisticated Buddhism.

431

King, W. *A Thousand Lives Away: Buddhism in Contemporary Burma*. Cambridge: Harvard University Press, 1964. A stimulating study on numerous aspects of the major social characteristic of Burma, its Theravada Buddhism.

432

Mendleson, E. Michael. "Religion and Authority in Modern Burma." *World Today* 16 (1960) 110-118. Relations between church and state, internal divisions within the Sangha, the question of religious and political allegiance and the control by laymen of the Order.

433

_____. "The Uses of Religious Scepticism in Modern Burma." *Diogenes* (1963) 94-116. An examination of a process whereby religious authority is achieved, and how religion can be manipulated for secular ends.

434

Htin Aung, Maung. *Folk Elements in Burmese Buddhism.* London: Oxford University Press, 1962. Pre-Buddhist cults, in which sorcery, alchemy, astrology and the worship of spirits, which flourished under the patronage of the brown-robed Ari monks, still have a strong life in Burma today.

435

Mendleson, E. Michael. "The King of the Weaving Mountain." *Journal, Royal Central Asian Society,* 48 (1961) 229-237. A sociologist describes a weikzas, part of an unorganized non-hierarchal aspect of contemporary Burmese religion.

436

Maung Maung. *Law and Custom in Burma and the Burmese Family.* The Hague: M. Nijhoff, 1963. Burmese Buddhist law is studied against the background of Burmese society, politics and government.

437

Mendleson, E. M. "A Messianic Buddhist association in Upper Burma." *Bulletin, School of Oriental and African Studies, University of London* 24 (1961) 560-580. An elaboration of his article in the JRCAS, describing certain beliefs and rituals which do not fit neatly into the category of either Buddhism or Animism.

438

Htin Aung, U. *Burmese Law Tales: The Legal Element in Burmese Folk Lore.* London: Oxford University Press, 1962. This publication of 65 tales is a sequel to his earlier anthology of folk tales (Oxford, 1948); here the relevance of each tale to an aspect of Burmese law is outlined.

439

_____. *Folk Elements in Burmese Buddhism.* London: Oxford University Press, 1962. Non-Buddhist elements incorporated in Burmese Buddhism are traced back to the village cults of the 11th century.

440

_____. *Burmese Folk Tales.* London: Oxford University Press, 1948. Some 75 stories collected from villages in Upper and Lower Burma, assembled in four groups; animal, romantic, wonder and humorous tales, together with a detailed introduction.

441

_____. *Burmese Drama: a Study, with Translations, of Burmese Plays.* London: Oxford University Press, 1937. In four parts; rise of the vernacular tongue as a modern literary medium; origin and development of modern Burmese drama; biographical sketches of playwrights; Burmese dramatic practice. Four major plays have their text in full.

442

Mi Mi Khaing. *Burmese Family.* Bloomington: Indiana University Press, 1962. Family life in Burma a generation ago with details of village and urban life, trade, education, the arts and customs of the people.

443

Slater, Robert Henry Lawson. *Paradox and Nirvana.* University of Chicago Press, 1951. A brief study of the theological-philosophical content of Burmese Buddhism and the social aspects; substantial bibliography as befitting a former Ph.D. thesis.

444

Sien Tu, U. "The Psychodynamics of Burmese Personality." *Journal, Burma Research Society* 47 (1964) 263-286. Groups together a number of distinct personality traits to help explain the characteristics of the Burmese; these include hospitality, aggressiveness, egocentricity, fear of shame and ridicule, and deprecatory habits.

445

Ba, Han. "The Burmese Complex: Its Roots." *Journal, Burma Research Society* 46 (1963) 1-10. The customs which affect a Burmese from earliest childhood shape his social character.

446

Griswold, Alexander B. and others. *The Art of Burma, Korea, Tibet.* New York: Methuen, 1964.

THAILAND

GENERAL

Thailand, once Siam, has a modern history far happier than that of its neighbors, for it, alone of all Southeast Asia, preserved independence in the face of the 19th-century flood from Europe that overwhelmed all else. Adroitly it accommodated itself, as did Japan (with which it has often been compared, and with which it feels a certain mutual appreciation). Its earlier history, as that of its neighbors, is known only sketchily. A picture of a small, static, agricultural Buddhist civilization is nearly all we have. Few records are available, other than archaeological ruins of temples at various early capitals, and like that of Burma and Vietnam, the ancient past of Thailand is difficult to trace in any detail. Various threads have remained as a continuity in the nation's culture, however, notably the monarchy, the Buddhist faith, and the Thai race and tongue. Today a homogeneous people finds national unity not merely desirable, but with an attitude in contrast to that of other peoples in Southeast Asia, perfectly feasible, for these threads of continuity hold them together. With this unity there is a gradual acceptance also of economic development as a goal in the nation's life, and modernization proceeds, assisted by a non-doctrinaire attitude to the outside world.

Bibliographies

447

Sharp, Lauriston, and associates. *Bibliography of Thailand.* Ithaca: Data Paper 20, Southeast Asia Program, Cornell University, 1956. A 64-page list of selected books, articles, and newspaper items, annotated by the staff of the Cornell Thailand Research Project; a general coverage, but of particular use to students concerned with sociological studies or contemporary developments.

448

Chulalongkorn University. *Bibliography of Material About Thailand in Western Languages.* Bangkok: Post Publishing Co., 1960. A 325-page alphabetical listing of authors, under various social science headings.

449

Embree, John F. and Lillian Ota Dotson. *Bibliography of the Peoples and Cultures of Mainland Southeast Asia.* New Haven: Southeast Asia Studies, Yale University, 1950. Thailand and the Thai are listed on pp. 461-558, with items in alphabetical order of authors, and particular emphasis on anthropology.

450

Halpern, Joel M. *An Annotated Bibliography on the Peoples of Laos and Northern Thailand*. Department of Anthropology, Brandeis University, 1961. Reproduced by Duopage Process, in the U. S. A. Micro-Photo Division, Bell and Howell Co., Cleveland 12, Ohio, U. S. A. As with other bibliographies on Laos, this six-page list contains many items relevant to northeastern Thailand.

451

Embree, John F. and William L. Thomas. *Ethnic Map and Gazetteer of Northern Southeast Asia*. New Haven: Southeast Asia Studies, Yale University, 1950. Considers the tribes of northern Thailand.

452

Mason, John B. and H. Carroll Parish. *Thailand Bibliography*. Gainesville: University of Florida Libraries, 1958.

453

Wyatt, David K. and Constance M. Wilson. "Thai Historical Materials in Bangkok." *Journal of Asian Studies* 25 (1965) 105-118. Indicates briefly the nature, origins, extent, accessibility and location of manuscript and archival materials relating to the Bangkok period of Thai history preserved in the Thai Department of Fine Arts and elsewhere.

454

Damrong Rajanubhah, Prince. "The Story of the Records of Siamese History." *The Siam Society, Fiftieth Anniversary Publication*, 1. Bangkok: The Siam Society, 1954. 79-98. Outlines Thai sources, including inscriptions, chronicles and other material, for pre-1800 history.

455

Bernath, Frances A. *Catalogue of Thai Language Holdings in the Cornell University Libraries through 1964*. Ithaca: Data Paper 54, Southeast Asia Program, Cornell University, 1954. A 5,000 item, 236-page listing of the cataloged cards.

Journals

456

Journal of the Siam Society (1904–   ). Published annually by an autonomous scholarly body with royal patronage, this includes articles on art, society, history, and archaeology. A series of volumes containing a collection of articles from earlier issues was produced to commemorate the fiftieth anniversary of the society.

457

Siam Rath Weekly Review. Bangkok. An English language weekly review associated with a Thai language daily, the *Sayam Rath*.

458

The Bangkok Post. A daily English language newspaper initiated in 1946, the best in Thailand.

Land, People, and Language

These three basic elements in Thailand are very simple. The land is essentially a plain, today a padi field, drained by one of Asia's more important rivers, the Menan or Chao Phrayo. The people are the Thai, who moved down from the north and settled by stages from perhaps the 13th-century or earlier. Their language is Tai. These are broad generalizations, and there are exceptions. There are non-Buddhist non-Thai peoples in the south, and there are others in the north and elsewhere who do not live on the plain or grow padi. These attract the study of specialists, as the items below indicate. Nevertheless, the popular view of Thailand as a vast green cup is correct. It is one of the more easily defined areas in Southeast Asia, a factor which has helped contribute to its stability and unity.

459

Fisher, Charles A. *South-East Asia*. 2nd ed. New York: E. P. Dutton, 1964. After earlier chapters in which traditional Siam is considered as part of "South-East Asia as an entity," modern Thailand is discussed on 484-528; the land and the people, its modernization, regional economies and urban and political geography being among the aspects covered. Useful bibliography.

460

Pendleton, Robert L., Robert C. Kingsberry, and others. *Thailand: Aspects of Landscape and Life*. New York: Duell, Sloan & Pearce, 1962. An internationally famous soil authority includes in this comprehensive study of the physical and economic geography of Thailand much of his research in agronomy and agricultural economics.

461

————. "Land Use in Northeastern Thailand." *Geographic Review* 33 (1943) 15-41. A detailed survey, accompanied by numerous photographs, of rice and other agriculture, cattle-raising and other land uses of the Korat region, comprising nearly a third of Thailand.

462

Zimmerman, Carle C. "Some Phases of Land Utilization in Siam." *Geographic Review* 27 (1937).

463

Seidenfaden, Erik. *The Thai Peoples*. Book I. *The Origins and Habitats of the Thai People, with a Sketch of their Material and Spiritual Culture*. Bangkok: Siam Society, 1958. Eight chapters describe the various Thai groups throughout Thailand, after explaining their origins in west central Asia and their slow migration to Thailand.

464

Young, Gordon. *The Hill Tribes of Northern Thailand: A Socio-Ethnological Report*. 2nd ed. Bangkok: The Siam Society, 1962. Concerned with the origins and habitats of the hill tribes; outlines significant changes in their social, cultural and economic patterns brought about by settlement and by contact with the Thai.

465

Brandt, John H. "The Negrito of Peninsula Thailand." *Journal, Siam Society* 49 (1961) 123-158. A detailed study of the nomadic aborigine of the mountains in the south, people who are linked to similar small groups crouching deep in the Malay jungle.

466

Bernatzik, H. A. *The Spirits of the Yellow Leaves*. London: Robert Hale, 1958. A description of various Thai groups, with comparative detail from Laos.

467

Blofield, John. "Some Hill Tribes of North Thailand (Miaos and Yaos)." *Journal, Siam Society* 43 (1955) 1-20. Hill people straddling the borders of China, Burma, Laos, Thailand, and Vietnam.

468

Shorto, H. L. and others. *Bibliographies of Mon-Khmer and Tai Linguistics*. London: Oxford University Press, 1963. Being volume 2 of London Oriental Bibliographies; half of these briefly annotated entries relate to Thai.

469

Haas, Mary R. *Thai-English Students Dictionary*. Stanford: Stanford University Press, 1964. A full-length dictionary, providing a comprehensive coverage for English-speaking students of Thai; with an accurate guide to pronunciation.

470

————. *The Thai System of Writing*. Washington: American Council of Learned Societies, 1956. A slim book of a little more than 110 pages which describes and explains the script and the writing system of Thailand.

471

Anuman Rajadhon, Phya. *Thai Language*. Thailand Culture Series 17. Bangkok: National Culture Institute, 1954. A clear outline by a well-known scholar of the general characteristics of the Thai language, its history and its alphabet.

HISTORY

Unlike the great Chinese civilization to the north, Thailand has no long and illustrious history. It has a record of continuous settlement, it has the ruins of several earlier capitals on its plain to indicate the existence of states and government, but not until Ayudhya was founded in the 14th century is there any clear picture. Indeed, it is centuries after that before a historical narrative can be sustained in any detail. Scholars have tried and are continuing to try to probe into the unknown history of Ayudhya and the earlier states, but relatively speaking, inquiry is still at the beginning in this respect.

Bangkok, the present capital, however, has maintained its history now for almost 200 years, and with this state we are on firmer ground. Both from the scholarship of the Thais themselves, including the illustrious work of the royal house, and from scholars of the Western World, the modern history of Thailand is known, and although much more inquiry must take place before a full account is recorded, comparatively speaking there is considerable material available.

General Works

472
Blanchard, Wendell (ed.). *Thailand, Its Peoples, Its Society, Its Culture.* New Haven: Human Relations Area Press, 1958. A large survey by a number of authors, of history, politics, economics, social patterns, etc., with maps, tables, and lengthy bibliography.

473
Wilson, David A. "Thailand," in G. McT. Kahin (ed.) *Government and Politics in Southeast Asia.* 2nd ed. Ithaca: Cornell Universary Press, 1964. A valuable survey in four parts; the historical background, the contemporary setting, the political process, and major problems. A useful reading list.

474
Thompson, Virginia. *Thailand, the New Siam.* New York: MacMillan, 1941. A substantial work, in three parts; human and land geography, 19th and 20th century history and government; economic developments of the 19th and 20th centuries; social characteristics.

475
Vella, Walter Francis. *The Impact of the West on Government in Thailand.* Berkeley: University of California Press, 1955. A penetrating account of the modernization of Thailand in the 19th and 20th centuries, with the changes brought by Western ideas and methods on the monarchy and administration.

476
Ingram, James C. *Economic Change in Thailand since 1950.* Stanford: Stanford University Press, 1955. A detailed examination, based on primary material of the nation's change from a subsistence economy to being part of the trading economy of the world; with particular emphasis on the role of rice.

477
Skinner, George William. *Chinese Society in Thailand: an Analytical History.* Ithaca: Cornell University Press, 1957. A detailed study of the Chinese community within the Thai State, with major emphasis on the 20th century developments of both parties.

478
Hall, D. G. E. *A History of South East Asia.* 2nd ed. New York: St. Martin's Press, 1964. In the absence of one overall historical study of the state, this provides a single source summary of its history.

479
Graham, Walter Armstrong. *Siam.* 2 vols. London: 3rd ed. Moring, 1924. An early survey by a long-time British officer and resident in Thailand, with still useful chapters on racial and social groups, the country's history, educational system, art, music, and much else.

Early History

480
Le May, Reginald. *A Cultural History of South East Asia.* London: Allen and Unwin, 1954. Five of the twelve chapters concern Thailand exclusively, discussing with numerous archaeological illustrations its cultural and to some extent political history from the early Mon period of 8-century A.D. to the founding of Ayudhya in 1350 A.D.

481
Wood, William Alfred Rae. *A History of Siam from the Earliest Times to the Year A.D. 1781. rev. ed.* Bangkok: The Siam Barnakich Press, 1933. A useful pioneer work.

482
Wales, Horace G. Quaritch. *Ancient Siamese Government and Administration.* New York: Paragon, 1965. Published originally in London in 1934, this is a study from Thai sources of traditional Thai political and administrative practice and belief.

483
Heine-Gelden, Robert. "Conceptions of State and Kingship in Southeast Asia." *Far Eastern Quarterly* 2 (1942) 15-30. Later revised and published as Cornell Data Paper 18 (1956) this is a succinct examination of the ancient belief, not completely dispelled, that the social order of a state was divine and was related to the comos as a whole.

484
Dhani Nivat, Prince. "The Old Siamese Conception of the Monarchy." *Journal, Siam Society* 36 (1947) 91-106. The basic purpose, powers and limitations of the monarchy.

485
Le May, Reginald. *A Concise History of Buddhist Art in Siam.* Cambridge: Cambridge University Press, 1938. Indicates the origins and comments on the schools of Buddhist art in Siam, with particular reference to the history of the period prior to 16th century.

486
Wales, H. G. Quaritch. *Siamese State Ceremonies. Their History and Function.* London: B. Quaritch, 1931. Religious festivals and court ceremonies, Hindu in origin, accepted and adapted by Buddhist rulers.

487
Briggs, L. P. "Draraavati, the Most Ancient Kingdom of Siam." *Journal, American Orientalist Society* 65 (1945) 98-107.

488
Wyatt, David K. (ed.). *The Nan Chronicle.* Ithaca: Data Paper 59. Southeast Asia Program, Cornell University, 1966. A local history of an ancient state in what is now north Thailand, written in 1894, translated by Prasoet Churatana, and dealing with events from the 14th to the 19th century.

489
The Siam Society. *Selected Articles from the Siam Society Journal.* Vol. 3. *Early History and Ayudhya Period.* Bangkok: Siam Society, 1959. Contains 11 articles on early Thai history.

490
_____. *Selected Articles from the Siam Society Journal.* Vol. 4. *Lophburi, Bangkok, Bhuket.* Bangkok: Siam Society, 1959. Contains 9 articles, including various notes on Lophburi, founded in the 5th century and for many centuries the heart of Thailand.

491

_____. *Selected Articles from the Siam Society Journal.* Vol. 5. *Relationship with Burma — Part I.* Vol. 6. *Relationship with Burma — Part II.* Bangkok: Siam Society, 1959. The volumes translate 2 Burmese histories that deal with Burmese invasions of Siam in the 16th and 17th centuries, and Siamese invasions of Burma in the 17th and 18th centuries, with Ava captured in 1752.

492

Grimm, T. "Thailand in the Light of Official Chinese Historiography." A chapter in the "History of the Ming Dynasty." *Journal, Siam Society* 49, (1961) 1-20. Interesting Chinese notes of Thailand from the 14th, 15th, and 16th century.

493

Carthew, M. "The History of the Thai in Yunnan, 2205 B.C.–1253 A.D." *Journal, Siam Society* 40, 1 (1952) 1-38. Extracts from *History of the Southern Princes* by Yangtsai, translated by G. W. Clark. Shanghai: Shanghai Mercury Press, 1894.

494

Hoontrakul, Likhit. *The Historical Records of the Siamese-Chinese Relations commencing from ancient times up to the time when the Siamese people formed themselves into a State called Siam with the town of Sukhotai as Capital.* Bangkok: Thai Bithaya Press, 1953. Consists in part of translations and excerpts from Chinese works, only some of which have relevance to Thailand.

495

Gerini, G. E. "Siam's Intercourse with China (Seventh to Nineteenth Centuries)." *Asian Review* 10 (1900) 365-394; 11 (1901) 155-170.

496

Damrong, Prince. "Our Wars with the Burmese." *Journal, Burma Research Society* 38 (1955) 121-196; 40 (1957) 135-240; 40 (1958) 241-347. Wars from the Sixteenth to the Nineteenth Century.

497

Thein, U Aung. "Intercourse Between Siam and Burma as Recorded in the 'Royal Autograph Edition' of the History of Siam." *Journal, Burma Research Society* 25 (1935) 49-108; 28 (1938) 109-176; 232.

498

Spinks, Charles Nelson. "Siam and the Pottery Trade of Asia." *Journal of the Siam Society* 44 (1956) 61-112. An outline of the part played by Thai pottery, particularly Sawankalok ware of the 14th to 15th centuries, in trade with Japan and elsewhere; author ranges widely, uses Japanese and other sources.

499

Wolters, O. W. "Chen-li-fu, A State on the Gulf of Siam at the beginning of the 13th Century." *Journal of the Siam Society* 48, 2 (1960) 1-36. Translation from a a Chinese text, and commentary, describing a small state which in A.D. 1200–1205 established relations with the Sung dynasty.

500

Briggs, L. P. "Siamese Attacks on Angkor Before 1430." *Far Eastern Quarterly* 8 (1948) 3-33. This article is referred to also in the section on Cambodia, as are others relevant to Thailand.

501

Luce, G. H. "The Early Syam in Burma's History." *Journal of the Siam Society* 46 (1958) 123-214, 47 (1959) 59-101. The Shan in east Burma and northwest Thailand, from before the Mongol conquest of Yunnan in the mid-13th to the mid-14th centuries.

502

Coedes, G. "The origins of the Sukhodaya dynasty." *Journal, Siam Society* 14 (1921).

Early Europeans

As with other parts of Southeast Asia we have to turn to accounts by or of travelers and traders for a picture of the early state. The lack of indigenous documentation forces us to use this secondary and alien material. It illustrates a weakness in Southeast Asian studies not felt by scholars of other areas, but which nevertheless is a prop on which, for the time being, we must lean.

503

The Siam Society. *Selected Articles from the Siam Society Journal.* Vol. 7. *Relations with Portugal, Holland and the Vatican.* Bangkok: Siam Society, 1959. Includes a survey of 17th and 18th century relations between Siam and Holland, a translation of a 17th century Dutch description of Siam, as well as other articles relating to the 16th and 17th centuries.

504

_____. *Selected Articles from The Siam Society Journal.* Vol. 8. *Relationship with France, England and Denmark.* Bangkok: Siam Society, 1959. Various articles by E. W. Hutchinson and others on 17th century relations.

505

Bassett, D. K. "English Relations with Siam in the Seventeenth Century," *Journal, Malaysian Branch, Royal Asiatic Society* 34, 2 (1961) 90-105. Concerned mainly with correcting Anderson and Hutchinson by scholarly use of primary East India Company material not consulted by them.

506

Anderson, John. *English Intercourse with Siam in the Seventeenth Century.* London: Kegan Paul, 1890. A large work, based on contemporary records.

507

Collis, Maurice. *Siamese White.* London: Faber & Faber, 1951. A well-written account of Samuel White, late 17th century trader.

508

Furnivall, J. S. "Samuel White, Port Officer of Mergui." *Journal, Burma Research Society.* 7 (1915) 241-249. Was the *shahbandar* for the King of Siam.

509

Hutchinson, E. W. *Adventurers in Siam in the Seventeenth Century.* London: Royal Asiatic Society, 1940. The adventurers were mainly English, with the exception of Constantine Phaulkon, a Greek who dominates the period.

510

Boxer, C. R. *A True Description of the Mighty Kingdoms of Japan and Siam,* by François Caron and Joost Schouten. London: Argonaut Press, 1935. Reprinted from the English edition of 1663, with scholarly notes and lengthy historical introduction.

511

De La Loubre. *A New Historical Relation of the Kingdom of Siam, by Monsieur de La Loubre, Envoy Extraordinary from the French King, to the King of Siam, in the years of 1687 and 1688.* 2 vols. London: 1693. Reproduced by Duopage Process in the U. S. A. Microphoto Division, Bell & Howell; Cleveland 12, Ohio. An interesting account of Siam in the 17th century.

Early Bangkok Period

With the destruction of Ayudhya in the late 18th century, and the subsequent establishment of Bangkok, Thailand enters into a period of continuous and recorded history. It preserves its unity, its faith and its crown during the tumultuous years of the 19th century when the European invader deprives its neighbors of all three. It preserves Bangkok as its royal capital, when Hue and Ava both vanish. It adjusts to the West, and preserves its culture. Today, as in the late 18th century, its king sits in Bangkok, the ruler of an independent nation.

512

Vella, Walter Francis. *Siam Under Rama III 1824–1851*. Monograph for the Association of Asian Studies 4. Locust Valley: J. J. Augustin, 1957. A critical examination based on Thai sources, of developments during the reign of Rama VI, giving a vivid picture of Siam before modernization, and illustrating the breakaway tendencies and other problems of the outlying regions of Laos, Cambodia and the Malay States.

513

Tregonning, K. G. *The British in Malaya: The First Forty Years 1786–1826*. Tucson: University of Arizona Press, 1965. Relations between Thailand and the British on Penang in this period are covered in chapters six and seven, pp. 75-108.

514

Tarling, Nicholas. "British Policy Towards Siam, Cambodia, and Vietnam 1842–1858." *Asian Studies* 4 (1966) 240-258. Contrasts the differing reactions of these states to British missions and the relative importance of these states to the British.

515

Simmonds, E. H. S. "The Thalang Letters 1773–94; political aspects and the trade in arms." *Bulletin School of Oriental and African Studies, University of London* 26, 3 (1963) 592-619. An episode of South Thailand and the British; another article of relevance by Simmonds appears in the Malaysia section.

516

Dhani Nivat, Prince. "The Reconstruction of Rama I of the Chakri Dynasty." *Journal, Siam Society* 43 (1955) 21-48. Outlines generally the revival of literature, drama, music, architecture and national life, initiated in the late 18th century by the founder of the Chakri dynasty.

517

Crawfurd, John. *The Crawfurd Papers, A Collective of Official Records Relating to the Mission of Dr. John Crawfurd Sent to Siam by the Government of India in the Year 1821*. Bangkok: Vajiranana National Library, 1915. Although the British mission was a failure, its published records give a useful picture of many aspects of the country.

518

Burney, Captain H. *The Burney Papers*. 8 vols. Bangkok: Vajiranana National Library, 1910–1914. A British mission from 1825–26 which failed, but whose records, even more than those of Crawfurd, provide a useful source of information.

519

Sewell, C. A. Seymour. "Notes on Some Old Siamese Guns." *Journal, Siam Society* 19 (1922) 1-43. Interesting information on 16th to 19th century history of armies and armaments.

520

Gerini, G. "Historical Retrospect of Junk Ceylon Island." *Journal, Siam Society* 2 (1905) 3-109. An island off the west coast of Thailand which appears constantly in history; with particular reference to the late 18th and 19th centuries.

Early Modernizers

With European pressures becoming ever stronger, there were two paths of action; either to close the door and retreat, a path chosen by China and Burma; or to open the door to accommodate oneself to the new forces, a path chosen by Japan. Thailand also put its house in an order sufficient to stay independent. In this, two rulers carried their elite and the nation with them; Mongkut and Chulalongkorn.

521

Moffat, Abbot Low. *Mongkut, the King of Siam*. Ithaca: Cornell University Press, 1961. A life of the nineteenth-century autocratic modernizer of Siam; describes his early Western contacts, his measures; makes liberal use of a selection of the king's letters and decrees.

522

Mongkut. *The King of Siam Speaks. A Collection of Writings by King Rama IV, better known as King Mongkut*. Bangkok: Central Library, Chulalongkorn University, 1958. A 250-page collection of the papers of the dynamic king, the founder of modern Thailand.

523

Griswold, Alexander B. *King Mongkut of Siam*. New York: Asia Society, 1961. A good biography of an outstanding leader who retained control while skilfully opening up his state to modernization.

524

Smith, Malcolm. *A Physician at the Court of Siam*. London: Country Life, 1946. Contains useful personal comments on the Thai elite at the courts of King Mongkut, Chulalongkorn and Vajiravudh.

525

Tarling, Nicholas. "The Mission of Sir John Bowring to Siam." *Journal, Siam Society* 50, 2 (1962) 92-118. The Anglo-Siamese Treaty of 1855 which opened Thailand to regular trade and brought her in contact with the western world.

526

Prachoom Chomchai. *Chulalongkorn The Great*. Tokyo: Centre for East Asian Cultural Affairs, 1965. A volume of readings, edited and translated from Thai sources, of a remarkable ruler overshadowed by an illustrious father.

527

Tarling, N. "Siam and Sir James Brooke." *Journal, Siam Society* 48 (1960) 66-70. Another British attempt to open the door, but a failure.

528

Dhani Nivat, Prince. "The Reign of King Chulalongkorn." *Journal of World History* 2 (1954) 446-466. Internal developments, cultural revival, and foreign relations of an outstanding successor to Mongkut who died in 1910.

529

Kiernan, V. G. "Britain, Siam and Malaya: 1875–1885." *Journal, Modern History* 28 (1956) 1-20. A careful study based on official records of diplomatic moves concerning the Siamese controlled Malay States.

530

Sternstein, Larry. "The Distribution of Thai Centres at Mid-Nineteenth Century." *Journal, Southeast Asian History* 7 (1966) 66-72. A brief piece of historical geography, pinpointing the towns of 19th century Thailand, with map.

531

Briggs, Lawrence Palmer. "Aubaret and the Treaty of July 15, 1867. Between France and Siam"; and "The Aubaret vs. Bradley Case at Bangkok 1866–67." *Far Eastern Quarterly* 6 (1947) 122-138, 266-282. Details of Anglo-French rivalry in Siam.

532

_____. "The Treaty of March 23, 1907 between France and Siam and the return of Battambang and Angkor to Cambodia." *Far Eastern Quarterly* 5 (1946) 439-454. An outline of 19th century disputes which were settled for 30-odd years by the 1907 Treaty.

533

Thomson, R. Stanley. "Siam and France, 1863–1870." *Far Eastern Quarterly* 5 (1945) 28-46. Siam's reaction to France's assumption of authority in Cambodia.

534

Le May, Reginald. *The Coinage of Siam* 2nd ed. Bangkok: The Siam Society, 1961. From this it is possible to extract material of relevance to economic conditions, concerning trade, finance, etc., of this period.

535

Nunn, W. "Some Notes upon the Development of the Commerce of Siam." *Journal, Siam Society* 15 (1922) 78-102. An examination of foreign trade from 200 A.D. to 1856; with particular emphasis on the Bangkok period.

536

Bowring, Sir John. *The Kingdom and People of Siam*. 2 vols. London: Parker, 1857. A detailed account of many aspects of the state as it seemed to the sympathetic officer who negotiated the 1855 Treaty.

537

Wong, Lin Ken. "The Trade of Singapore 1819–1869." *Journal, Malayan Branch, Royal Asiatic Society* 33, 4 (1960). A scholarly monograph that contains a section on trade with Siam in this period, pp. 134-158.

538

Landon, Margaret. *Anna and the King of Siam*. London: Hamilton, 1956. A novel, carefully based on fact, making use of historical material, of the life of an English governess at King Mongkut's court.

539

Minney, R. J. *Fanny and the Regent of Siam*. London: Collins, 1962. A sequel to the previous work, dealing with the son of Anna Leonowens, and King Chulalongkorn; again based on documents and recollections of the time.

The Chinese

540

Skinner, George William. *Chinese Society in Thailand: an Analytic History*. Ithaca: Cornell University Press, 1957. A historical study of the Chinese community from the time of Ayudthia, with the concluding five chapters dealing with the 20th century; the economic importance of the Chinese and their assimilatory tendencies receive attention.

541

_____. *Leadership and Power in the Chinese Community of Thailand*. Ithaca: Cornell University Press, 1958. Another major work, which gives a comprehensive survey to the social background, values and influences, authority and alignments, the economic position and the politics of the Chinese, with 1951–1955 being the major period of assessment.

542

_____. "Change and Persistence in Chinese Culture Overseas: A Comparison of Thailand and Java." *Journal of South Seas Society* 16 (1960) 86-100. Challenges the "fact" that Chinese minorities in Southeast Asia never assimilate, by giving substantial evidence of such assimilation in Thailand.

543

Purcell, Victor. *The Chinese in Southeast Asia*. 2nd ed. London: Oxford University Press, 1965. The history and social and economic conditions of the Chinese in Thailand discussed on 81-165.

544

Skinner, G. William. "Chinese Assimilation and Thai Politics." *Journal of Asian Studies* 16 (1957) 237-250. Outlines earlier assimilation of Chinese until Thai policy from 1910 discouraged it; discusses also policy fluctuations to 1957.

545

Jiang, Joseph P. L. "The Chinese in Thailand: Past and Present." *Journal, Southeast Asian History* 7 (1966) 39-65. Discusses their changing status and role, with their economic and social position of the 19th century contrasted with the present.

546

Freedman, Maurice. "Chinese Communities in Southeast Asia: A Review Article," *Pacific Affairs* 31 (1958) 300-304. Interesting comments on current research by other scholars.

547

Coughlin, Richard J. "The Chinese in Bangkok." *American Sociological Review* 20 (1955) 311-316. Stresses the strength of the Chinese community, and emphasizes its resistance to assimilation.

548

_____. "The Status of the Chinese Minority in Thailand." *Pacific Affairs* 25 (1952) 378-389. Thai discriminatory policies towards the urban Chinese are examined.

549

_____. *Double Identity: The Chinese in Modern Thailand*. Hong Kong: Hong Kong University Press, 1960. A sociological study, based on 1951 and 1952 field work, ranging over a wide area of Chinese life particularly in Bangkok.

550

Landon, Kenneth P. *The Chinese in Thailand*. New York: Oxford University Press, 1941. An earlier work still valuable for its material on pre-war conditions and government attitudes and actions.

The Pre-Pacific War

The great lacunae in the history of Thailand are the sparsity of accounts of economic development (although there are some references on this subject in the section on economic patterns) and the almost complete absence of records dealing with the Japanese occupation period of 1942-1945. We do have, however, some accounts of political and other events, particularly from the watershed of 1932. Indeed it is this date that perhaps would serve more effectively in a truly Thai pattern of periodization.

551

Crosby, Sir Josiah. *Siam, the Crossroads*. London: Hollis and Carter, 1945. A brief but informative survey by a long-time British ambassador, of the country, the people, the pre-1932 politics and coup d'état, and the foreign relations of Thailand before the war.

552

Landon, Kenneth Perry. "Siam" in Lennox A. Mills and Associates. *The New Work of Southeast Asia*. Minneapolis: University of Minnesota Press, 1950. 246-272. An outline of events from 1932 to 1948.

553

_____. *Siam in Transition: a Brief Survey of Cultural Trends in the Five Years Since the Revolution of 1932*. Shanghai: Kelly & Walsh, 1939. An account of the events preceding and following the 1932 coup d'état, when the absolute monarchy was replaced.

554

_____. "Thailand's Struggle for National Security." *Far Eastern Quarterly* 4 (1944) 5-26. The survival flexibility of the Thai is illustrated by surveying relations with Europe in the 19th and 20th centuries, and with Japan from 1933 onwards.

555

Coast, John. *Some Aspects of Siamese Politics*. New York: Institute of Pacific Relations, 1953. Surveys in a personal, animated way the exciting developments of two decades: 1932 to 1952.

556

Martin, James V. "Thai-American Relations in World War II." *Journal, Asian Studies* 22 (1963) 451-467. Pre-Pacific-War developments as well as 1942–1945 activities are sketched in.

557

Purcell, Victor. "The Relinquishment by the United States of Extraterritoriality in Siam," *Journal, Malayan Branch, Royal Asiatic Society* 37, 1 (1964) 99-120. Britain relinquished its extra-territorial rights in 1909, but America did not follow suit until 1920. Reasons for the delay are explained.

558

Christian, John L. & Nobutake Ike. "Thailand in Japan's Foreign Relations," *Pacific Affairs*. 15 (1942) 195-221. An historical study of Japanese-Siamese contacts from 1635; but with major emphasis on the 1930's, and the Japanese arrival and occupation.

559

_____. "Thailand Renascent," *Pacific Affairs*. 14 (1941) 185-197. A review of Thailand's foreign relations of the 1930's, with emphasis on developments with French Indo-China.

560

Chakrabongse, Prince Chula. *Lords of Life: The Paternal Monarchy of Bangkok, 1782–1932*. New York: Taplinger, 1960. A history of the Chakkri Dynasty from its foundation in 1782, by one of those involved.

561

Landon, Kenneth Perry. "The Thailand's Quarrel with France in Perspective." *Far Eastern Quarterly* 1 (1941) 25-42. Cambodia as a bone of contention in the 19th and 20th centuries.

562

Zinkin, Maurice. *Asia and the West*. London: Chatto & Windus, 1951. A critical survey of the development of the socio-economic problems of 20th century Thailand, on pp. 169-177.

563

Vadakarn, L. V. *Thailand's Case*. Bangkok: Thai Commercial Press, 1941. A strongly-worded Thai protest against France for the territories such as Cambodia which it wrenched away from a weak 19th century Thailand.

564

Sayre, Francis B. "The Passing of Extraterritoriality in Siam." *American Journal of International Law*. 22 (1928) 70-88.

565

_____. *Siam: Treaties with Foreign Powers, 1920–1927*. Bangkok: Royal Siamese Government, 1928. French and English language versions of the treaties which cancelled the earlier, unequal treaties, and which established Thailand as an equal in the international world.

566

Wheatcroft, R. *Siam and Cambodia, in pen and pastel*. London: Constable, 1928. Deals largely with the Siamese scene.

567

Le May, Reginald. *An Asian Arcady*. Cambridge: Heffer & Son, 1926. A reflective book on the history, customs, and religion of the Lao people in north Thailand.

POLITICAL PATTERNS

The long traditions of the Thai are nowhere better evidenced than in its political patterns. Thai political leadership has been basically authoritarian throughout history. Although this authority was widened after 1932, it remains essentially the same pattern. This non-democratic system has worked effectively in achieving its main goals — national unity, independence, and now development. With so many of the world's scholars belonging to a cultural milieu that includes democracy, this pattern has attracted at times a non-scholarly and emotional antipathy. The fact that the country is non-Christian has aroused less feeling than the fact that it is non-democratic. Both factors are irrelevant, and fortunately this has been recognized by a number of scholars whose work is listed here.

568

Insor, D. Thailand: *A Political, Social and Economic Analysis*. New York: Praeger, 1963. Contemporary Thailand is depicted by an intimate and detailed study of social, religious, economic and, in particular, political life, with the roles of the major elements outlined with care.

569

Wilson, David A. *Politics in Thailand*. Ithaca: Cornell University Press, 1962. A study of the contemporary political patterns, with emphasis on such major factors in political power as the kingship, national leadership, the cabinet and bureaucratic government, the military, the political organizations; with a brief historical background.

570

_____. "Thailand," in G. McT. Kahin (ed.) *Governments and Politics in Southeast Asia*. 2nd ed. Ithaca: Cornell University Press, 1964. An informative and authoritative survey.

571

Simmonds, Stuart. "Thailand — A Conservative State" in Saul Rose (ed.) *Politics in Southern Asia*. New York: St. Martins Press, 1963. 119-142. Illustrates how the main goal of all, national unity, has produced a conservative and non-doctrinaire attitude.

572

Kruger, Rayne. *The Devil's Discus*. London: Casswell, 1964. In June, 1946, the young King of Thailand was found dead with a bullet wound in his head. The activities of this man and many near him among the political elite, in particular, Pridi Banomyong, are seriously and objectively examined.

573

Darling, Frank C. "Modern Politics in Thailand." *Review of Politics* 24 (1962) 163-182. A detailed examination of the administration of Field Marshal Sarit.

574

Nuechterlein, Donald E. "Thailand: Year of Danger and Hope." *Asian Survey* 6 (1966) 119-124. A brief survey of 1965.

575

Darling, Frank C. "Marshal Sarit and Absolutist Rule in Thailand." *Pacific Affairs* 33 (1960) 347-360. Considers that the overthrow of Phibun Songkhram in 1951 marked a major turning point in Thai political patterns. Compares Sarit's attitudes to the very different type of rule existing in the 1930's.

576

Wilson, David A. and Herbert, P. Phillips. "Elections and Parties in Thailand." *Far Eastern Survey* 27 (1958) 113-119.

577

Pickerell, Albert and Daniel E. Moore. "Elections in Thailand." *Far Eastern Survey* 26 (1957) 103-111. The February, 1957, elections to the National Assembly.

Administration

578

Siffin, William J. *The Thai Bureaucracy. Institutional Change and Development*. Honolulu: East-West Center Press, 1966. Portrays the institutional characteristics of the Thai bureaucracy, and the evolution of this system, with a coherent tradition; as in all developing nations the bureaucracy is much more than merely an instrument of administration, as Riggs has shown. As a complementary work to Riggs, it is administrative instrumentality, and its development is examined.

579

Riggs, Fred W. *Thailand: The Modernization of a Bureaucratic Polity*. Hawaii: East-West Center Press, 1966 Traces the processes of change that have occurred in Thai government and administration from the mid-nineteenth century; then examines contemporary Thai government, and the broad influence of the civil service on social and cultural changes.

580

Sutton, Joseph L. (ed.). *Problems of Politics and Administration in Thailand.* Bloomington: Department of Government, Indiana University, 1962. Seven papers on the working of municipal, provincial, and central government, by American scholars associated with the establishment of an Institute of Public Administration at Thammasat University, Bangkok.

581

Mosel, James N. "Thai Administrative Behaviour," in William J. Siffin (ed.) *Toward the Comparative Study of Public Administration.* Bloomington: Indiana University, 1957. 278-331.

582

Udyanin, Kasem and Rufus D. Smith. *The Public Service in Thailand. Organization, Recruitment and Training.* Brussels: International Institute of Administrative Sciences, 1954. A brief but useful 60-page study.

583

Evers, Hans-Dieter. "The formation of a social class structure: Urbanization, Bureaucratization and a Social Mobility in Thailand." *Journal, Southeast Asian History* 7, 2 (1966) 100-115. Lack of social mobility among Thai bureaucrats in Bangkok.

584

Reeve, W. D. *Public Administration in Siam.* London: Royal Institute of International Affairs, 1952. An outline of the development of the civil service and its major functions since 1932.

585

Chap Tharamathaj. *A Study of the Composition of the Thai Civil Service.* Bangkok: Institute of Public Administration, Thammasat University, Bangkok, 1962. An M.A. thesis, prepared under the supervision of W. J. Siffin.

586

Arsa, Meksawan. *The Role of the Provincial Governor in Thailand.* Bangkok: Institute of Public Administration. Thammasat University, 1962. A competent study.

587

Choop Karnjarsaprakorn. *Municipal Government in Thailand as an Institution and Process of Self Government.* Bangkok: Institute of Public Administration. Thammasat University, 1962.

588

Wira Wimonnit. *Historical Patterns of Tax Administration in Thailand.* Bangkok: Institute of Public Administration, Thammasat University, 1961.

Village Political Patterns

589

Sharp, Lauriston, "Local initiative and central government in Thailand," in Vu Quoc Thuc (ed.) *Social Research and Problems of Rural Development in South-East Asia.* Paris: UNESCO, 1963. 95-111. A penetrating discussion of new factors that might create and support village and government initiative, as well as a consideration of existing roadblocks that restrict such initiative. Emerson's *Representative Government* is quoted with approval.

590

Phillips, Herbert P. "The Election Ritual in a Thai Village." *Journal of Social Issues.* 14 (1958) 38-50. The whole process of electing a representative becomes a ritual to the villages.

591

Sharp, Lauriston. "Peasants and Politics in Thailand." *Far Eastern Survey* 19 (1950) 157-161. Unsophisticated attitudes and ideas of rural villagers towards the westernized administrators of faraway Bangkok.

Foreign Relations

The basic role of Thai foreign relations is to work for the preservation of the state. In Thailand's recent history, this has implied above all a fear of international communism directed from China, and a hope that the U.S.A. would protect it. Both elements are expressed in the works listed here.

592

Darling, F. C. *Thailand and the United States.* Washington: Public Affairs Press, 1965. Assesses the interaction of American foreign policy on the domestic policies of Thailand in the post-war period; the author, a former CIA employee, stresses the influence on the Thai political system of international forces.

593

Nuechterlein, Donald E. *Thailand and the Struggle for Southeast Asia.* Ithaca: Cornell University Press, 1965. An able study of Thailand's post-war attempt to link American power with the preservation of its own national security in an unstable region. Chief attention focuses on Laos and the ebb and flow of U.S.-Thai relations.

594

Brimmell, J. H. *Communism in South East Asia.* London: Oxford University Press, 1959. The activities of the international movement affecting Thailand, and Thailand's counter-measures, are well-studied here, from 1927 to SEATO.

595

Fifield, Russell H. *The Diplomacy of Southeast Asia 1945–1958.* New York: Harper, 1958. A factual survey of Thailand's post-war international relations is given on 230-273, and in further chapter on regionalism and the UN; SEATO figures throughout.

596

Modelski, George (ed.). *SEATO. Six Studies.* Melbourne: Cheshire, 1962. The participation of Thailand in this organization is dealt with in part three, pp. 88-128.

597

Stanton, Edwin F. "Spotlight on Thailand." *Foreign Affairs* 33 (1954) 72-85. Uneasy Thailand in the wake of the Geneva Conference watches 1953-54 developments and fears a communist dagger at its throat.

598

_____. *Brief Authority.* New York: Harper & Brothers, 1956. Former U. S. Ambassador writes on the major political changes and international developments from 1946 to 1953.

599

Darling, Frank C. "British and American Influence in Post-war Thailand." *Journal, Southeast Asian History* 4 (1963) 88-102. Different reactions of U.S.A. and Britain to Thailand's war declaration in 1942 produced a different response to Thailand from 1945 to 46.

600

Peterson, Alec. "Britain and Siam: The Latest Phase." *Pacific Affairs* 19 (1946) 364-372. Post-war negotiations between the two, to restore the status quo.

General Works

601

Busch, Noel F. *Thailand: An Introduction to Modern Siam.* 2nd ed. Princeton: Van Nostrand, 1964. General information for the casual reader.

602

Wood, W. A. R. *Consul in Paradise. Sixty-Nine Years in Siam.* London: Souvenir Press, 1965. A former British consul recalls in 15 chapters anecdotes about his life in Siam from 1896 to 1965.

603

King, John Kerry. "Thailand's Bureaucracy and the Threat of Communist Subversion." *Far Eastern Survey* 23 (1954) 169-173. A brief assessment of an unresolved problem: Will Thailand go Red in the provinces?

604

MacDonald, Alexander. *Bangkok Editor.* New York: Mac-Millan, 1949. Editor of a leading English-language paper gives a graphic picture of political life in post-war Bangkok.

605

Thompson, Virginia and Richard Adloff. "Thailand (Siam)" in Lawrence K. Rosinger and Associates. *The State of Asia: A Contemporary Survey.* New York: Alfred A. Knopf, 1951. 268-291. A detailed but concise account of immediate post-war political developments.

606

_____. "The State's Role in Thai Economy." *Far Eastern Survey* 21 (1952) 123-127. The greater participation by the government after the war in development economics.

607

Thompson, Virginia. "Governmental Instability in Siam." *Far Eastern Survey* 17 (1948) 185-189. The April, 1948 coup d'état.

608

Bartlett, Norman. *Land of the Lotus Eaters.* London: Jar-rold's, 1959. A substantial book on numerous aspects of near contemporary Thailand, including politics, by a former press attaché.

609

Chakrabongse, Prince Chula. *The Twain Have Met: or An Eastern Prince Came West.* London: Foulis, 1957. Some interesting comments on Thai politics in a gentle auto-biography.

610

Kemp, Peter. *Alms for Oblivion.* London: Cassell, 1961. Highly dangerous political activity immediately prior to and after the end of the war, with Thai and Lao nationalists, communists, French, Americans and others, in northern Thailand and Laos.

611

Jumsai, Manich. *Compulsory Education in Thailand.* Paris: UNESCO, 1951. A historical survey of education from 1871, with major emphasis on current characteristics; the most complete record available.

ECONOMIC PATTERNS

Comparatively little has been written on Thailand's economic patterns, possibly because until very recently it has been basically a single-crop economy, dependent largely on rice. Throughout modern times, however, there have been other crops and products, and today considerable material is available for work on all aspects of its economy. Its trade, its communications, its banking and finance, its various industrial and agricultural products as well as other aspects of the economic pattern all present opportunities to the scholar, for at present they are little-recorded. Students seeking contemporary information, however slight, are advised to consult Hong Kong's weekly, *Far Eastern Economic Review.*

General Works

612

Ingram, James C. *Economic Change in Thailand Since 1850.* Stanford: Stanford University Press, 1955. Thailand's modern century is examined; in 1850 it exported nothing, had virtually no currency or financial facilities, and was struggling on a barter subsistence economy. The author surveys the change to a modern state. A substantial survey.

613

International Bank for Reconstruction and Development, Economic Mission to Thailand. *A Public Development Program for Thailand.* Baltimore: Johns Hopkins Press, 1959. A survey of the economics of the state, and its potential for growth; with recommendations which became the basis of the 1960 economic and social plan.

614

Muscat, Robert J. *Development Strategy in Thailand. A Case Study of Economic Modernization,* New York: Praeger, 1966. Post-war economic development examined in the light of the need for further rapid and sustained development, and aimed at defining a strategy to maximize growth-producing decisions.

615

Judd, Laurence Cecil. *Dry Rice Agriculture in Northern Thailand.* Ithaca: Data Paper 52, Southeast Asia Program, Cornell University, 1964. A study of shifting cultivation, the "slash and burn" or "swidden farming" long used in uplands or non-irrigated areas all over Southeast Asia, and commonly practiced among the northern Thai.

616

Prachoom Chomchai. "Development and Trade: An Appraisal of Thailand's Recent Experience." *Asian Studies* 4 (1966) 259-267. Assesses the impact of Thailand's first National Economic Development Plan 1961–1966, on her foreign trade and payments position.

617

Ayal, Eliezer B. "Thailand's Six Year National Economic Plan." *Asian Survey* 1 (1962) 33-43. A summary of the 1961–66 plan.

618

Pombhejara, Vichitvong N. "The Second Phase of Thailand's Six-Year Economic Development Plan, 1964–1966." *Asian Survey* 5 (1965) 161-168. A brief outline of economic progress.

619

Ingram, James C. "Thailand's Rice Trade and the Allocation of Resources" in C. D. Cowan (ed.) *Economic Development of South-East Asia.* London: Allen & Unwin, 1964. 102-126. A survey of various aspects relating to rice exports from 1855.

620

Ayal, Eliezer. "Value Systems and Economic Development in Japan and Thailand." *The Journal of Social Issues,* 19 (1963) 35-51. A comparative study of differing social norms and contrasting group ideals of hard and not-so-hard work.

621

Kassebaum, John C. *Thailand Economic Farm Survey, 1953.* Bangkok: Ministry of Agriculture, 1955. A rather forbidding UN report, being entirely statistical, but a valuable source for Thai agricultural data.

622

Thailand. *Thailand and Her Agricultural Problems.* Bangkok: National FAO Committee, Ministry of Agriculture. rev. ed. 1950. Information on soils, climate, and other geographical and economic aspects of agriculture — with numerous maps.

623

Gould, Joseph S. "Thailand, a Developing Economy." *India Quarterly,* 8 (1952) 311-334. A useful outline of the economic base of the Thailand of 1952, and its plans for development.

Pre-War Patterns

624

Report of the FAO Mission for Siam. Washington: Food and Agriculture Organization of the United Nations, 1948. A 125-page survey of the agricultural and forest resources of Thailand, with recommendations for their development. Numerous illustrations by Pendleton.

625

Andrews, James M. *Siam. Second Rural Economic Survey, 1934–1935.* Bangkok: Times Press, 1935. A comprehensive assessment of the state of agricultural economics in Thailand at that time.

626

Zimmerman, Carle C. *Siam. Rural Economic Survey 1930–1931.* Bangkok: Bangkok Times Press, 1931. The author, a Harvard professor, presents here an unrivaled collection of data arising out of a nation-wide survey of income and its sources, expenditure, investment and credit patterns, as well as numerous other aspects of life, particularly in rural Thailand.

627

Siam. Nature and Industry. Bangkok: Ministry of Commerce and Communications, 1930. A comprehensive 300-page volume of 22 chapters, covering most aspects of the country's commerce, trade, industry, banking, public services.

628

Williams, Leigh. *Jungle Prison.* London: Andrew Melrose, rev. ed. 1954. Twenty years with the teakwood industry in northern Thailand.

Labor

629

Fogg, Ernest L. "Labor Organization in Thailand." *Industrial and Labor Relations Review* 6 (1953) 368-377. An outline of the post-war organization of labor and its position in Thailand today.

630

Lasker, Bruno. *Human Bondage in Southeast Asia.* Chapel Hill: University of North Carolina, 1950. Thailand appears throughout this survey while, in addition, an appendix, "Historical Forms of Human Bondage in Siam," is useful.

631

Pillai, P. P. (ed.). *Labor in Southeast Asia: A Symposium.* New Dehli: Indian Council of World Affairs, 1947. Includes a paper on Thailand.

632

Thompson, Virginia M. *Labor Problems in Southeast Asia.* New Haven: Yale University Press, 1947.

SOCIAL AND CULTURAL PATTERNS

The social patterns in recent years have attracted a number of outstanding scholars. Cornell in particular has concentrated on Bang Chan village where research pioneered by Professor Lauriston Sharp has probed keenly and deeply into the social patterns of a Buddhist village. Other work, on the Muslims of the south, the hill tribes of the north and the urbanized peoples of Bangkok, have added to our knowledge. In addition, translations of the indigenous literature, and studies of art (also recorded in the earlier section of history) help portray this basically agrarian and Buddhist land.

General Works

633

Kaufman, Howard Keva. *Bangkhaud; a Community Study in Thailand.* Monograph 10, Association of Asian Studies. Locust Valley: J. J. Augustin, 1960. A village in the rice growing area of central Thailand has its social patterns and its daily life meticulously examined.

634

Kingshill, Konrad. *Kudaeng — The Red Tomb, a Village Study in Northern Thailand.* Bangkok: The Siam Society, 1960. A detailed study of a Lao Buddhist village, in which the family, the economy, education, social patterns, government and acculturation is examined.

635

Textor, Robert B. *From Peasant to Pedicab Driver: A Social Study of Northeastern Thai Farmers Who Periodically Migrated to Bangkok and Became Pedicab Drivers.* 2 ed. New Haven: Cultural Report 8, Southeast Asia Studies, Yale University, 1961. An 83-page enquiry.

636

De Young, John. *Village Life in Modern Thailand.* Berkeley: University of California Press, 1955. A detailed study of the social patterns, the agricultural way of life, and the religions of the villagers of northern Thailand; as with other works, of relevance to Laos.

637

Phillips, Herbert P. *Thai Peasant Personality. The Patterning of Interpersonal Behavior in the village of Bang Chan.* Berkeley: University of California Press, 1965. An extended examination of the research design and method used, and an analysis of the psychological attitudes to life of Thai peasants.

638

Goldsen, Rose K. and Max Ralis. *Factors Related to Acceptance of Innovations in Bang Chan, Thailand.* Ithaca: Data Paper 25, Southeast Asia Program, Cornell University, 1957. Two contrasting studies on aspects of the social pattern of a village community.

639

Sharp, Lauriston, and others. *Siamese Rice Village: A Preliminary Study of Bang Chan, 1948–49.* Cornell Research Center, 1953. Studied from many angles by a team of U.S. scholars, this village in central Thailand produced a wealth of information on social patterns.

640

Hanks, Lucien M. and Herbert P. Phillips. "A Young Thai from the Countryside," in B. Kaplan (ed.) *Studying Personality Cross-Culturally.* Evanston: Row, Peterson, 1961. 637-656. The city's impact on a villager — modernization meeting traditionalism.

641

Phillips, Herbert. "Relationships between Personality and Social Structure, in a Siamese Peasant Community." *Human Organizations* 22, 2 (1963) 105-108. Five social units to which the villager is linked, and a few of his major personality characteristics.

642

Bernatzik, H. A. *The Spirits of the Yellow Leaves.* London: Robert Hale, 1958.

643

Fraser, Thomas M. *Rusembilan: A Malay Fishing Village in Southern Thailand.* Ithaca: Cornell University Press, 1960. A comprehensive study of a non-Thai Moslem minority in a Buddhist Land, and their fishing economy.

644

Benedict, Ruth. *Thai Culture and Behavior; an Unpublished Wartime Study Dated September 1943.* Ithaca: Data Paper 4. Southeast Asia Program. Cornell University, 1952. A penetrating study by a distinguished cultural anthropologist of the characteristic pattern in Thai behavior, as expressed in family and national affairs.

645

Moerman, Michael. "Ban Ping's Temple: The Center of a 'Loosely Structured' Society," in *Anthropological Studies in Theravada Buddhism.* New Haven: Cultural Report Series 13, Southeast Asia Studies, Yale University, 1966. 137-174. A stimulating corroboration of the principle that village society is centered round the temple, and that this society permits considerable conduct variations from the norm.

646

Embree, John F. "Thailand, a Loosely Structured Social System." *American Anthropologist* 52 (1950) 181-193. Considerable variations of individual behavior are accepted by the Thai without comment; a casual and relaxed attitude permits individualistic conduct. A basic paper for anyone interested in Thai social patterns.

647

Haas, Mary R. "The Declining Descent Rule for Rank in Thailand." *American Anthropologist* 53 (1951) 585-587. A letter to the editor, correcting Embree.

648

Anuman Rajadhon, Phya. *Life and Ritual in Old Siam: Three Studies of Thai Life and Customs.* New Haven: Human Relations Area Files Press, 1961. Translated and edited by William J. Gedney, 3 related articles by a Thai writer on: the life of a farmer; Buddhism in Thailand, and child customs. The first paper, on the farmer's life, and the annual round of activities associated with rice growing published previously in English by Yale in 1955.

649

Moerman, Michael. "Western Culture and The Thai Way of Life." *Asia* 1 (1964) 31-50. Specific material, social, and intellectual innovations from the West, and their adaption in one small northern Thai village.

650

Hanks, Jane Richardson. *Maternity and Its Rituals in Bang Chan, Thailand*. Data Paper 51, Southeast Asia Program, Cornell University, 1963. A study of the economic, social, religious, and cosmological attitudes involved, and ethnographic data concerning childbirth.

651

Tirabutana, Prajuab. *A Simple One: the Story of a Siamese Girlhood*. Ithaca: Data Paper 30, Southeast Asia Program, Cornell University, 1958. The early life and thoughts of a Thai girl in a northeast provincial town.

652

Anuman Rajadhon, Phya. "Fertility Rites in Thailand." *Journal, Siam Society* 48, 2 (1960) 37-42. The water-throwing feast and other rites to end the dry season and to hasten the monsoon.

653

_____. *The Story of Thai Marriage Customs*. Bangkok: National Culture Institute, 1954. This work, being No. 13 of the Thailand Culture Series, outlines briefly the various customs attached to a Buddhist wedding.

654

Lingat, R. "Evolution of the Conception of Law in Burma and Siam." *Journal, Siam Society* 19 (1925) 115-128.

655

Wells, Kenneth Elmer. *Thai Buddhism, Its Rites and Activities*. Bangkok: Christian Bookstore, 1960. Published originally in 1939 and begun as a Columbia Ph.D. thesis, this large volume makes frequent use of Siamese texts to outline religious practices and traditions in Thailand; one of the few comprehensve works on this subject.

656

Moerman, Michael. "Ethnic Identification in a Complex Civilization: Who Are The Lue?" *American Anthropologist* (October 1965) 1215-1230. The Lue are among the tribal Thai of the north — but it is far more complicated than that.

657

Landon, Kenneth P. *Southeast Asia, Crossroad of Religions*. Chicago: University of Chicago Press, 1949.

Literature and Art

658

Mosel, James N. *Trends and Structure in Contemporary Thai Poetry*. Ithaca: Data Paper 43, Southeast Asia Program, Cornell University, 1961. Serious literature in Thailand is almost exclusively equated with poetry, which enjoys an active life; here 11 poems are given, with commentary and background information.

659

Sunthorn, Bhu. *The Story of Phru Abhai Mani*. Bangkok: Chatra Books, 1952. A translation by Prem Chaya and a rendering in prose of a romantic poem of the early 19th century written by a famous poet.

660

Le May, R. *Siamese Tales, Old and New*, London: Noel Douglas, 1930. Translation and commentary of a small volume of Siamese tales, collected by Phya Manunet Banham, which help illustrate the Thai character.

661

Bowrie, Theodore R. *The Arts of Thailand. A Handbook of the Architecture, Sculpture and Painting of Thailand*. Bloomington: University of Indiana Press, 1960. A comprehensive survey.

662

Hurlimau, Martin. *Bangkok*. New York: The Viking Press, 1963. A book of vivid photographs illustrating the Bangkok scene.

CAMBODIA

GENERAL

Until recently, Cambodia had no ocean port of its own, and it remained inside its lip of mountains, one of the lands of mainland Southeast Asia that perpetuated an earlier tradition, shunning the coast. Its ring of mountains helped keep its people homogeneous. Cambodia, almost alone among the countries of Southeast Asia, has no minority group of any significance, the Chams being the only non-Khmer group inside the kingdom. A fertile plain, drained by the great Mekong River, offers land enough for all, and fish for everyone is in the great lake of Tonle Sap. But envious neighbors surround it, and the pressures of contemporary life crowd in. Little of this has been studied in detail.

Journals

663

Sangkum. Phnom Penh. Monthly. Editor Prince Norodom Sihanouk. Official commentary on contemporary political affairs.

664

Kambuja. Phnom Penh. 1964– Monthly; articles by Norodom Sihanouk and others; semi-official descriptions of contemporary Cambodia; illustrated.

665

Realités Cambodgiennes. Phnom Penh, 1956– A weekly; semi-official news and comments.

HISTORY

Cambodia has had no long continuous history. Rather, like Rome or Mexico, it has seen barbarians destroy an ancient civilization and a great culture. Much later a new civilization arose under new conquerors. Cambodia's great Khmer Empire has been studied by modern scholars, but much of the past remains unrecorded. So, too, the peoples and the 20th-century scene have been little investigated. As in other parts of Southeast Asia, most of the research on Cambodia has occurred within the last 20 years; large gaps remain.

General Works

666

Henz, Martin. *A Short History of Cambodia from the Days of Angkor to the Present*. New York: Praeger, 1958. An outline of the modern political history of Cambodia linked rather tenuously to the Angkor period; intended for the general reader.

667

Steinberg, David J. and Others (eds.). *Cambodia: Its People, Its Society, Its Culture*. New Haven: Human Relations Area Files Press, 1957. A handbook of history, economics, politics and society, compiled by a team rather pre-occupied with the cold war.

668

Buttinger, J. *The Smaller Dragon*. New York: Praeger, 1958. Although Cambodia appears in this major work only incidently, it is very useful as a regional survey.

669

Hall, D. G. E. *A History of Southeast Asia.* 2nd ed. New York: St. Martins Press, 1964. An outline of Cambodian history from its earliest period to the present is given in several chapters.

670

Imbert, Jean. *Histoire des Institutions Khmers. Annales de la Faculté des Droit de Phnom Penh.* 2 vols. Phnom Penh, 1961. The evolution of Cambodian monarchy, together with other aspects of the state, such as land tenure, administration and religion, between 800 A.D. and 1960; a valuable study.

Angkor

Between the 9th and 15th centuries a great tropical civilization rose, flourished, and died on the Cambodian plain. The Khmer Empire at its height controlled part of what is now Thailand and Vietnam, and drew tribute from the Malaya Peninsula as well. At Angkor, its capital, huge temples were built as part of a god-king cult that had the center of the universe established there. Destroyed finally by invading Thai in the fourteenth century, and its capital abandoned, Angkor and the Khmer civilization became almost forgotten until modern times.

GENERAL WORKS

671

Briggs, L. P. *The Ancient Khmer Empire.* Transactions of the American Philosophical Society. New Series, 41, 1. Philadelphia: The American Philosophical Society, 1951. With a meticulous listing of sources, and a 550-item bibliography, this remains the most detailed English language history of ancient Cambodia from its beginnings until its final extinction.

672

Coedes, G. *The Making of South East Asia.* London: Routledge and Kegan Paul, 1966. A major part of this classic French work, now translated, on mainland Southeast Asia prior to the 13th century, deals with Cambodia.

673

Groslier, B. P. *Indochina. Art in the Melting Pot of Races.* Vol. ix of *Art of the World.* London: Methuen, 1962. A detailed commentary of Cambodia accompanying a beautifully illustrated work.

674

Giteau, Madaleine. *Khmer Civilization and the Angkor Civilization.* London: Thames & Hudson, 1965. An outstanding study; a profusely illustrated and scholarly text.

675

LeMay, Reginald. *The Culture of South-East Asia.* London: Allen and Unwin, 1954. Major attention is given to Cambodia in this study of Buddhist and other Indian-derived art and civilization from 500 to 1500 A.D.

676

Frederic, Louis. *The Temples and Sculpture of Southeast Asia.* London: Thames and Hudson, 1965. Cambodia's magnificent temples, particularly those at Angkor, receive considerable attention in this beautiful coffee-table book.

677

Coedes, G. *Les etats hindouises d'Indochine et d'Indonesie.* Paris: E. de Boccard, 1964. The Khmer civilization receives major attention in this classic study by the eminent French scholar.

678

————. *Angkor: An Introduction.* London: Oxford University Press, 1963. Eight lectures on Angkor Wat, the Bayon, Jayavarman VII, and other aspects of Angkor.

679

MacDonald, Malcolm. *Angkor.* London: Jonathan Cape, 1958. A brilliant series of photographs by Loke Wan Tho.

680

Groslier, P. and Jacques Arthaud. *Angkor: art and civilisation.* rev. ed. New York: Praeger, 1966. A monument to a remarkable civilization considered and illustrated with insight.

681

Aymonier, E. T. *Le Cambodge.* 3 vols. Paris: E. Leroux, 1900–04. Embodies the content of French archaeological research at that time on early Cambodia; still useful.

682

Maspero, G. *L'Empire Khmer.* Phnom Penh: Imprimerie du Protectorat, 1904. Still a standard reference for the Angkorean days.

SPECIALIZED STUDIES

683

Wolters, O. W. "The Khmer King at Basan (1371–3) and the Restoration of the Cambodian Chronology During the Fourteenth and Fifteenth Centuries." *Asia Major* 12 (1966) 44-89. A major contribution to our understanding of this period.

684

Groslier, B. P. "Our Knowledge of Khmer Civilization. A Re-Appraisal." *Journal, Siam Society* 48 (1960) 1-28. A stimulating survey of general issues, commenting on the main characteristics of this civilization.

685

Minsky, Jeannette (ed.). *The Great Chinese Travelers.* New York: Random House, 1964. A celebrated 13th century Chinese account of many aspects of Angkor, by Chou Ta-kuan, 203–33 A.D.

686

Sullivan, Michael. "The Discovery of Angkor." *History Today* 10 (1960) 169-179. Narrates the work of discovery, restoration, and elucidation at Angkor of the École Française d'Extreme Orient, from 1898.

687

Coe, M. D. "Social typology and the tropical forest civilizations." *Comparative Studies in society and history* 4 (1961) 65-85. Makes numerous comparisons between two tropical, non-urban civilizations, the Khmer and the Maya.

688

Wales, H. G. Quaritch. *The Mountain of God.* London: B. Quaritch, 1953. Chapter 6, 131-170, entitled "Khmer Temple-Mountains," outlines the religious significance, and the derivatory aspects of the Angkorean civilization.

689

Briggs, Lawrence P. "The Syncretism of Religions in Southeast Asia, Especially in the Khmer Empire." *Journal of the American Oriental Society* 71 (1951) 230-249.

690

Willmott, W. E. "The History and Sociology of the Chinese in Cambodia prior to the French Protectorate." *Journal, Southeast Asian History* 7 (1966) 15-38. Chinese contacts with pre-Angkorean Cambodia, with Angkor, and from the end of Angkor civilization to the 19th century.

691

Briggs, L. P. "The Khmer Empire and the Malay Peninsula." *Far Eastern Quarterly* 9 (1950) 256-305. Contacts and control from Cambodia during three main periods; Funan 150–550 A.D.), Chen-la (550–802 A.D.) and Angkor (802–1431 A.D.).

692

————. "Spanish Intervention in Cambodia 1593–1603." *T'oung Pao* 39 (1950) 132-160. A Cambodian embassy to Malacca and Manila initiates a train of events that leads to a massacre of Spanish in Cambodia, the assassination of the king, and the supremacy of the Thai.

693

_____. "Siamese Attacks on Angkor before 1430." *Far Eastern Quarterly*, 8 (1948) 3-33. Although Siamese attacks on Cambodia date from 1250 A.D., the author refutes the suggestion that they captured Angkor or over-ran Cambodia before 1430-31 A.D.

694

Bassett, D. K. "The Trade of the English East India Company in Cambodia 1651–1656." *Journal, Royal Asiatic Society* (1962), 35-61. An appendix (55-61) prints verbatim a contemporary report on the kingdom, with details of the country, government, people and trading commodities.

The Period of French Subjection

From the middle of the 19th to the middle of the 20th century Cambodia was under effective French control. French authority clashed with Thai pretensions in establishing its borders and power. The one-hundred year period has been little recorded; French scholarship was concentrated on the archaeological work of Angkor, and Cambodian scholarship was never encouraged.

GENERAL WORKS

695

Ennis, T. E. *French Policy and Developments in Indochina.* University of Chicago Press, 1936. The French penetration of Indochina and an analysis of economic, social and administrative problems. Cambodia figures in this and in other general studies, but rather as a poor, little-noticed relative. It receives little attention.

696

Roberts, S. H. *Indochina: History of French Colonial Policy, 1870–1925.* London: P. S. King, 1929. After a general section on principles of French colonial policy throughout its empire, Indochina is dealt with in chapter II.

697

Robequain, C. *The Economic Development of French Indo-China.* London: Oxford University Press, 1944. Cambodian agriculture, communications, financing, industries, population and trade during the colonial period; although the major attention is given to Vietnam.

698

Vella, Walter. *Siam Under Rama III.* New York: J. J. Augustin, 1947. Includes a good account (pp. 94-108) of Cambodia's unhappy relations with Siam in the first half of the 19th century.

699

Thompson, V. *French Indo-China.* London: Allen and Unwin, 1937. Forty pages (pp. 321-362) are devoted to Cambodia's social and political organization, its economy, administration, and French-Khmer relations.

SPECIALIZED STUDIES

700

Thomson, R. S. "Establishment of the French Protectorate over Cambodia. " *Far Eastern Quarterly,* 4 (1945) 313-340. An outline of events from the Montigny mission of 1855 leading to the French protectorate of 1863 and the coronation of the King in 1864.

701

_____. "Siam and France, 1863–1870." *Far Eastern Quarterly* 1 (1945) 28-46. The Siamese and French competition for Cambodia from France's protectorate treaty of 1863 until 1867, when another treaty clinched the issue.

702

Briggs, L. P. "Aubaret and the Treaty of July 15, 1867 between France and Siam." *Far Eastern Quarterly* 6 (1947) 122-138. An outline of the rivalry that led to the cession of part of Cambodia to Siam.

703

_____. "A Sketch of Cambodian History." *Far Eastern Quarterly* 6 (1947) 345-363. A suggested periodization, from earliest times until the coming of the French.

704

_____. "The Treaty of March 23, 1907 between France and Siam, and the return of Battambang and Angkor to Cambodia." *Far Eastern Quarterly* 5 (1946) 439-454. To explain the significance of the return of Angkor and Battambang to Cambodia, reference is made to the Khmer empire and the coming of the Thai conquerers; then, in detail, 19th century history, and the role of Chulalongkorn of Siam.

705

Vadakarn, L. V. *Thailand's Case.* Bangkok: Thai Commercial Press, 1941. A strongly-worded Thai protest against France for the territories, such as Cambodia, which it took from Siam in the 19th century.

706

Brodrick, A. H. *Little Vehicle. Cambodia and Laos.* London: Hutchinson, 1949. A visit in 1939 produces a detailed account of many aspects of life.

707

Ponder, H. W. *Cambodian Glory.* London: T. Butterworth, 1938. Observations and Angkor.

708

Pannetier, A. *Notes Cambodgienues: Au coeur du pays Khmer.* Paris: Payot, 1921. A French doctor in Cambodia is critical of the paternal administration of his compatriots; and of the Chinese in Cambodia.

709

Morizon, Rene. *Monographie du Cambodge.* Hanoi, 1931. Details of French colonial administration, education and economics.

710

Pym, Christopher (ed.). *Henri Mouhot's Diary. Travels in the Central Parts of Siam, Cambodia and Laos during the Years 1858–61.* Kuala Lumpur: Oxford University Press, 1966. The report by Mouhot, which first aroused western interest in Angkor, together with his illustrations of Cambodia over one hundred years ago.

711

Levy, R. and Roth, A. *French Interests and Policies in the Far East.* New York: Institute of Pacific Affairs, 1941. The 1937-41 pressure on the French in Cambodia by Thailand for the return of its "lost provinces" is treated on pp. 171-75.

712

Landon, Kenneth P. "Thailand's Quarrel with France in Perspective." *Far Eastern Quarterly* 1 (1941) 25-42. French 19th century movements into Cambodia seen as they affected Thai interests, with the 1940–1941 Thai-French war seen as Thailand's effort to recover territory yielded before 1907.

POLITICAL PATTERNS

The political patterns of Cambodia have been dominated by the personality of one man, Prince Norodom Sihanouk. In the face of French reluctance and dilatory inclinations, he secured the independence of his country before the pro-communist extremists were able to secure effective support for their pretensions to be the champions of national liberty. Following independence it has been his drive, astuteness, and political subtlety that has kept Cambodia united and peaceful. Nevertheless, beneath the surface of his one-party system, dissident elements still operate, and here, as elsewhere in Southeast Asia, the political pattern has not hardened into anything that can be called permanent.

General Works

713

Smith, Roger M. *Cambodia's Foreign Policy*. Ithaca: Cornell University Press, 1965. A 50-page outline of Cambodian history, and then a clear and scholarly study of the difficult non-alignment path being pursued by Sihanouk. His country's relations with his near neighbors illustrates how traditional Thai and Vietnamese pretensions and ambitions weaken the stability of the region. The presence and influence of the major powers, China and America in particular, also is examined.

714

_____. "Cambodia" in G. McT Kahin (ed.) *Governments and Politics of Southeast Asia* 2 ed. Ithaca: Cornell University Press, 1964. A study of the historical background, the contemporary setting, the political process and major problems; perhaps the most useful single work for the student of Cambodian political patterns.

715

Lancaster, Donald. *The Emancipation of French Indo-China*. London: Oxford University Press, 1961. Although Vietnam occupies the central position in this major study, Cambodian political patterns after 1945 are treated throughout, and the role of Sihanouk in particular is studied with care.

Specialized Studies

716

Devillers, Philippe. "The Dynamics of Power in Cambodia" in Saul Rose (ed.) *Politics in Southern Asia*. New York: St. Martin's Press, 1963. An outline of the post-war political evolution, with an inquiry into the intentions and motives of Sihanouk, with some disturbing comments on ancient Asian rivalries and hatreds.

717

Armstrong, John P. *Sihanouk Speaks*. New York: Walker and Co., 1964. A collection of the prince's speeches, used as the basis for a sympathetic appreciation of his policies.

718

Field, Michael. *The Prevailing Wind: Witness in Indo-China*. London: Methuen, 1965. A valuable pen portrait of Sihanouk and an analysis of Cambodian-Chinese relations.

719

Osborne, Milton E. "History and Kingship in Contemporary Cambodia." *Journal of Southeast Asian History* 7 (1966) 1-14. A perceptive study of past influences on the attitudes of Sihanouk.

720

Thompson, Virginia and Adloff, Richard. *Minority Problems in Southeast Asia*. Stanford: Stanford University Press, 1955. A section (pp. 170-97) deals with the Khmer Issarak movement.

721

_____. "Cambodia Moves Towards Independence." *Far Eastern Survey* 22, 9 (1953) 105-111. Immediate post-war history, including relations with Thailand and France, and internal developments such as the Issarak movement, the Vietminh, and Sihanouk's exile.

722

Hammer, E. J. *The Struggle For Indochina*. Stanford: Stanford University Press, 1954. Concerned mainly with Vietnam; Sihanouk and Cambodia appear on pp. 294-297 and elsewhere.

723

Cole, A. B. (ed.). *Conflict in Indochina and International Repercussions, A Documentary History 1945-1955*. Ithaca: Cornell University Press, 1956. Cambodia figures in four of the one hundred key documents reproduced here.

724

Eden, Anthony. *Memoirs of Anthony Eden: Full Circle*. Boston: Houghton Mifflin, 1960. Refers briefly to Cambodia at the Geneva Conference of 1954.

725

Szaz, Zoltan M. "Cambodia's Foreign Policy." *Far Eastern Survey* 24 (1955) 151-158. Covers development particularly from the post-Geneva period, 1954-55, when Indian support for a neutralist stand was solicited.

726

Sihanouk, Norodom. "Cambodia Neutral: The Dictate of Necessity." *Foreign Affairs* 36, 4 (1958) 582-586. Neutrality as a necessity for Cambodian survival during the anti-communist crusade of the West.

727

Leifer, M. "Cambodia, the politics of Accommodation." *Asian Survey* 4 (1964) 674-679. Surveys Sihanouk's actions in 1963 in preserving national unity and in avoiding offense to China. See also his "Cambodia — In Search of Neutrality," in *Asian Survey* 3 (1963).

728

Lacouture, Jean and Devillers, Philippe. *La Fin d'une guerre: Indochina 1954*. Cambodia's role in the Geneva Conference is included in this study.

729

Fifield, R. H. *The Diplomacy of Southeast Asia: 1945-1958*. New York: Harper & Brothers, 1958. Cambodia's relations with its neighbors, with other involved powers, and the role of Sihanouk, occupy 30 pages (366-95).

730

Kahin, G. McT. *The Asian-African Conference, Bandung, Indonesia, April 1955*. Ithaca: Cornell University Press, 1956. Sihanouk at Bandung, and his fears of communism, with China's attitude being considered by all Asia.

731

Crozier, Brian. "The International Situation in Indochina." *Pacific Affairs* 29 (1956) 309-323. The beginnings of the communist policy of subversion, and Cambodian response in 1955.

732

Smith, Roger M. "Cambodia's Neutrality and the Laotian Crisis." *Asian Survey* 1 (1961) 17-24. The problem created by communist infiltration in Laos, and Cambodia's efforts to safeguard itself.

733

Black, John. "The Lofty Sanctuary of Khao Phra Viharn." *Journal, Siam Society* 54, 1 (1956) 1-31. With photographs and maps, this is a description of the remarkably sited temple, on the tip of a mountain precipice, which has been an object of international dispute.

734

Nakhanat, P. S. and Duangthisan, Chamrat. *The Khao Phra Viharn Case*. Bangkok: Sansawan Press, 1962. A statement of the Thai position concerning a temple on the border, the object of a serious dispute.

735

Singh, L. P. "The Thai-Cambodian Temple Dispute." *Asian Survey* 2 (1962) 23-26. The origins of the Khao Phra Viharn temple dispute and the struggle between the two to possess it.

736

Leifer, M. "Cambodia and her Neighbours." *Pacific Affairs* 34 (1961-62) 361-374. The then-current disputes between Cambodia, Thailand and Vietnam, and the background to them.

737

_____. "The Cambodian Elections." *Asian Survey* 2 (1962) 20-24. The 1962 elections were intended to promote national unity.

738

Simon, Jean-Pierre. "Cambodia: Pursuit of Crisis." *Asian Survey* 5 (1965) 49-53. Developments in foreign affairs during 1964 ably outlined.

739

Leifer, M. "The Cambodian Opposition." *Asian Survey* 2 (1962) 11-15. Deals with Son Ngoc Thanh, who organized an anti-French demonstration in 1942 and then the Khmer Issarak movement, and who contributed to the Democratic Party and the Pracheachon Party, which participated in the 1955 and 1958 elections.

740

Burchett, W. T. *Mekong Upstream*. Berlin: Seven Seas Publishing, 1959. An experienced Australian-communist journalist describes the Khmer Issarak and other aspects of Cambodia.

741

Lewis, Norman. *A Dragon Apparent*. London: Jonathon Cape, 1951. In these travels, the Khmer Issarak groups are encountered and Sihanouk interviewed.

742

Modelski, G. (ed.). *SEATO. Six Studies*. Melbourne: F. W. Cheshire, 1962. Cambodia is discussed here briefly.

743

Leifer, M. "Cambodia and SEATO." *International Journal* XVII (1962) 122-132. Sihanouk's reactions to SEATO and the reasons for them.

744

Newman, B. *Report on Indochina*. London: R. Hale, 1953. A brief survey of politics in Cambodia (pp. 153-77) and the country as it looked in 1952.

745

Sihanouk, Norodom. *La monarchie cambodgienue et la croisade royale pour l'independance*. Phnom Penh: Imprimerie Rasmey, 1961. In two parts; the first deals with the monarchy, from 802 to 1904, as a symbol of greatness and unity; the second deals with Sihanouk's efforts to secure independence. Required reading in Cambodian schools.

746

Preschez, Philippe. *Essai sur la democratie du Cambodge*. Paris: Foundation Nationale des Sciences Politiques, Centre d'Études des Relations Internationales, 1961. Covers the political history from 1945 to 1960, and observes the return to royal authoritarianism.

747

Khoi, Le Thanh. *Le Viet-Nam: Histoire et civilisation, le milieu and l'histoire*. Paris: Editions de Minuit, 1955. Cambodian affairs as seen from Vietnam.

748

Clubb, O. E. Jnr. *The United States and the Sino-Soviet Bloc in Southeast Asia*. Washington: The Brookings Institution, 1962. Cambodia is considered in a discussion on the possibility of a neutral zone in Southeast Asia.

749

Tooze, Ruth. *Cambodia: Land of Contrast*. New York: The Viking Press, 1963. A pleasant introduction.

LAOS

GENERAL

The smallest state in Southeast Asia, in population if not in size, and the most underdeveloped, this isolated country clings to the eastern bank of the upper Mekong. Its people, the Lao in particular, inhabit both sides of the great river, which has been more of a main highway than a boundary. Until the French and the Thai between them settled the modern border, the ancient Laos covered part of eastern Thailand.

With no coastline, with few people, with many mountains and few plains, no great civilization has been recorded here; nor indeed do we have records of anything much at all, until the Cold War of the modern age thrust this little state and its tribal peoples and its flimsy administration into world prominence. The bibliography reflects this interest in the political patterns of the contemporary scene, and the little that has been attempted on the economic, social, or historical patterns.

Bibliographies

750

McKinstry, J. *Bibliography of Laos and Ethnically Related Areas, to 1961*. Berkeley: University of California Press, 1962.

751

Lafont, Pierre B. *Bibliographie Du Laos*. Paris: École Française D'Extreme Orient, 1964. Covers the earth sciences, social sciences, and humanities in 1867 entries; items mainly in French, but also English, Russian, Japanese, and other languages.

752

Embree, J., and Thomas, W. L. Jr. *Ethnic Groups of Northern Southeast Asia*. New Haven: Yale University Press, 1950.

Land, People, and Language

753

Halpern, Joel M. *Government, Politics and Social Structure in Laos. A Study of Tradition and Innovation*. New Haven: Southeast Asia Studies, Monograph Series 4, Yale University, 1964. An analysis of Lao society and government, with useful statistical data, and with insights into the lives, careers and thoughts of various Lao.

754

Tissot, R. "Geographical and Human Aspects" in René de Berval (ed.). *Kingdom of Laos*. Saigon: France-Asie, 1959. 9-15. The tablelands, the valleys, the Mekong; and then the rains.

755

Benedict, Ruth. *Thai Culture and Behaviour*. Ithaca: Data Paper 4, Southeast Asia Studies, Cornell University, 1963. Material used is relevant to Lao adult and child life, traditional background, religion, and some major characteristics; a sensitive and stimulating study.

756

Kingshill, Konrad. *Kudaeng — The Red Tomb. A Village Study in Northern Thailand*. Bangkok: The Siam Society, 1960. As with other research on northern Thailand, this is relevant to Lao village studies.

757

Halpern, Joel M. "Observations on the Social Structure of the Lao Elite," in *Asian Survey* 1, 5 (1961) 25-32. Descendents of the courtier class, French-educated, urban-centered, inter-related.

758

Izikowitz, K. G. *Lamet: Hill Peasants in French Indo-China*. Etnografisca Studier 17. Goteborg: Etnografiska Museet, 1951. A sound description of the Lamet tribe in the mountains of northwest Laos.

759

Halpern, Joel M. "Traditional Medicine and the Role of the *Phi* in Laos." *Eastern Anthropologist* 16, 3 (1963) 191-200. The role of the bonzes, shamans, herbalists and other traditional healers of the sick in Laos.

760

Roffe, G. Edward and Roff, Telma W. *Spoken Lao: Books I and II.* Washington: American Council of Learned Societies, 1956-58.

761

Briggs, L. P. "The Appearance and Historical Usage of the Terms Tai, Thai, Siamese and Lao," in *Journal of the American Oriental Society* 69 (1949) 60-73.

762

Le May, Reginald. *An Asian Arcady.* Cambridge: Heffer, 1926. On the Lao people of northern Thailand.

HISTORY

Very little has been recorded of Lao history prior to the 19th century, when the area came gradually under French influence and control. Prior to that, a monarchy ruled over a Buddhist people who watched Thai encroachments; but the details of this history still await the scholar.

General Works

763

Le Boulanger, Paul. *Histoire du Laos français: Essai d'une étude chronologique des principantes laotiennes.* Paris: Plon, 1930. An outline history from 1353 to the establishment of the French protectorate; the most comprehensive single work on Lao history; bibliography.

764

Smith, Roger M. "Laos" in G. McT. Kahin (ed.) *Governments and Politics of Southeast Asia.* 2nd ed. Ithaca: Cornell University Press, 1964. 527-592. The historical background, the contemporary setting, the political process and major problems. Again, as with other states in Southeast Asia, a most valuable contribution.

765

De Berval, René (ed.). *Kingdom of Laos: The Land of the Million Elephants and of the White Parasol.* Saigon: France-Asie, 1959. A distinguished group contributes to this special issue of *France-Asie*, with articles on religion, ethnography, history, arts, economy, external relations, and other aspects of Laos today.

766

Lebar, Frank and Others. *Laos: Its Peoples, Its Society, Its Culture.* New York: Taplinger, 1960. One of the series of the "Human Relations Area Files," this has 21 compact sections dealing comprehensively with Lao affairs; bibliography.

767

Thompson, V. *French Indo-China.* London: Allen & Unwin, 1937. A section of one chapter (pp. 363-390) on the people, religions, arts and economy of Laos, and the contact of ideas introduced through French education.

768

Viravong, Maha Sila. *History of Laos.* New York: Paragon, 1964. Translated from Lao, this history becomes factual from the 16th century onwards. It concludes with Siamese supremacy and then French control in the 19th century.

Specialized Studies

769

Wyatt, David K. "Siam and Laos, 1767–1827." *Journal, Southeast Asian History* 4, 2 (1963) 13-32. The increasing active involvement of the Thai government in Lao affairs for sixty years prior to the Vientiane rebellion of 1827.

770

Vella, Walter. *Siam Under Rama III.* New York: J. J. Augustin, for the Association of Asian Studies, 1957. The Vientiane rebellion of 1827 against its suzerain, the Thai ruler, and the tightening of Thai control which followed, is handled on pp. 78-93.

771

Briggs, Lawrence P. "The Treaty of March 23, 1907 between France and Siam and the return of Battambang and Angkor to Cambodia." *Far Eastern Quarterly* 5 (46) 439-54. Treats the French treaty of 1893 with Laos on pp. 444-446.

772

Brodrick, A. H. *Little Vehicle: Cambodia and Laos.* London: Hutchinson, 1949. The detailed report of a keen-eyed observer who toured Laos in 1939.

773

Mouhot, M. H. *Travels in the Central Parts of Indochina (Siam) Cambodia and Laos during the years 1858, 1859 and 1860.* 2 vols. London, J. Murray, 1864. Laos is described in the concluding chapter of vol. 2.

774

Sukhabanij, Kachorn. "The Thai Beachhead States in the 11th and 12th Centuries." *Silapakon Journal* (Bangkok) 1, 3 and 4, (1957).

775

Lasker, Bruno. *Human Bondage In Southeast Asia.* Chapel Hill: University of North Carolina Press, 1950. Slavery, debt bondage, serfdom, peonage, compulsory public services and other forms of social inequality throughout historic times in all Indochina, including Laos.

POLITICAL PATTERNS

General Works

776

Fall, Bernard B. "The Pathet Lao — A 'Liberation' Party," in Robert A. Scalopino (ed.). *The Communist Revolution in Asia: tactics, goals and achievements.* Englewood Cliffs, N. J.: Prentice-Hall, 1965. A study of the communist Pathet Lao in which references to ancient ethnic differences and hatreds are made, as well as an outlet of communist organizational moves from the Lao Issara of 1945 to the near communist control of 1965.

777

Dommern, Arthur J. *Conflict in Laos: the politics of Neutralization.* New York: Praeger, 1964. The cold war in Laos, from 1945, but with particular reference to the crises of the late fifties and early sixties.

778

Champassak, Sissouk Na. *Storm Over Laos: a Contemporary History.* New York: Praeger, 1961. The Laotian representative on the International Control Commission presents, in particular, an account of events from the Geneva Conference of 1954.

779

Simmonds, Stuart. "Independence and Political Rivalry in Laos, 1945–1961" in Saul Rose (ed.) *Politics in Southern Asia.* New York: St. Martins Press, 1963. 163-199. An outline of post-1945 history, with consideration of the small elite groups which disputed power.

780

Burchett, Wilfred G. *The Furtive War: The United States in Vietnam and Laos.* New York: International Publishers, 1963. An experienced pro-communist reporter interprets 1954-1962 developments.

781

Brimmell, J. H. *Communism in South East Asia.* London: Oxford University Press, 1959. Laos appears from 1945 onwards; a useful reference.

782

Trager, Frank N. "Laos and the Defense of Southeast Asia." *Orbis* VII, 3 (1963) 550-582. Outlines Laotian developments and U. S. anti-communist measures from 1954.

783

Thompson, V. and Adloff, Richard. "Laos: Background of Invasion." *Far Eastern Quarterly* 22, 6 (1953) 62-66. A survey of the changing 1941–1952 political scene in Laos, leading to the Vietminh invasion in 1953 and the formation of the Pathet Lao.

784

Hammer, Ellen J. *The Struggle for Indochina.* Stanford: Stanford University Press, 1954. Laos from 1941 until 1953 is dealt with as incidental to the main French interests in Vietnam.

785

Burchett, Wilfred T. *Mekong Upstream.* Berlin: Seven Seas Publishers, 1959. The second half of this book deals with the happy people of Laos working with their kind Pathet Lao brethren for a worker's paradise; biographical data of Meo and Kha leaders is included.

786

Fifield, Russell H. *The Diplomacy of Southeast Asia: 1945–1958.* New York: Harper & Brothers, 1958. The modern international relations of Laos, pp. 344-366.

787

Fall, Bernard B. "Re-Appraisal in Laos." *Current History* 42 (1962) 8-14. A lack of information led to unwise decisions by the U.S.A.; surveys four major developments in U. S. policy in Laos from 1955 to 1962.

788

Crozier, Brian. "Peking and the Laotian Crisis: An Interim Appraisal." *China Quarterly* 7 (1961). See also his "Peking and the Laotian Crisis: A Further Appraisal," *ibid.* 11, 1962). The role of China at the Geneva Conference on Laos; with implications to the rest of Southeast Asia.

789

Dooley, Thomas A. *The Edge of Tomorrow.* New York: Farrar, Straus and Cudahy, 1958. A U. S. medical team at work in a village in northern Laos; outline of customary medicine.

790

Lewis, Norman. *A Dragon Apparent.* London: Jonathan Cape, 1951. A pleasant account by a perceptive Englishman.

791

Leach, Edmund. "The Frontiers of 'Burma'." *Comparative Studies in Society and History* 3 (October 1960) 49-68.

792

Jonas, A. and Tanham, G. "Laos: A Phase in Cyclic Regional Revolution." *Orbis* V (1961). 64-73.

793

Czyzak, John J. and Salans, Carl F. "The International Conference on Laos and the Geneva Agreement of 1962." *Journal of Southeast Asian History* 7, 2 (1966) 27-47. A detailed account of how the Geneva Conference functioned, and the tactics which made it successful.

794

Modelski, G. *International Conference on the Settlement of the Laotian Question, 1961–2.* Canberra: Australian National University, Research School of Pacific Studies, Department of International Relations, 1962. An outline of the Geneva Conference, together with the texts of the agreements "reached on Laos" neutrality.

795

Zagoria, Donald S. *The Sino-Soviet Conflict, 1956–1961.* Princeton: Princeton University Press, 1962. Laos as a minute pawn is involved in this clash between the giants.

796

Nuechterlein, Donald E. *Thailand and the Struggle for Southeast Asia.* Ithaca: Cornell University Press, 1965. Post-war crises in Laos, and its penetration by communist forces commands attention.

797

Meeker, Oden. *The Little World of Laos.* New York: Charles Scribner's Sons, 1959.

Documents

798

Great Britain. *Documents Relating to the Discussion of Korea and Indo-China at the Geneva Conference, April 27–June 1954.* Parliamentary Papers XXXI. Miscellaneous No. 16 (1954). Cmd. 9186. London: Her Majesty's Stationery Office, 1954. Part 2, on Indo-China (105-168) gives speeches of delegates and proposals submitted at the Geneva Conference, while CMD 9239, Miscellaneous 20 (1954) *Further Documents Relating to the Discussion of Indo-China at the Geneva Conference June 16–July 21, 1954,* gives the final declaration, together with the U. S. and Vietnam statements; as well as final text of the Treaty.

799

_____. *International Conference on the Settlement of the Loatian Question, May 12, 1961–July 23, 1962.* Cmd. 1828. Laos No. 1 (1954). London: Her Majesty's Stationery Office, October 1962.

800

_____. *Vietnam and the Geneva Agreements. Documents concerning the discussions between representatives of Her Majesty's Government and the Government of the Union of Soviet Socialist Republics held in London in April and May 1956, March 30–May 8, 1956.* Parliamentary Papers XLV. Cmd. 9763. Vietnam No. 2 (1956). London: Her Majesty's Stationery Office, 1956.

801

_____. *First Interim Report of the International Commission for Supervision and Control in Laos, August 11–December 31, 1954.* Cmd. 9445. Laos No. 1 (1955). London: Her Majesty's Stationery Office, 1955. These reports are published annually.

ECONOMIC PATTERNS

802

Halpern, Joel M. "Capital, Saving and Credit among Lao Peasants," in Raymond Firth and B. S. Yamey (eds.) *Capital Saving and Credit in Peasant Societies.* London: Allen and Unwin, 1964, 82-103. A sparse population which practices subsistence agriculture, has little capital and saves rarely; credit involves the Chinese.

803

_____. *Economy and Society of Laos.* New Haven: Monograph Series 5, Southeast Asia Studies, Yale University, 1964. Integrates earlier work on northern and central Laos of a socio-economic nature with additional material on various aspects of the economy and the people. One of the most useful of the few detailed surveys available.

804

Solheim, William G. and Hackenberg, Robert A. "The Importance of Anthropological Research to the Mekong Valley Project." *France-Asie* 169 (1961) 2459-2474. The socio-economic system in the basin is described, changes forecast and research urged.

805

Schaaf, C. Hart and Fifield, Russell H. *The Lower Mekong: Challenge to cooperation in Southeast Asia.* New York: Van Nostrand, 1963. In two sections; Fifield examines the political currents of Laos (and the other countries concerned — Cambodia, Vietnam and Thailand) and Schaaf explains the economics involved in the harnessing of the Mekong River now under way.

806

Halpern, J. M. "Trade Patterns in Northern Laos." *Eastern Anthropologist* XII, 2 (1958) 119-24. A general survey of geographic and ethnographic facts, the institution of *Lam,* transport, pattern of business, silver currency and the role of opium.

807

_____. "The Role of the Chinese in Lao Society." *Journal, Siam Society* 49 (1961) 21-46. Small urban groups of South Chinese with a dominant role in commerce; with five tables.

808

Robequain, C. *The Economic Development of French Indo-China.* London: Oxford University Press, 1944. Lao pre-war agriculture, communications, financing, population and trade receive brief consideration.

VIETNAM

GENERAL

Vietnam is perhaps the best-known country in Southeast Asia today. Until recently it was the least-studied. This dichotomy shows up clearly in any bibliography. It has an ominous similarity to Serbia, where, at little known Serajevo, the first World War began. Suddenly Serbia was a household word to millions who had never heard of it before, millions who could find little to explain its background or why it had become world-famous.

Lying alongside the South China Sea, with inland mountains separating it from countries further west, Vietnam's lines of communications are from the north. Thus it is almost a part of East Asia, rather than Southeast Asia. Particularly is this true of its northern bag of rice, the river valley area of Tonkin, which today is the Democratic Republic of Vietnam. For hundreds of years this fertile area was the south-ernmost river of China, and the Chinese influence in the culture of its people is strong. The southern bag of rice, separated from the north by a long narrow strip of plains and mountains, is the delta region of the Mekong River. This north-south division has lasted throughout its history, and is of course a basic factor in its development today.

The drift of settlement has been always from north to south. The later immigrants caused the earlier settlers to move farther southward, or alter-natively off the plains and into the mountains; or to intermarry and merge with those coming behind.

Relatively little of its past has been written that can be used here, for although Vietnamese records of the state centered at Hue date back in detail to the 18th century, this is a language few people, other than Vietnamese, are able to use. French occupation of this area in the 19th century promoted scholar-ship in some directions, notably archaeology, but little that might encourage nationalism was per-mitted. For the last 20 years a fierce and unpredic-table war has kept scholarship at a minimal level. The following is a bibliography of works that indi-cate the gaps, and reveal the absence of the type of research undertaken in other parts of Southeast Asia. The bibliography may also indicate how very much Vietnam was considered on the fringe of Sino-logical studies.

Bibliographies

809

Hobbs, Cecil C. and others. *Indochina. A Bibliography of the Land and the People.* Washington: Library of Con-gress, 1950. A 1850-item bibliography, largely of French works, some in English; and a section each on Russian and Vietnamese language items. Major attention on Viet-nam.

810

Embree, John F. and Dotson, Lillian O. *Bibliography of the Peoples and Cultures of Mainland Southeast Asia.* New Haven: Southeast Asia Studies, Yale University, 1950. An 800-page book, with two major sections on Vietnam: "Vietnam and the Vietnamese," and "Vietnam Tribal and Ethnic Minority Groups;" very largely French language items.

811

Auvade, Robert. *Bibliographe Critique Des Oeuvres Parues Sur L'Indochine Francaise.* Paris: G-P Maisonneuve and Larose, 1965. Generous annotation is given to 150 books, nearly all French, listed under bibliography, culture, sociology, social and economic structure, history and politics, and the war.

812

Chen Ching-Ho. "The Imperial Archives of the Nguyen Dynasty 1802–1945." *Journal, Southeast Asian History* 3, 2 (1962) 111-127. An outline of that which still sur-vives, and the valiant attempt to publish it.

813

Hobbs, Cecil. *Southeast Asia. An Annotated Bibliography of Selected Reference Sources in Western Languages. Revised and Enlarged.* Washington: Library of Congress, 1964. As with other general bibliographies listed elsewhere relating to the Southeast Asian region, this contains a section on Vietnam.

Journals

814

Bulletin de L'Ecole Francaise d'Extreme-Orient. Paris and Hanoi, 1901– . For over sixty years, articles on archa-eology, art, ethnology and history of "IndoChina," cover-ing all the former French possessions.

815

France-Asie. Saigon and Tokyo, 1946– . An enterprising bi-annual, on cultural, economic, political and historical aspects of "Indochina;" occasionally articles and special issues in English.

Land, People, and Language

"Two bags of rice on a pole," is a description of Vietnam not without merit. The Tonkin area, or North Vietnam, is one rice bowl, where indeed rice has been irrigated for millennia, and where perhaps the very idea of tropical rice cultivation may have been developed. The Mekong River basin and its broad alluvial plains is the southern rice bowl. Be-tween the two, the north-south mountain chain crowds close to the coast, and the communicable land link is restricted. Hue, the ancient capital of this land, was strategically placed in the center. The two new capitals of Hanoi and Saigon reflect the shift of balance to a one-rice-bag country.

816

Indo-China. London: Geographical Handbook Series, Naval Intelligence Division, British Admiralty, 1943. Over 500 pages of detailed information prepared during the Pacific War by leading geographers headed by H. C. Darby, on the geology, climate, fauna, coastlines, rivers and other physical features, and the political, economic and social geography of the Indochinese area.

817

Dobby, E. H. G. *Southeast Asia*. London: University of London Press. 8 ed. 1964. Includes a sound, comprehensive survey of the geography of Vietnam.

818

Fisher, Charles A. *Southeast Asia. A Social, Economic and Political Geography*. New York: E. P. Dutton, 1964. The modern states of Indochina, including Vietnam, are considered on pp. 529-80; useful maps, tables and bibliography.

819

Lebar, Frank M., Hickey, Gerald C. and Musgrave, John K. *Ethnic Groups Of Mainland Southeast Asia*. New Haven: Human Relations Area Files Press, 1964. In this major work of ethnography, a description is given of various basic characteristics of the Vietnamese people, such as: their location; settlement patterns; economy; kin groups; marriage and family; sociopolitical organization; and religion, pp. 161-75; minority groups in Vietnam also receive attention. Comprehensive bibliography.

820

Gourou, Pierre. *The Peasants of the Tonkin Delta: A Study of Human Geography*. 2 vols. New Haven: Human Relations Area Files Press, 1955. Published originally in French in 1936; a description of the land, the people and the way of life of the delta peasants in northern Vietnam; bibliography.

821

Janse, Olov R. T. *The Peoples of French Indo-China*. Washington: Smithsonian Institution, 1944. A brief monograph, giving some description in a succinct page or two, of the various races; many photographs.

822

Condominas, Georges. "The Mnong Gar of Central Vietnam," in George P. Murdock (ed.) *Social Structure in Southeast Asia*. Viking Fund Publications in Anthropology 29. Chicago: Quadrangle Books, 1960. 15-23. A Mon-Khmer tribe of the mountainous interior which resorts to shifting cultivation and practices matrilineal descent. (Article is in French).

823

Zelinsky, Wilber. "The Indochinese Peninsula: A Demographic Anomaly." *Far Eastern Quarterly* 9 (1950) 115-145. A description and explanation of the puzzle that Indochina, while close to overpopulated areas, is underpopulated.

824

Broek, Ruth. *Indochina*. New York: Doubleday, 1960. A brief survey of its cultural geography, prepared with the cooperation of the American Geographical Society.

825

Benedict, P. K. "Languages and Literatures of Indochina." *Far Eastern Quarterly* 6 (1947) 379-389. Vietnamese (then called Annamese), Lao, Cham and Khmer the indigenous tongues are discussed.

826

Jones, Robert B. and Huynh sanh Thong. *Introduction to Spoken Vietnamese*. Washington: American Council of Learned Societies, 1960. In three parts: pronunciation, with six lessons; the Vietnamese system of writing, with another six lessons; more dialogue and reading newspapers.

827

Thompson, Laurence C. and Nguyen duc Hiap. *A Vietnamese Reader*. Seattle: University of Washington Press, 1961. Intended for the student with a basic knowledge of spoken Vietnamese; a follow-up to Jones and Huynh sanh Thong.

828

Nguyen-Dinh-Hoa. *Speak Vietnamese*. Publication of the School of Languages 1. Saigon: Vien Khao, 1957. First prepared for Columbia University in 1953, with 30 graded lessons on the colloquial language of Saigon, this is a useful introduction to spoken Vietnamese.

829

Le Van Hung. *Vietnamese-English Dictionary*. Paris: Editions Europe-Asie, 1955. Over 30,000 words included in this work; her English-Vietnamese dictionary is promised.

830

Le-Bah-Khanh and Le-Bah-Kong. *Standard Pronouncing English-Vietnamese and Vietnamese-English Dictionary*. New York: F. Ungar, 1955. Designed for Vietnamese-speaking users rather than English-speaking users, but nevertheless adequate.

831

Nguyen-Dinh-Hoa. *Vietnamese - English Dictionary*. Rutland: Tuttle, 1966. Considered by many as the best dictionary available. First published in Saigon in 1959.

HISTORY

Although the history of Vietnam is known to us in outline form, there are insufficient works in the English language to permit any study in depth. This applies particularly to the many centuries before the 19th. The Dong-s'on bronze age culture is a part of Southeast Asian prehistory, so it is dealt with there. Some work has been done in that area, but very little, relatively speaking, is devoted to the long centuries of Chinese occupation or domination, or to the early states such as Funan and Champa, which even then had a strongly nationalist attitude. The later states, the growth of Hue as a political center of some sophistication, the early reactions of the Vietnamese to the 18th century French, the Vietnamese wars with Cambodia, and the internal developments, are known to us only in a tantalizingly skimpy manner. Even 19th and 20th century history leaves much to be desired, and the serious scholar seeking amplification for many points must still refer to the work which has been done in French.

Early Centuries

GENERAL WORKS

832

Buttinger, J. *The Smaller Dragon. A Political History of Vietnam*. New York: Praeger, 1958. A major work of scholarship, alone in its field; deals in detail with the history of Vietnam from 207 B.C. until the end of the 19th century A.D. A comprehensive survey.

833

Burling, Robbins. *Hill Farms and Padi Fields. Life in Mainland Southeast Asia*. Englewood Cliffs: Prentice-Hall, 1966. Not a political history, but an examination of the various cultural changes and developments within the area, including Vietnam, which over the millennia have affected the way of life of the villagers.

834

Coedes, G. *The Making of South East Asia*. London: Routledge and Kegan Paul, 1966. In this survey of mainland Southeast Asia up to the watershed period of the 13th century A.D., the early states on the Vietnamese peninsula are outlined, while Part II, chapter one deals specifically with "The Chinese conquest of the Red River Delta and the birth of Vietnam."

835

_____. *Les etats hindouises d'Indochine et d'Indonesie*. Paris: E. de Boccard, 1964. Funan and other peninsula states are studied in this classic work.

836

Wang Gungwu. "The Nanhai Trade, a study of the early history of Chinese trade in the South China Sea." *Journal, Malayan Branch Royal Asiatic Society,* 31, 3 (1958). A scholarly monograph which uses Chinese sources to describe Chinese contacts with Vietnam throughout this period.

837

Reischauer, Edwin O. and Fairbank, John K. *East Asia. The Great Tradition.* Boston: Houghton Mifflin, 1960. Vietnam, particularly the north, has been almost as much a part of East Asia as Southeast Asia. It is a part, if a neglected part, of Sinological studies, for Chinese influence during the early millennia became for centuries Chinese control. References to this are in the index of this excellent survey of China, p. 736.

838

Groslier, Bernard Philippe. *Indochina. Art in the Melting Pot of Races.* London: Methuen, 1962. As with other works listed under "Cambodia," the bronze civilization of Dong-s'on, and the early states of Vietnam such as Funan, Champa and Chen-la, are described here.

839

Majumdar, R. C. *Ancient colonies in the Far East.* 1. *Champa.* Lahore: Punjab Sanskrit Book Depot, 1927. One of the very few works devoted to this Malaysian race and their ancient state.

SPECIAL STUDIES ON PRE-NGUYEN DYNASTY

840

Janse, Olov R. T. *Archaeological Research in Indo-China.* Harvard-Yenching Institute Monograph Series 7 and 10. 2 vols. Cambridge: Harvard University Press, 1947. Describes excavation of the Chiu-Chen district of the Han dynasty finds. Other scholarly contributions on this and earlier periods are listed in the Southeast Asia section, as they belong, more properly, to the region as a whole.

841

Wheatley, Paul. "Discursive Scholia on Recent Papers on Agricultural Terracing and on Related Matters pertaining to Northern Indochina and Neighbouring Areas." *Pacific Viewpoint* 6, 2 (1965) 123-144. Issued also in the reprint series of Berkeley's Center for International Studies; this examines the nature and origins of tropical agricultural terracing in northern Vietnam.

842

Briggs, Lawrence Palmer. "The Hinduized States of Southeast Asia: A Review." *Far Eastern Quarterly* 7 (1948) 376-393. An article in its own right, which summarizes the views of Coedes, and which presents alternative hypotheses on the early history of Vietnam.

843

Chan Hok-Lam. "Chinese Refugees in Annam and Champa at the end of the Sung Dynasty." *Journal, Southeast Asian History* 7, 2 (1966) 1-10. Thousands fleeing from the collapsing court from 1276 onwards found shelter in Vietnam.

844

Woodside, A. B. *Early Ming expansionism 1406–1437. China's Abortive Conquest of Vietnam.* Cambridge: Papers on China 17, Center for East Asian Studies, Harvard University, 1963.

845

Murakami, Hideo. " 'Viet Nam' and the Question of Chinese Aggression." *Journal, Southeast Asian History* 7, 2 (1966) 11-26. Looks into the meaning of the words "Viet Nam," a matter of some importance.

846

Luce, G. H. "Countries Neighbouring Burma." *Journal, Burma Research Society* 14 (1924) 138-205. A series of translations from Chinese histories dealing with southward voyages in the early centuries A.D., some of which have relevance to Vietnam.

847

Le Tac, Manh-Nghi and Tran-Kinh-Hoa (eds.). *An-Nam-Chi-Lu'oc.* Hue: University of Hue, 1961. Le Tac, who lived in 1285, when the Mongols invaded Vietnam, wrote this account of Vietnamese life and institutions after returning with the Mongols to China. It is the oldest surviving historical document written by a Vietnamese. It is presented here in its original Chinese together with a translation in modern Vietnamese.

French Penetration and Occupation

The major factor in modern Vietnamese history has been the French impact and the nationalist reaction against it. French missionaries in the 18th century became French conquerors in the 19th. France, disappointed or unassuaged in China, involved itself heavily in Vietnam, particularly in the late 19th century, once it had recovered from its humiliating defeat in Europe at the hands of Prussia. Vietnam resisted, was conquered, but never fully surrendered. Deep down it preserved its soul, and as France became weaker in the 20th century, the colonial edifice became more and more unacceptable to those who had to live there. But much from France was transmitted to Vietnam, and for several generations at least a French legacy will remain.

GENERAL WORKS

848

Cady, J. F. *The Roots of French Imperialism in Eastern Asia.* Ithaca: Cornell University Press, 1954. French early 19th century relations with China and its penetration of "Indochina" until imperialism had taken root there in the 1870's; with detailed annotated bibliography.

849

Buttinger, Joseph. *A Dragon Embattled: A History of Colonial and Postcolonial Vietnam.* 2 vols. New York: Praeger, 1967. A successor to his earlier work, this discusses the impact of French colonial rule, the beginnings and growth of modern nationalism, the rise to power of the communists, the Japanese occupation and the post-war period; a substantial contribution to our knowledge of Vietnam.

850

Thompson, V. *French Indo-China.* London: Allen and Unwin, 1937. Discusses the history and numerous other aspects of colonial administrative institutions; the economy, the contacts between Vietnamese and French civilizations, and the varied reaction by Vietnamese and others to the French.

851

Robequain, C. *The Economic Development of French Indo-China.* London: Oxford University Press, 1944. A substantial work, dealing with the new factors introduced by the French, or the latent possibilities utilized by them which transformed the economy of Vietnam in the first 40 years of the 20th century, in particular.

852

Chesneaux, Jean. *Contribution A L'Histoire De La Nation Vietnamienne.* Paris: Editions Sociales, 1962. An outline history with chapters on the land and the people, the early period, the 16th to the 18th centuries, and then in more detail the 19th (5 chapters) and the 20th century (5 chapters); with a brief bibliography for each chapter.

853

Roberts, S. H. *History of French Colonial Policy, 1870–1925.* London: F. Cass, 1963. First published in 1929. After general principles and theories of French policy, Vietnam receives consideration on pp. 419-98. Useful in understanding French attitude and actions.

854

Nguyen Van Thai and Nguyen Van Mung. *A Short History of Vietnam*. Saigon: Times Publishing, for the Vietnamese-American Association, 1958. A simple factual account in six sections, five of which deal with the 19th and 20th centuries; the first history of Vietnam written in English by a Vietnamese.

855

Ennis, T. E. *French Policy And Developments in Indochina*. Chicago: Chicago University Press, 1936. A description of French penetration and an analysis of economic, social and administrative problems since French occupation in the 1850's.

856

Maspero, Georges (ed.). *Un empire colonial français l'Indochine*. 2 vols. Paris: Les Editions G. Van Oest, 1929. A number of specialists contribute to this major work on the geography, history, administration, economics, peoples and literature of the area; extensive bibliography to each chapter.

SPECIALIZED STUDIES, 19TH CENTURY

857

Lamb, A. "British Missions To Cochin China." *Journal, Malayan Branch, Royal Asiatic Society* 34, 3-4 (1961). A scholarly monograph which accompanies the original accounts of six 18th and 19th century missions with a valuable preface.

858

Thomson, R. Stanley. "France in Cochin China: the question of retrocession 1962–65." *Far Eastern Quarterly* 6 (1947) 364-78. The Cochin Chinese treaty of 1862 was argued fiercely in the Paris parliament.

859

_____. "The Diplomacy of Imperialism: France and Spain in Cochin China 1858–63." *Journal Modern History* 12 (1940) 334-356.

860

Saxena, Sri Krishna. "Causes Leading to the Deputation of a Burmese Political Mission to the Court of Cochin-China (1822–1824) and its Results." *Bulletin de L'Ecole Française d'Extreme-Orient* 45 (1951) 373-379. This minor incident is referred to also by another article included in the section on Burma.

861

Lasker, Bruno. *Human Bondage In Southeast Asia*. Chapel Hill: University of North Carolina, 1950. Slavery, debt bondage, serfdom, compulsory labor, and other forms of economic and social injustice as recorded throughout historic times all over Indo-China.

862

Langer, W. L. *The Diplomacy of Imperialism, 1890–1902*. New York: Knopf, 1956. Within the context of world wide European rivalry for colonies, Indochina is treated briefly (pp. 43-5, 390-96).

863

Lyautry, M. *Intimate Letters From Tonkin*. London: The Bodley Head, 1932. The translated letters of one of France's great pro-consuls, relating to the momentous achievements of 1894–1896, in the north.

864

Morse, Hosea B. *The International Relations of the Chinese Empire*. 3 vols. London: Longmans Green 1910–18. "France and Tongking." in Vol. 2, 340-367, is an account of Sino-French relations during the French conquest of Vietnam.

865

Orleans, H. D. *Around Tonkin and Siam*. London: Chapman and Hall, 1894. Hanoi and other towns visited while journeying from Tonkin to Siam. See also his *From Tonkin to India*. London: Methuen, 1898, an overland trip to the Irrawaddy River.

866

Scott, J. G. *France and Tongking*. London: Unwin, 1885. A narrative of the 1884 campaign of the French by Sir George Scott, the Burmese scholar.

867

Gaultier, Marcel. *Minh-Mang*. Paris: Larosse, 1935. The internal politics, Christian missions, wars and revolutions, social organization and foreign relations during the reign of the emperor Minh Mang, from 1791 to 1841.

868

Roberts, Edmund. *Embassy to the Eastern Courts of Cochin-China, Siam and Muscat*. New York: Harper and Brothers, 1837. Appointed by U. S. Government to secure commercial treaties, Roberts tells here of his mission; Vietnam is described on pp. 171-226.

869

Barrow, John. *A Voyage To Cochinchina, in the years 1792 and 1793*. London: T. Cadell and Davies, 1806. A detailed account from pp. 243-362 of the people and leaders of Vietnam, together with a historical sketch and an outline of the French foothold there.

870

Norman, C. B. *Tonkin, or France In The Far East*. London: Chapman and Hall, 1884. Describes in detail the occupation of North Vietnam from 1882, and the fighting against the Vietnamese that was involved, as well as French-Chinese relations of this period.

TWENTIETH CENTURY—PRE-PACIFIC WAR

871

Thompson, Virginia and Adloff, Richard. *The Left Wing in Southeast Asia*. New York: Sloane, 1950. Chapter II devoted to Vietnam; deals with early career of Nguyen ai-Quoc, now known as Ho Chih Minh.

872

Sacks, Milton. *Political Alignments of Vietnamese Nationalists*. Washington: Department of State, No. 3708, 1949. A detailed study of the Vietnamese nationalist movement, with major emphasis on its pre-war history.

873

Purcell, Victor. *The Chinese In Southeast Asia*. 2nd ed. London: Oxford University Press, 1965. An outline of the Chinese in the three Indochinese States, on pp. 167-221.

874

Thompson, Virginia and Richard Adloff. *Minority Problems in Southeast Asia*. Stanford: Stanford University Press, 1955. In two small sections, the Chinese and Indians in Vietnam are discussed.

875

Langlois, Walter G. *Andre Malraux. The Indochina Adventure*. London: Pall Mall Press, 1966. As a young liberal from 1926–27, France's present Minister of Foreign Affairs became involved in Vietnamese nationalist endeavors. A revealing picture of colonial injustice and autocracy.

876

Chesneaux, Jean. "Stages in the Development of the Vietnam National Movement 1862–1904." *Past and Present* 7 (1955) 63-75. A communist view.

877

Handler, J. "Indochina: Eighty Years of French Rule." *Annals, American Academy of Political and Social Science*. 226 (1943) 129-136. A non-communist view, somewhat briefer.

878

Thompson, V. M. "Indochina. France's great stake in the Far East." *Far Eastern Survey* 6 (1937) 15-22. Historical, political, economic and social aspects of the French position.

879

Brodrick, Allan H. *Little China, the Annamese Lands*. London: Oxford University Press, 1942. A travel book, written by an observant correspondent, critical of colonial Europeans, interested in Asians and their lands.

880

Coolidge, H. J. and Roosevelt, T. *Three Kingdoms of Indo-china.* New York: Crowell, 1933. The Kelly-Roosevelt expedition of the Chicago Field Museum; maps and photographs.

881

Levy, Roger. "Indochina in 1931–1932." *Pacific Affairs* 5 (1932) 205-217. Tumultuous years, with riots, risings, and repressions.

882

Rouband, Louis. *Viet Nam.* Paris: Valois, 1931. An early study of nationalism and communism in Vietnam.

883

Dorsenne, Jean. "Le peril rouge en Indochine." *Revue de deux mondes* (Paris). April 1932. 519-556.

Japanese Intervention

884

Levy, Roger, and Roth, Andrew. *French Interests And Policies In The Far East.* New York: Institute of Public Relations, 1941. Part two of this work, "French Indochina In Transition, 1938–41," largely concerns relations between France and Japan.

885

Uhalley, Stephen. "Japan's Southern Advance: The Indochina Phase." *Asian Studies* 4 (1966) 84-102. The unexpected ease of initial occupation of Vietnam was a basic factor tempting Japan in 1941 to consider, for the first time, moving into Southeast Asia.

886

Feis, Herbert. *The Road To Pearl Harbour.* New York: Atheneum, 1965. Published originally by Princeton in 1950, describing the gradual collision course of Japan and America, Vietnam from 1940 to 41 receives a mention as an object in the way.

From 1941 to the Geneva Conference

This period and subsequent developments have been studied in detail. These are dramatic events, and tragic too. France loses its self respect during the humiliating years of Japanese occupation, just as in France itself, for a time, all was shame. In the years after, when it tried to reimpose its 19th century authority on a nation that had the will to resist, it seemed blind to the great changes wrought by that occupation and by developments elsewhere in Asia. The world outside became involved, and scholars, at the coattails of the great, reflected that involvement. A desert of scholarship became a jungle of literature, through which an uncertain path has been picked.

GENERAL WORKS

887

Lancaster, Donald. *The Emancipation of French Indochina.* London: Oxford University Press, 1961. Perhaps the single most useful source dealing with Vietnam up to the Geneva Conference and the independence of 1954; a subtle, intelligent book which covers the nationalist movement of the 20th century in depth.

888

Hammer, Ellen J. *The Struggle For Indochina.* Stanford: Stanford University Press, 1954. Another work equally valuable for its pre-war material and its coverage of the post-war decade; a thorough review of French and nationalist activities from their beginnings in Vietnam; and the inexorable movement towards a militant crisis after the Japanese surrender.

889

Sacks, I. Milton. "Marxism in Viet Nam," in Frank N. Trager (ed.). *Marxism In Southeast Asia.* Stanford: Stanford University Press, 1960. 102-170. A detailed, careful survey of the indigenous roots of Vietnamese nationalism, the emergence of Marxism and its rise in the 1920's and 1930's in the face of pre-war weaknesses, and the Vietminh movement and the war, to 1954.

890

Brimmell, J. H. *Communism In South East Asia.* London: Oxford University Press, 1959. An outline of the ideology as well as the action of communists and nationalists in Vietnam, from the beginnings of Asian communism.

891

Decoux, Jean. *A la barrede l'Indochine; histoire de mon governement general, 1940–1945.* Paris: Plon, 1949. General Decoux gives the story of his wartime government in a large volume. De Gaulle, in his memoirs, has different views.

892

Shaplen, Robert. *The Lost Revolution.* New York: Harper and Row, 1965. Considers that the real tragedy of Vietnam occurred in the 1947–54 period, when the French and their acts of puppetry, rather than the nationalists, were supported.

893

Fall, Bernard B. *Street Without Joy.* enl. ed. New York: Praeger, 1964. The history of insurgency in Vietnam, in detail; a writhing snakes' nest of confused fighting, to Dien Bien Phu and Geneva, 1954; and in a less elaborate treatment, to 1964.

894

Gettleman, Marvin E. (ed.). *Vietnam: History, Documents and Opinions on a Major World Crisis.* New York: Fawcett Publications, 1965. A selection of reportage, scholarly analysis, and documentary material, covering Vietnam from 1943 to 1965.

895

O'Ballance, Edgar. *The Indo-China War, 1945–54. A Study in Guerrilla Warfare.* London: Faber, 1964. A 12-chapter history of the war, its stages of development clearly marked; useful list of relevant sources.

896

Cole, A. B. *Conflict in Indochina and International Repercussions. A Documentary History 1945–55.* Ithaca: Cornell University Press, 1956. Approximately one hundred key documents illustrating viewpoints, policies, and trends of the conflict; and attitudes of interested powers, from post-war beginnings to the Geneva Agreement of 1954.

897

Devillers, Philippe. *Histoire Du Viet-Nam de 1940 a 1952.* Paris: Editions du Seuil, 3rd ed. 1952. A thorough study by a recognized authority, on the nationalist-communist movement and French resistance.

898

Mus, Paul. *Vietnam, sociologue d'une guerre.* Paris: Editions du Seuil, 1962. A penetrating historico-sociological study. The impact of Marxism and other political ideologies on the peasant is considered, and the strength of nationalism is reviewed.

SPECIALIZED STUDIES

899

Devillers, Philippe. "Vietnamese Nationalism And French Policies," in W. L. Holland (ed.) *Asian Nationalism And The West.* New York: MacMillan, 1953. 197-265. A detailed examination of the immediate post-war period in Vietnam, actually the final three quarters of his work *Le Viet-Nam Contemporain.*

900

Dai, Shen-yu. "Peking And Indochina's Destiny." *Western Political Quarterly* 7 (1954) 346-368. An outline of the Chinese-French confrontation in Vietnam which began in the latter half of the 19th century; the beginnings of communism in Vietnam-China; the Vietminh; the conflict, and China's role throughout, to the Geneva Conference.

901

Clementin, J. R. "The Nationalist Dilemma in Vietnam." *Pacific Affairs* 23 (1950) 294-310. Describes the nationalist organizations linked to Ho Chih Minh in 1950, at the time that China became communist.

902

Sharp, Lauriston. "Paradoxes in the Indochinese dilemma." *Annals, American Academy of Political and Social Science* 294 (1954) 89-98.

903

Hammer, Ellen J. "The Bao Dai Experiment." *Pacific Affairs* 23 (1950) 46-58. The buttressing of this monarch after 1945: an examination of the parties involved and the futile hopes entertained.

904

Micaud, Charles A. "Post-War Governments and Politics of French Indo-China." *Journal of Politics* 9 (1947) 731-744. A lucid summary of the complicated developments in France and Vietnam immediately after the war.

905

Dang-chan-Lieu. "Annamese nationalism." *Pacific Affairs* 20 (1947) 61-66. An outline of the Vietnamese nationalist movement.

906

Gourou, Pierre. "For a French Indo-Chinese Federation." *Pacific Affairs* 20 (1947) 18-29. A French presence was necessary to protect the weaker races and to help the Vietnamese.

907

Lasker, Bruno (ed.). *New Forces In Asia*. New York: Wilson, 1950. Contains major portions of three articles on Vietnam: by Bruno Lasker, (background of Indochinese nationalism), Ellen Hammer and R. Laurel.

MINOR WORKS

908

Hammer, Ellen J. "Indochina," in Lawrence K. Rosinger and others. *The State of Asia*. New York: Knopf, 1951. 221-267.

909

Sacks, M. "Communism and Regional Integration," in P. Talbot (ed.) *South Asia in the World Today*. Chicago: Chicago University Press, 2nd imp. 1951.

910

Hammer, Ellen J. *The Emergence of Vietnam*. New York: Institute of Pacific Relations, 1947.

911

Lewis, N. *A Dragon Apparent — Travels in Indo-China*. London: Jonathan Cape, 1951. An observant traveler, interested in politics and contemporary affairs, writes on the Vietminh, the religious sects, and much else.

912

Isaacs, Harold R. (ed.). *New Cycle in Asia; selected documents on major international developments in the Far East, 1943-1947*. New York: MacMillan, 1947. Issued under the auspices of the Institute of Pacific Relations, six major documents (pp. 156-174) on Vietnam, and a summary of events.

The Geneva Conference: 1954

This was the international conference held in 1954 when the French, wearied by the years of unsuccessful war, with their own homeland in disarray, sought to negotiate terms for their withdrawal. Russia and Great Britain were among the interested nations of the world also anxious to see an end to the fighting and a reduction in world tensions. Their presence helped France, and produced a settlement whereby Vietnam was divided in two, with both sections regaining — as did Cambodia and Laos — their lost independence.

913

Eden, Anthony. *Memoirs of Anthony Eden: Full Circle*. Boston: Houghton Mifflin, 1960. In this volume of his autobiography, the former British Prime Minister discusses in detail the working and achievements of the 1954 Conference on Indochina.

914

Roy, Jules. *The Battle of Dienbienphu*. London: Faber & Faber, 1965. A detailed study, published originally as *La Bataille de Dien Bien Phu* (Paris: Julliard, 1963), of the battle that ended French hopes of re-establishing themselves in Vietnam, and ensured French acquiescence in withdrawal negotiations then under way at Geneva.

915

Great Britain. *Documents Relating to British Involvement in Indochina, 1945-1965*. Cmd. 2834. London: Her Majesty's Stationery Office, 1965. Includes most of the important communications involving Britain as co-chairman of the Geneva Conference; with 20-year summary of events.

916

Fall, Bernard B. "Indochina Since Geneva." *Pacific Affairs* 28 (1955) 3-25. Outlines political and economic developments in the north and south during the six months that had elapsed after the Geneva Agreements of 1954.

917

Murti, B. S. N. *Vietnam Divided. The Unfinished Struggle*. London. Asia Publishing House, 1964. Indian member of the International Commission in Vietnam, created by Geneva Conference, records the events that followed on that conference; an Asian view of Diem.

POLITICAL PATTERNS

No coherent contemporary political pattern is discernable in Vietnam. There is merely an agonized search for stability. Peaceful progress seems far off, as communists and non-communists, locked together, struggle for mastery. In areas where the war penetrates, but only occasionally, indigenous elements of the country are attempting to shape a pattern different from that devised by those who have inherited a pattern discernably influenced by France, or even America. Buddhist monks, young students, members of the military, perhaps represent the real Vietnam more accurately than other groups now in political control. Certainly their presence is becoming more effective; but, in the midst of this whirlwind, it is hardly the time to observe set patterns.

The political pattern as of 1968 was dominated by the war and by the American presence. No government, in the south or in the north, could ignore either. Change was slow, movement was almost frozen, and meaningful political development was rendered most difficult because of this.

The Diem Regime, 1954—63

GENERAL WORKS

918

Jumper, Roy and Marjorie Weiner Normand. "Vietnam," G. McT. Kahin (ed.). *Governments and Politics of Southeast Asia*. 2nd ed. Ithaca: Cornell University Press, 1964. A major analysis of the political patterns of both north

Jumper, Roy and Marjorie Weiner Normand (con't.)
and south Vietnam, dealing with the historical background, the contemporary setting, the political process
and the major problems of both states; with useful
reading list.

919

Fall, Bernard B. *The Two Vietnams. A Political and Military Analysis.* 3rd rev. ed. New York: Praeger, 1966.
Written by an informed scholar who has maintained his
interest in Vietnam for many years, this comprehensive
survey of the complicated French-Vietminh-Vietnam-
American involvement is a major work, essential for
both the north and the south; particularly concentrated
on the Diem period.

920

Bouscaren, Anthony T. *The Last of the Mandarins: Diem
of Vietnam.* Pittsburgh: Duquesne University Press, 1965.
A biography of the President of South Vietnam by an
admirer.

921

Warner, Denis. *The Last Confucian.* New York: MacMillan,
1963. Diem's biography by a long-time Southeast Asian
correspondent who appears critical of everyone, but
particularly Diem.

922

U. S. Army Area Handbook for Vietnam. Washington:
Pamphlet 550-40, Department of the Army, 1962.
Prepared by the Foreign Area Studies Division of the
American University, this is an objective, detailed, and
comprehensive work on contemporary Vietnam, with
attention focused on political, social, and economic
institutions; extensive bibliography of contemporary
material.

923

Scigliano, Robert. *South Vietnam: Nation Under Stress.*
Houghton Mifflin, 1963. The people, political patterns,
and economic efforts of a land where south resists the
north, where anti-communism restrains popular freedom,
and where Vietnamese and Americans are in an unequal
alliance; culminates in the 1963 coup against Diem.

924

Fall, Bernard B. *Vietnam Witness: 1953–66.* New York:
Praeger, 1966. A selection of his writings based on six
lengthy periods spent in the area from 1953 onwards, in
which the follies of all: French, Vietnamese and Americans, are cataloged, and an assessment made of the
future.

925

Gettleman, Marvin E. *Vietnam: History, Documents and
Opinions on a Major World Crisis.* New York: Fawcett
Publications, 1965. A selection of documentary material
covering 1945–65; a useful guide and survey.

926

Field, Michael. *The Prevailing Wind: Witness in Indo-
China.* London: Methuen, 1965. Interesting analysis of
Vietnamese national character; the Vietnamese predis-
position towards ideologies that provide complete
answers, and their fanaticism; describes Diem and his
family with insight.

SPECIALIZED STUDIES

927

Carver, George A. "The Faceless Viet Cong." *Foreign
Affairs* 44 (1966) 347-372. Gives names and substance
to the faceless Viet Cong, the southern branch of the
Viet Minh in Hanoi.

928

Weinstein, Franklin B. *Vietnam's Unheld Elections: The
Failure to Carry Out the 1956 Reunification Elections
and the Effect on Hanoi's Present Outlook.* Ithaca: Data
Paper 60, Southeast Asia Program, Cornell University,
1966. Endeavors to straighten the record over the confused story of the failure to hold the Vietnamese
re-unification elections scheduled for 1956; considers it
a vital cause of the present conflict.

929

Carver, George A. "The Real Revolution In South Vietnam." *Foreign Affairs* 43 (1965) 387-408. A penetrating
assessment of the social revolution under way in Vietnam,
with the French-educated and foreign-orientated mandarinate losing political power to a more militantly "Vietnamese" group, including students, monks and the
military.

930

Nguyen Tuyet Mai. "Electioneering: Vietnamese Style."
Asian Survey 11, 9 (1962) A participant in the 1959 elections gives an illuminating account of her experiences
which made a mockery of democracy.

931

Scigliano, Robert. "The Electoral Process in South Vietnam:
Politics in an underdeveloped state." *Midwest Journal of
Political Science* 4 (1960) 138-161.

932

Lindholm, Richard W. (ed.). *Vietnam: The First Five
Years. An International Symposium.* East Lansing, Mich:
Michigan State University Press, 1959. One of a series
of annual reviews by a group that was involved in Vietnam; 25 brief articles give a broad picture of Vietnam
between 1954 and 1959.

933

Scigliano, Robert. "Political Parties in South Vietnam under
the Republic." *Pacific Affairs* 33 (1960) 327-346. The
Revolutionary Labor Personalism Party, the National
Revolutionary Movement, the civil servants, and other
political groups.

934

Fall, Bernard B. "The Political-Religious Sects of Vietnam."
Pacific Affairs 28 (1955) 235-253. An outline of the
history of Cao-Daism, the Hoa Hao sect and the Binh-
Xuyen, the three sects suppressed by Diem.

935

Jumper, Roy. "The Communist Challenge to South Vietnam." *Far Eastern Survey* 25 (1956) 161-168. South
Vietnam under Ngo Diem by 1956 was reacting against
the Vietminh and the north; the techniques of the Vietminh among the peasants and the intellectuals outlined.

936

Fishel, Wesley R. (ed.). *Problems Of Freedom: Vietnam
Since Independence.* Glencoe: Free Press, 1961. Twelve
scholars examine partition, administration, personalism,
education, land reform, minorities and other socio-political problems.

937

Honey, P. J. "The Problem of Democracy in Vietnam."
World Today 16 (1960) 71-79. Examines Vietnam to see
whether the concept of a State exists, as well as political
freedoms; and decides they do not.

938

Nguyen Thai. *Is South Vietnam Viable?* Manila: Carmelo &
Bauermann, 1962. Yes, if . . . Has interesting bibliography
of nongovernment publications in Vietnam.

939

Marr, David. "Political Attitudes of Young Urban Intellectuals in South Viet Nam." *Asian Survey* 6 (1966) 249-
263. Frustrated youth, anti-American in many ways.

940

Scigliano, Robert and Snyder, Wayne W. "The Budget
Process in South Vietnam." *Pacific Affairs* 33 (1960)
48-60. Outlines the power of the executive and weakness
of the assembly.

941

Hammer, Ellen J. "Progress Report on Southern Vietnam."
Pacific Affairs 30 (1957) 221-235.

942

Grant, J. A. C. "The Vietnam Constitution of 1956." *American Political Science Review* 52 (1958) 437-463.

943

Dowdy, H. E. *The Bamboo Cross. Christian Witness in the
jungles of Viet Nam.* New York: Harper, 1964.

Village Patterns

944

Hickey, Gerald C. *Village in Vietnam*. New Haven: Yale University Press, 1964. A detailed study of the settlement pattern, village organizations and associations, social stratification and mobility, religion, health and education in the delta village of Khanh Haw, in Long An province.

945

Osborne, Milton E. *Strategic Hamlets In South Viet-Nam. A Survey and a Comparison*. Ithaca: Data Paper 55, Southeast Asia Program, Cornell University, 1965. An examination of the strategic hamlet program, an assessment of its effectiveness, and a comparison with the successful resettlement operation in Malaya.

946

Mus, Paul. "The role of the village in Vietnamese politics." *Pacific Affairs* 22 (1949) 265-272. The basic problems of Vietnam can be understood only if they have been viewed from the standpoint of the village.

947

Zasloff, Joseph. "Rural Resettlement in South Vietnam: The Agroville Program." *Pacific Affairs* 35 (1962-63). 327-340. The predecessor to the strategic hamlet project introduced in 1961, this 1959-61 scheme was an attempt to regroup southern peasants into rural centers; it failed.

948

O'Daniel, John W. *The Nation That Refused to Starve: The Challenge of the New Vietnam*. New York: Coward-McCann, 1960. An illustrated account of the resettlement of the refugees from communist North Vietnam after 1954.

Administration

949

Dang, Nghiem. *Viet-Nam: Politics And Public Administration*. Honolulu: East-West Center Press, 1966. Traces the historic pressures that have shaped the Vietnamese concept of the civil servant; nine centuries of Chinese domination, together with the French impact, as well as Buddhist and Indian influences; "how the administrator faces up to modern demands" is considered; the first systematic study of public administration in Vietnam.

950

Jumper, Roy. "Mandarin Bureaucracy and Politics in South Vietnam." *Pacific Affairs* 30 (1957) 47-58. The cultural background of the Vietnamese civil servant, his loss of power; and the involvement of administration and army in politics.

951

Dorsey, John T. "South Vietnam in Perspective." *Far Eastern Survey* 27 (1958) 177-182. An assessment of the administrative stability of 1958 as compared with the anarchy of 1954.

952

Jumper, Roy. "Problems of Public Administration in South Vietnam." *Far Eastern Survey* 26 (1957) 183-190. The list is long.

953

Carver, George A. "The Real Revolution In South Viet Nam." *Foreign Affairs* 43 (1965) 387-408. The more foreign-influenced and less indigenous groups, such as the French-educated mandarinate, are losing power to those with a more militant nationalism, such as students, monks and military.

954

Viet Nam Government Organization Manual 1957-58. Saigon: Institute of Administration Research and Documentation Division, Saigon, 1958. A 270-page manual on the organization of the Vietnamese administration, with details of all the departments involved.

The American Presence

955

Mecklin, John. *Mission In Torment. An Intimate Account of the U.S. role in Vietnam*. New York: Doubleday, 1965. Two years, 1962-1964, spent in a troubled land, disturbed by much of American policy and action.

956

Higgins, Marguerite. *Our Vietnam Nightmare*. New York: Harper, 1965. The gradually escalating involvement of America in the war in Vietnam is critically examined, and the U. S. is censured for its part in the overthrow of Diem in 1963.

957

Halberstam, David. *The Making of a Quagmire*. New York: Random House, 1965. The New York Times correspondent describes the fall of Diem in 1963 and the folly of the official American position in Vietnam.

958

Montgomery, John D. *The Politics of Foreign Aid. American Experience in Southeast Asia*. New York: Praeger. Vietnam receives the major attention of the four countries considered; the emphasis is on U. S. politics and actual successes achieved by aid.

959

Taylor, Milton C. "South Vietnam: Lavish Aid, Limited Progress." *Pacific Affairs* 34 (1961) 242-256. Aid is no guarantee of growth, particularly if the aid is clumsily conceived and applied.

960

Moore, Robert Lowell. *The Green Berets*. 14th imp. New York: Crown, 1966. An account of the U. S. Special Forces.

961

Browne, Malcolm W. *The New Face of War*. Indianapolis: Bobbs-Merrill, 1965.

The War

962

Fall, Bernard B. *Street Without Joy*. enl. ed. New York: Praeger, 1964. Perhaps the most complete account of the fighting of this 20-year war; a classic.

963

Tanham, George K. *Communist Revolutionary Warfare. The Vietminh in Indochina*. New York: Praeger, 1961. The Vietminh military doctrine, military organization and political motivation, logistics, personnel, operations and tactics.

964

Thompson, Sir Robert. *Defeating Communist Insurgency. Experiences from Malaya and Vietnam*. London: Chatto and Windus, 1966. Sir Robert draws wisely on his experiences in the Malayan Emergency, 1948-60, and 1961-65 and as head of the British Advisory Mission in Vietnam; emphasizes the non-military measures necessary to win a country.

965

Trager, Frank. "Vietnam: The Military Requirements for Victory." *Orbis* 8 (1964) 563-583. A scholar influential with the government outlines the three different kinds of war in Vietnam, and recommends measures for success.

966

Burchett, Wilfred G. *Vietnam: Inside Story of the Guerrilla War*. New York: International Publishers, 1965. A communist publicist gives first-hand descriptions of the Viet Cong from 1963 to 65; a brave and resourceful fighter.

967

Tringuier, Roger. *Modern Warfare; A French view of counter-insurgency*. New York: Praeger, 1963. Translated from the French by Daniel Lee; with an introduction by Bernard B. Fall.

968

Cross, James Eliot. *Conflict In The Shadows. The Nature and Politics of Guerrilla War*. New York: Doubleday, 1963.

969

O'Ballance, Edgar. *The Indo-China War, 1945–54. A Study in Guerrilla Warfare*. London: Faber, 1964. A useful survey of the first 10 years of this modern 20-year war.

ECONOMIC PATTERNS

Vietnam has the economy of a Southeast Asian colony enduring 20 years of unfinished war. It is a mess, scarcely a pattern. In the 19th century it was a non-developing static economy, a subsistence pattern that maintained a non-increasing population. French colonial control brought economic penetration in the 20th century. Roads linked areas hitherto isolated, ocean ships removed the products of colonial agricultural and extractive industries, and health measures encouraged a steady increase in population. The years of submission to the Japanese, and the war that began thereafter, ended the peace and ended the colonial pattern. Nothing has come in its place to suggest what stable economic pattern of the future will follow, and all that can be surmised is that in some way, the future will inherit the past.

970

United Nations. *Toward the Economic Development of the Republic of Viet-Nam*. Report Economic Survey Mission to the Republic of Viet Nam. New York: UN, 1959. A 300-page survey by U.N. Agencies of the country's basic data; and then a realistic planning outline given for all aspects of its economy.

971

Lindholm, Richard W. (ed.). *Vietnam: The First Five Years. An International Symposium*. East Lansing, Mich.: Michigan State University Press, 1959. Among the 25 articles published here, agricultural development, finance, industrial development, and other aspects of the nation's economy are included.

972

Fall, Bernard B. *The Two Viet-Nams. A Political and Military Analysis*. New York: Praeger, 1963. Chapter 14, "The Economic Base," surveys the economic pattern of modern Vietnam.

973

Robequain, C. *The Economic Development of French Indo-China*. London: Oxford University Press, 1944. A detailed description of how a static, underdeveloped region received the classic colonial treatment of all Southeast Asia, and emerged with good roads and miles of plantations.

974

Gourou, Pierre. *Land Utilization in French Indochina*. New York: Institute of Pacific Relations, 1945. A large work which deals in depth with the land, population, and rural economic activities; numerous tables and maps.

975

Hendry, James B. "Land Tenure in South Vietnam." *Economic Development and Cultural Change* 9 (1960) 27-40. Data collected in a delta village on land ownership, agrarian reform, land values and other aspects of land; tables and graphs.

976

Trued, M. N. "South Vietnam's Industrial Development Center." *Pacific Affairs* 33 (1960) 250-267. Founded in 1957, outlines problems and two-year achievements of the I.D.C. in its efforts to assist economic development.

977

Wurfel, David. "Agrarian Reform in the Republic of Vietnam." *Far Eastern Survey* 26 (1957) 81-92. A survey of the tenancy position and a consideration of the 1956 Ordinance aimed at land re-distribution and other reforms.

978

Miller, E. W. "Industrial Resources of Indochina." *Far Eastern Quarterly* 6 (1947) 396-408. The discouragement of industry by the French led to agricultural efforts receiving the main consideration; rice, tea, coffee, rubber, coal, and timber surveyed.

979

Bun Hoan. "Vietnam: Economic Consequences of the Geneva Peace." *Far Eastern Economic Review,* December 11, 1958. 753-57; "Vietnam: Structure of a Dependent Economy," *ibid.* December 18, 1958, 789-90, 793-94, 797-98; "Impact of Military Expenditure on the South Vietnamese Economy," *ibid.* December 25, 1958, 839-43. This Hong Kong weekly is a useful source for contemporary economic developments throughout East and Southeast Asia.

980

Bilodeau, Charles, Somlith Pathammavong and Le Quang Hong. *Compulsory Education in Cambodia, Laos and Vietnam*. Paris: UNESCO, 1955. A survey of existing educational facilities, with a view to their improvement.

SOCIAL AND CULTURAL PATTERNS

Little has been written concerning the social patterns of the people of Vietnam. The individual Vietnamese and the minority races have not been studied to the extent to which the Indonesians or Thai have been studied. His characteristics as an individual, a member of a family, a village or other group are scarcely recorded. Perhaps the most glaring blank is the current lack of scholarly works on Vietnamese Buddhism, for his religion today, and perhaps always, has direct political significance. Perhaps nothing more clearly reflects the pioneering stage of Southeast Asian studies than the small amount of readily available scholarship relating to the social patterns of Vietnam. Far off on the remote flank of Sinological studies, some Japanese and others have written on the Vietnamese, as have some French scholars; but their work is little known in the English-speaking world. Modern post-war research has been difficult, for it is not a post-war period at all in Vietnam, and the field work in village or monastery is the work of a war correspondent, not a research student. The situation may improve, but Vietnamese social patterns, of village or monastery, city or country, remain little studied.

981

Hickey, Gerald C. *Village in Vietnam*. New Haven: Yale University Press, 1964. A detailed study of the settlement pattern, village organization and associations, social stratification and mobility, religion, health and education, social relations and the family and household, in a south Vietnamese village. An outstanding work.

982

Mus, Paul. "Foreword" in Gerald C. Hickey. *Village in Vietnam*. This foreword (xi-xxiii) warrants a listing on its own.

983

Gourou, Pierre. *The Peasants of the Tonkin Delta: A Study of Human Geography.* 2 Vols. New Haven: Human Relations Area Files, 1955. Published originally in 1936, in French, this deals with the land, the people and the cultural patterns of the peasants in North Vietnam.

984

Mus, Paul. "The role of the village in Vietnamese politics." *Pacific Affairs* 22 (1949) 265-272. Another penetrating insight into village attitudes and behavior patterns.

985

Bilodeau, Charles, Somlith Pathammavong and Le Quang Hong. *Compulsory Education in Cambodia, Laos and Vietnam.* Paris: UNESCO, 1955. A review of the existing pattern and possible developments.

986

McAleavy, Henry. "Dien in China and Vietnam." *Journal, Asian Studies* 17 (1958) 403-415. The legal institution of *dien* — pledging or pawning — is outlined.

987

Carver, George A. "The Real Revolution In South Viet Nam." *Foreign Affairs* 43 (1965) 387-408. The social pattern in the cities is changing violently, with the more basically Vietnamese groups, such as monks, students and military, assuming more power from those less rooted in indigenous patterns; the French-educated and foreign-oriented civil servants.

NORTH VIETNAM

GENERAL

The Democratic Republic of Vietnam (DRV) was created in 1954, following the Geneva Agreements that ended the long war between the Vietnamese and the French. North Vietnam, as the new state came to be called, quickly established a communist way of life. Almost insurmountable difficulties were raised against visitors to deter nearly all non-communists. Research has been made most difficult. As a result, little sustained scholarship has been undertaken thus far.

Bibliography

988

Keyes, June Godfrey. *A Bibliography of North Vietnamese Publications in the Cornell University Library.* Ithaca: Data Paper 17, Southeast Asia Program, Cornell University, 1962. A 116-page, briefly annotated, list of materials on North Vietnam, mainly — but not entirely — post 1954.

General Works

989

Jumper, Roy and Normand, Marjorie Weiner. "Vietnam." George MacT. Kahin (ed.). *Governments and Politics of Southeast Asia.* Ithaca: Cornell University Press, 2nd ed. 1965. The contemporary setting, political process, and major current problems of North Vietnam are here treated, 460-524.

990

Fall, Bernard B. *The Viet-Minh Regime: Governments and Administration in the Democratic Republic of Vietnam.* rev. ed. Ithaca: Institute of Pacific Relations, 1956. Outlines and interprets events surrounding the birth of the state, and discusses developments re: North Vietnam, including the Geneva Conference, from 1941 to 1954.

991

Honey, P. J. *Communism In North Vietnam: Its role in the Sino-Soviet dispute.* Cambridge: Massachusetts Institute of Technology Press, 1964. Beginning with a history of the North Vietnam Communist Party, the author traces the policies pursued by various members of the leadership; Sino-North Vietnamese relations, and the role played by North Vietnam in Sino-Russian relations also are examined.

992

_____. (ed.). *North Vietnam Today: Profile Of A Communist Satellite.* New York: Praeger, 1962. A detailed picture of life in Ho Chi Minh's new state, as presented in 10 essays by Vietnamese, European, and American scholars.

993

Ho Chi Minh. *Selected Works.* 3 vols. Hanoi: Foreign Languages Publishing House, 1960–61. Articles and speeches by Ho between 1920 and 1954.

994

Vo Nguyen Giap. *People's War, People's Army: The Viet Cong Insurrection Manual for Under-developed Countries.* New York: Praeger, 1962. A series of articles by the North Vietnamese military leader, covering various aspects of the war against the French, to 1954; Bernard Fall contributes a biographical sketch of Giap.

995

Starobin, Joseph. *Eyewitness in Indochina.* New York: Cameron and Kahn, 1954. An ex-communist interviews Ho Chi Minh and writes re: a jungle base in 1953, and the administration of communist-controlled territory.

996

Hoang Van Chi. *From Colonialism to Communism.* New York: Praeger, 1964. One who was there — but not with them — writes of the first years of communist North Vietnam.

POLITICAL PATTERNS

General Works

997

Fall, Bernard B. "A Straight Zigzag:" The Road to Socialism in North Viet-Nam," in A. Doak Barnett (ed.) *Communist Strategies in Asia.* New York: Frederick A. Praeger, 1963. 199-227. North Vietnam, along with Yugoslavia, imposed its communist system from within; can stand on its own feet as a military power; and has never experienced a major purge; all unique features which are explained here in a useful resumé covering events from 1941.

998

Fischer, Ruth. "Ho Chi Minh: Disciplined Communist." *Foreign Affairs* 33, 1 (1954) 86-97. An outline of his career confirms the writer's view of Ho as basically a nationalist.

999

Lacouture, Jean. *Vietnam: Between Two Truces.* New York: Random House, 1966. The discussion of differences between North Vietnam and the National Liberation Front in the south is particularly interesting.

1000

Honey, P. J. "The Position of the DRV Leadership and the Succession to Ho Chi Minh," in P. J. Honey (ed.) *North Vietnam Today.* New York: Praeger, 1962. 47-60. The nature of the leadership in North Vietnam, and the position of Vo Nguyen Giap, Truong Chinh and others, as possible successors to power.

1001

Fall, Bernard B. "North Vietnam's Constitution and Government." *Pacific Affairs* 33 (1960) 282-290. A survey of the 1960 elections, and the individuals affected, with biographical material on new appointments.

1002

McVey, Ruth. *The Calcutta Conference and the Southeast Asian Uprisings.* Ithaca: Modern Indonesia Project, Southeast Asia Program, Cornell University, 1958. The North Vietnamese delegation took a controversial position.

1003

Burchett, Wilfred G. *North of the Seventeenth Parallel.* Delhi: Peoples Publishing House, 1956. An experienced pro-communist describes a jungle base of Ho Chi Minh, shortly before the battle of Dien Bien Phu; other useful information can be sifted from the chaff.

1004

Murti, B. S. *Vietnam Divided. The Unfinished Struggle.* London: The Asia Publishing House, 1964. Ho Chi Minh's success from 1945 to 1954 is described on pp. 93-112 by the author, an Indian member of the International Commission in Vietnam.

Foreign Relations

1005

Honey, P. J. *Communism in North Vietnam: Its Role in the Sino-Soviet Dispute.* Cambridge: Massachusetts Institute of Technology Press, 1964. Stresses factors such as geography and leadership that have influenced communism in the Sino-Soviet dispute; also a history of its differing relationship with the two.

1006

Hinton, Harold. *Communist China in World Politics.* Boston: Houghton Mifflin, 1966. Contains a useful section on China's relations with the Democratic Republic of Vietnam.

1007

Donnell, John C. "North Vietnam: A Qualified Pro-Chinese Position," in Robert A. Scalopino (ed.) *The Communist Revolution In Asia.* New Jersey: Prentice-Hall, 1965 140-172. Traces the gradual ascendancy over the pro-Soviet elements of the pro-China element in North Vietnam from 1954 to 1965, with the stand of individual central committee members examined.

1008

Hinton, Harold L. "Sino-Vietnamese Relations," in Harold L. Hinton (ed.) *China's Relations with Burma and Vietnam: A Brief Survey.* New York: Institute of Pacific Relations, 1958. The Chinese Nationalist move into North Vietnam from 1945-46, and North Vietnamese relations with Communist China after 1949.

1009

Beloff, Max. *Soviet Policy in the Far East 1944–1951.* London: Oxford University Press, 1953. Russian relations with Ho Chi Minh are described on pp. 221-228.

1010

Shen Yu Dai. *Peking, Moscow and the Communist Parties of Colonial Asia.* Cambridge: M.I.T., 1954.

ECONOMIC AND SOCIAL PATTERNS

The little that is known of the economic and social pattern of North Vietnam reveals a tight state control over all economic activity, and a heavy, monolithic ideology pressing on the people. Doctrinaire handling of the land issue, in which peasants were dispossessed, and authoritarian controls have produced crises and discontent; yet nationalism and social cohesion maintain the state.

1011

Fall, Bernard B. "Crisis in North Vietnam." *Far Eastern Survey* 26 (1957) 12-15. Heavy emphasis placed upon the total elimination of the land owners, and the bungling of this by the prime minister, Pham Van Dong, produced a violent agrarian reaction.

1012

Kaye, William. "The Economy of North Vietnam," in P. J. Honey (ed.) *North Vietnam Today.* New York: Praeger, 1962. A survey of economic developments in North Vietnam since 1954; with numerous tables.

1013

Shabad, Theodore. "Economic Developments in North Vietnam." *Pacific Affairs* 31 (1958) 36-53. Outlines the economic rehabilitation of the area between 1954 and 1958.

1014

Gittinger, J. Price. "Communist Land Policy in North Vietnam." *Far Eastern Survey* 28 (1959) 113-126. Outlines the problems of land tenure in the Tonkin delta and the efforts, in 1953, and then those organized in 1955 by Truong Chinh which led to serious agrarian unrest, and the public "mistakes correction movement" from 1957.

1015

Fall, Bernard B. "The Labor Movement in the Communist zone in Vietnam." *Monthly Labor Review* (USA) 57 (May, 1965) 534-47. A brief biographical sketch of Hoang Quoc Viet, together with a short outline of the labor movement's history, from the strikes of the 1930's.

1016

Gittinger, J. Price. "A Note on the Economic Impact of Totalitarian Land Tenure Change: the Vietnamese Experience." *Malayan Economic Review,* 5, 2 (1960) 81-84. The process of land tenure and reform is contrasted between North and South Vietnam.

1017

Tongas, Gerard. "Indoctrination Replaces Education," in P. J. Honey (ed.) *North Vietnam Today.* New York: Praeger, 1962. 93-104. An outline of the communist educational system in North Vietnam.

1018

Nhu Phong. "Intellectuals, Writers and Artists." *China Quarterly* 9 (1962). The mixed fortunes of the non-communist intellectuals who rallied in 1946 to the nationalist Ho Chi Minh, only to be disillusioned, to rebel, and to be suppressed.

MALAYSIA

GENERAL

Perhaps nothing illustrates the differences between Southeast Asia on the one hand, and East and South Asia on the other, better than the shifting, temporary, and contemporary manner in which states are being formed. In comparison to the ancient states of East Asia, for example, with their territories known and recognized for millennia, Malaysia is just one — the most recent — of Southeast Asian states whose boundaries are only beginning to be firmed. Malaysia as a single state is only a few years old. The nucleus, formerly known as Malaya, only became a political unit in its own right after the Pacific War. Before that, but only for 150 years, it had been a collection of separate states grouped under British control. The same applies to the Borneo states, Sarawak and

Sabah, which joined Malaya to create Malaysia in 1963.

The island of Singapore also joined in 1963, it having been under British control since 1819; but left Malaysia in 1965, and today is the newest and smallest of the independent states of Southeast Asia. Singapore is included here because it would be impossible to separate definitively material which relates exclusively to that small state, nor would any useful purpose be served by attempting this separation.

The mixture of states is reflected in the mixture of peoples that inhabit this region. Malays and Chinese predominate in almost equal proportions in Malaysia; but in East Malaysia — that is the Borneo states — there are many non-Moslem native peoples, while in West Malaysia a sizeable Indian minority, and interior aborigines, share the peninsula with the other inhabitants.

This political grouping has been formed so recently that there are very few works indeed covering the new federation. The Borneo states led lives that impinged but rarely on the life of the Malay Peninsula. There was little contact between the two. Their history for the most part developed separately. It is possible to find similarities of growth, and the tropical environment imposed a similar pattern, but the student will find as yet few broad studies, and of necessity will be forced to advance up two or three or four widely separated paths that only at the top come together to form Malaysia.

Bibliographies

1019

Cheeseman, H. A. R. *Bibliography of Malaya*. London: Longmans, Green, 1959. Not annotated, but substantial and useful; arranged by topics in alphabetical order.

1020

Lim, Beda. *Malaya, A Background Bibliography*. Singapore: Journal, Malayan Branch, Royal Asiatic Society, (hereafter JMBRAS) 35 (1962). Particularly strong in history, administration, economic conditions and the Malayan peoples; not annotated.

1021

Andrews, Isobel. "Post War Bibliographies Containing Malayan Material" in *Singapore Library Journal* 2, 2 (1962) 2-16. Some 75 bibliographies are listed under: general and historical; social sciences; language and literature; science and technology; concludes with a discussion of a national bibliography.

1022

Srinivasagam, E. "Guide to Singapore Government Departments and Serials" in *Singapore Library Journal* 3, 2 (1964) 79-90. Outlines the structure of Singapore government and lists its publications, as of 1963.

1023

Lim Wong Pui Huen. "Current Malayan Serials" in *Singapore Library Journal* 2, 2 (1962) 75-94. Annual reports, directories, professional and research journals, and Malay language serials; arranged in sections.

1024

P. Lim Pui Huen. "Malaysian Newspapers Currently Published," in *Perpustakaan Malaysia* 1, 1 (1965) 56-61. Details of English, Malay, Chinese and Indian newspapers in Malaya, Sarawak, Singapore, Sabah and Brunei.

1025

De Silva, Lucien. "Sabah and Sarawak Materials" in *Perpustakaan Malaysia* 1, 2 (1965) 103-127. Outlines the Sarawak Museum holdings, with a 14 page check-list.

1026

Tregonning, K. G. *Malaysian Historical Sources*. 2nd ed. Singapore: Malaysia Publishing House, 1965. Eighteen bibliographical essays, on Chinese, Dutch, Malay, Portuguese and English language sources, mainly in Malaysia.

Journals

1027

Journal, Malayan Branch, Royal Asiatic Society. (1923–). Published quarterly by an autonomous society formed originally in 1878 (and with journal entitled 1878–1922 *Journal Straits Branch, R.A.S.*); articles and monographs on history, sociology, zoology and other aspects of the Malaysian region.

1028

Journal of Tropical Geography (1952–). Published annually by the Department of Geography, Universities of Singapore and Malaya; contains scholarly articles on the political, historical, economic and other aspects of the geography of Malaysia.

1029

Malayan Economic Review (1956–). Published twice annually by the Department of Economics, University of Singapore; contains scholarly articles dealing with the economics of Malaysia and neighboring regions.

1030

Sarawak Museum Journal (0000–). Published annually by the Sarawak Museum; a fascinating and idiosyncratic hodge-podge of everything and anything about Sarawak.

Land, People, and Language

GENERAL WORKS

1031

Fisher, C. A. *Southeast Asia; a Social, Economic and Political Geography*. London: Methuen, 1964. 583-690. Gives substantial coverage in four chapters to Malaysian physical, economic, social and political geography.

1032

Ooi Jin Bee. *Land, People and Economy in Malaya*. London: Longmans, 1963. A study in three parts, on climate, geography, economics and population; a 400-title bibliography.

1033

Dobby, E. H. G. *Southeast Asia*. London: University of London Press, 7th ed., 1960. Detailed attention is given to Malaysia by a former professor of geography at Singapore University.

1034

Ingham, F. T. and Bradford, E. F. *The Geology and Mineral Resources of the Kinta Valley, Perak*. Kuala Lumpur: Government Printer, 1960. Number 9 and the most recent, in the District Memoirs of the geological survey of Malaya; lists all official geological publications since 1946.

1035

Hodder, B. W. *Man In Malaya*. London: University of London Press, 1959. A brief study of human settlement in the Malay Peninsula from the geographer's viewpoint.

1036

Ho, R. "The Environment," in Wang Gungwu (ed.). *Malaysia*. New York: Praeger, 1964. 25-43. Malaysian climate, evolution, topography and soils outlined; emphasizes the importance of environment. See also: Lord Medway, "The Fauna" in *Malaysia*, 55-66, an outline of the characteristic zoological life, from invertebrates to mammals; and M. E. D. Poore. "Vegetation," *Malaysia* 44-54, which deals with the lowland rain forest which covers nearly all of the area.

1037

Merrill, E. D. "The Vegetation of Malaysia." *Far Eastern Quarterly* 2 (1942–43) 66-79. An introductory coverage.

1038

Ginsberg, Norton and Roberts, Chester F. *Malaya*. Seattle: University of Washington Press, 1958. A survey of the peoples of the Malay Peninsula is given in "Demographic Patterns," pp. 47-79, and "Patterns of Settlements," pp. 80-102.

1039

Malaysia. Official Year Book. 1963. Kuala Lumpur: Government Printer, 1964. Chapter 11, pp. 18-50, "The People" gives an historical and demographic outline; numerous tables.

1040

Winstedt, R. O. *An Unabridged English-Malay Dictionary*. Kuala Lumpur: Marican & Sons. 4th ed. 1965; together with: *An Unabridged Malay-English Dictionary*. Kuala Lumpur: Marican & Sons. 5th ed. 1963. The standard works, based on Sir Richard Winstedt's lifetime compilation.

1041

Teeuw, A. *A Critical Survey of Studies on Malay and Bahasa Indonesia*. Koninklijk Instituut Voor Taal-, Land-En Volkenkunde. Bibliographical Series 5. S. Gravenhage: M. Nijhoff, 1961. Virtually all publications wholly or party devoted to Malay or Bahasa Indonesia, or important for the study of these languages, are included; text with a 67-page bibliography.

1042

_____. "The History of the Malay Language." *Bijdragen lot de Taal- Land- en Volkankunde* 11S (1959) 138-156. Traces the language from old Malay inscriptions of the 7th century; refers to scholarly works of the 20th century; discusses linguistic data and regional variations.

1043

Shorto, H. L. and others. *Bibliographies of Mon-Khmer and Tai Linguistics*. London Oriental Bibliographies, 2. London: Oxford University Press, 1963. The languages of the aborigines of the Malay Peninsula are treated in 42 entries, pp. 30-32.

SARAWAK PEOPLE

1044

Richards, A. (ed.). *The Sea Dyaks and Other Races of Sarawak*. Kuching: Borneo Literature Bureau, 1963. A collection of articles on the various peoples which first appeared in the *Sarawak Gazette* between 1880 and 1930.

1045

Harrisson, T. (ed.). *The Peoples of Sarawak*. Kuching: Borneo Literature Bureau, 1959. Ten radio talks on most of the races of Sarawak, organized and edited by the curator of the Sarawak Museum.

1046

_____. "The Peoples of North and West Borneo," in Wang (ed.) *Malaysia* 163-178. Describes the Melanus, Kelabits, Kayans, Dyaks and others, in what he stresses as a non-Malay country; has some astute comments on the Kedayans, who revolted in Brunei in 1962.

1047

_____. "Borneo Writing" in *Bijdragen tot de Taal- Land-en Volkenkunde*. 121 (1965) 1-57. A substantial review of wooden boards containing traditional Iban records.

1048

Hose, C. and McDougall, W. *The Pagan Tribes of Borneo*. London: MacMillan, 2 vols., 1912. A most detailed work of two experienced scholars; deals almost entirely with Sarawak.

1049

Sarawak. Annual Report, 1965– . This annual government report contains chapters on the land, the peoples, and much else; bibliography, maps, illustrations.

1050

Cense, A. A. and Uhlenbeck, E. M. *Critical Survey of Studies on The Languages of Borneo*. Koninklijk Instituut Voor Taal-, Land- en Volkenkunde. Bibliographical Series 2. S. Gravenhage; M. Nijhoff, 1958. This essay, with a 323-item bibliography, covers all the major languages of the island, Sarawak and Sabah as well as Kalimantan.

1051

Reijffert, Fr. A. comp. *Vocabulary of English and Sarawak Land Dyak*. Kuching: Government Printing Office, 1956.

SABAH PEOPLE

1052

Jones, C. W. *Report on the Census of Population, 1960*. Kuching: Government Printer, 1962. Like his 1951 Census, this provides a detailed survey of the population, in towns, areas, by race and religion; with many tables and commentary.

1053

Lee Yong Leng. *North Borneo (Sabah): A Study In Settlement Geography*. Singapore: Eastern Universities Press, 1965. This deals with the physical environment, the population, and the historical and economic aspects of the various types of settlement in Sabah; extensive bibliography.

1054

Rutter, O. *The Pagans of North Borneo*. London: Hutchinson, 1928. A comprehensive work on the distribution, customs, ceremonies, arts, social organization and folk law of the Muruts and the Kadazans (then named Dusuns).

1055

Antonissen, Rev. A. comp. *Dictionary. Kadazan-English, English-Kadazan*. Canberra: Government Printing Office, 1958.

HISTORY

Unlike the mainland states of Southeast Asia, the islands have been an area of shifting boundaries and varying political entities. For millennia there have been recognizable states with a fairly continuous history evolving in the great river basins of mainland Southeast Asia. On the islands however, states have appeared here, then there; political power has been assumed by one island, then another, and by one port and another.

Malaysia is a state whose heart is the Malay Peninsula, and the major thread in its history is the development of that peninsula. For the most part, it did not develop, yet at a few places its river settlements passed through the great phases of history that affected the Indonesian Islands as well. A pre-Islamic millennium or more, when a culture emanating originally from India spread throughout the area as far as the southern Philippines, was followed by an Islamic period; and this in turn, hundreds of years later, gave place to colonial domination by a European power.

European influence, being the most recent and the most penetrating in many ways, has been the most recorded. The Islamic centuries saw also the British, Dutch and before them the Portuguese, and they too have left their records. These, unfortunately, are largely of themselves, and the conquered have to try and tell their history from the records of the conquerors. The pre-Islamic centuries, alas, yield little, other than third-rate archaeological remains and scanty Chinese references, and on this a 1,000 years of history must rely. How different from China, or India!

General Works

1056

Tregonning, K. G. *A History of Modern Malaya*. London: University of London Press, 1964. The most substantial of the recent general historical works, with major space devoted to the 19th and 20th centuries.

1057

Gullick, J. M. *Malaya*. London: Ernest Benn, 1963. A thorough and well-written work, describing clearly the people and the country, and the political, economic and social changes, particularly since 1945.

1058

Kennedy, J. *A History of Malaya*. London: Macmillan, 1962. A useful general text covering the period from the Malacca Sultanate to independence in 1957.

1059

Ryan, N. J. *The Making of Modern Malaya*. Kuala Lumpur: Oxford University Press, 1963. A synthesis of published material, presented with the insight and experience of teaching in Malayan schools.

1060

Ginsberg, Norton and Roberts, Chester F. *Malaya*. Seattle: University of Washington Press, 1958. Sponsored by the HRAF, a coverage of the geography, ethnology, economics, history and politics of the area.

1061

Wang Gungwu. (ed.). *Malaysia*. New York: Praeger, 1964. A large volume, five specialist authors contribute sections on: natural and human structure; historical background; society and culture; the economy; politics and government.

1062

Purcell, V. *Malaysia*. London: Thames & Hudson, 1965. With 98 illustrations, many of considerable historic interest, this sketch of the 19th and 20th centuries contains also a useful "who's who" of Malaysia's leaders.

1063

Miller, H. *The Story of Malaysia*. London: Faber & Faber, 1965. A historical outline from the 15th century for the general reader.

1064

Hall, D. G. E. *A History of South-East Asia*. London: MacMilan, 1964. Malaysia is dealt with in parts of eight chapters — extensive bibliography.

1065

Moore, Donald (ed.). *Where Monsoons Meet. The Story of Malaya in the form of an anthology*. London: Harrap, 1956. An excellent collection of contemporary accounts of the peoples, their life and history from rare or unobtainable books.

1066

Bastin, John & Winks, Robin W. (ed.). *Malaysia: Selected Historical Readings*. London: Oxford University Press, 1966. A large collection of recent articles and extracts from readily available books relating to the history of the Malaysian region from the 15th century.

1067

Silcock, T. H. and Fisk, E. K. (eds.). *The Political Economy of Independent Malaya*. Melbourne: Cheshires, 1963. A number of research papers of varying significance presented by scholars at the Australian National University, on the politics and economics of Malaya.

Pre-history

1068

Tweedie, M. W. F. *Prehistoric Malaya*. Singapore: Donald Moore, 1957. A non-specialist account of the three main prehistoric periods of Malaya, the stone, bronze, and iron age.

1069

_____. *The Stone Age in Malaya*. Journal, Malayan Branch, Royal Asiatic Society 26, 2 (1953). A fully documented study of the paleolithic, mesolithic and neolithic periods; with bibliography.

1070

Harrisson, Tom. "New Archaeological and Ethnological Results from Niah Caves, Sarawak." *Man*, LIX (1959) 1-8. A survey of paleolithic, mesolithic and neolithic discoveries dating before 40,000 B.C.

1071

_____. "The Caves of Niah: a History of Prehistory." *The Sarawak Museum Journal*, 8 (1957–58). 549-595. A major survey of Sarawak's prehistory.

1072

Mathews, John. *A Check List of Hoabinhian Sites Excavated in Malaya, 1860–1939*. Singapore: Eastern Universities Press, 1961. Details together with bibliographical references, of pre-historic archaeology.

1073

Sieveking, G. De G. "The Iron-Age Collections of Malaya." *Journal, Malayan Branch, Royal Asiatic Society* 29, 2 (1956) 79-138. A discussion on the Malayan Iron Age, with detailed diagrams.

1074

Lineham, W. "Traces of a Bronze-Age Culture Associated with Iron Age Implements in the Region of Klang and the Tembeling, Malaya." *JMBRAS*, 24, 3 (1957) 1-59.

1075

Lowenstein, J. "The Origin of the Malayan Metal Age." *JMBRAS;* 29, 2 (1956). 5-78. A sustained study of the origins of the metal, with detailed diagrams and photos.

Pre-Islamic

1076

Wheatley, P. *The Golden Kersonese*. Kuala Lumpur: University of Malaya Press, 1966. Chinese, Malay, French, Greek, English and other sources used to give flashes of light into the historical geography of the Malay Peninsula before 1500 A.D.

1077

_____. *Impressions of the Malay Peninsula in Ancient Times*. Singapore: Eastern Universities Press, 1964. A simplified and rearranged version of his earlier work, together with a more relaxed commentary and some new material.

1078

Coedes, G. "The Empire of the South Seas (Srivijaya from the 7th to the 13th centuries)." *Journal, Siam Society* 35, 1 (1944) 1-16. An outline of Srivijaya contacts with China and its possessions on the Malayan Peninsula.

1079

Wheatley, P. "Desultory Remarks on the Ancient History of the Malay Peninsula" in J. Bastin (ed.) *Malayan and Indonesian Studies*. Oxford: The Clarendon Press, (1964) 33-75. Discusses sources, identifies place-names and investigates amongst other aspects the radical changes in authority during the first millennium.

1080

_____. "Lankasuka." *T'oung Pao* 44 (1956) 387-412. Chinese, Arab, and other sources are used in this examination of an important kingdom on the Malaya Peninsula during the first 1500 years of the Christian era.

1081

_____. "The Malay Peninsula as known to the Chinese of the Third Century A.D." *JMBRAS*, 1 (1955) 1-23. Based on Chinese sources.

1082

_____. "Tun Sun." *Journal, Royal Asiatic Society* (1956) 17-30. Chinese sources describe an east coast state in the first millennium after Christ.

1083

Tibbetts, G. R. "The Malay Peninsula as Known to the Arab Geographers." *Journal of Tropical Geography* 9 1956) 21-60. A large number of Arabic texts shed light on a period before 1000 A.D.

1084

Wang Gungwu. *The Nanhai Trade. A Study of the Early History of Chinese Trade in the South China Sea.* *JMBRAS* 31, 2 (1958). Malaya figures only slightly in this study dealing with pre-1,000 A.D. Chinese trade.

1085

Sullivan, Michael. "Raja Bersiong's Flagpole Base. A Possible Link Between Ancient Malaya and Champa." *Artibus Asiae* 20, 4 (1957) 289-295. A 9th century link.

1086

Linehan, W. "The Kings of 14th Century Singapore." *JMBRAS* 20, 2 (1947) 117-127. Singapore's misty connections with Sri Vijaya.

Early Islamic

In Malaysian history, the role of Malacca assumes major prominence during this period. Beginning early in the 15th century, a combination of political, economic and social factors thrust Malacca into a role of Southeast Asian importance. Malacca figures in Indonesian history as well, and nothing indicates more clearly the late stage of nation shaping, and the fact that the island states of Southeast Asia are basically the work of the Colonialists of the last few hundred years, than that Malacca at this period, from the 15th and 18th centuries, is as essential to Indonesian development as it is to Malaysian. The national boundaries dividing the two had not then been drawn. References to it then appear in both sections.

1087

Brown, C. C. *Sejarah Melayu, or Malay Annals. Journal, Malayan Branch, Royal Asiatic Society,* 25 2-3 (1952). A translation, with copious notes, of the most famous of all Malay histories, which describes the 15th century Malacca Sultanate.

1088

Cortesao, A. Z. (trs.). *The Suma Oriental of Tome Pires.* London: The Hakluyt Society, 2 vols. 1944. This account of the East, written in Malacca in 1511–1515, has its second volume devoted to an account of the 15th century history of the Sultanate. It is the most important description of Southeast Asia available to us from the 16th century.

1089

Fatimi, S. Q. *Islam Comes to Malaysia.* Singapore: Malaysian Sociological Research Institute, 1963. Arabic, Dutch, Chinese and other references to the spread of Islam provide a controversial study.

1090

Marrison, G. E. "Persian Influence on Malay Life." *JMBRAS* 28, 1 (1955). 52-69.

1091

Johns, A. H. "Malay Sufism; as illustrated in an anonymous collection of 17th century tracts." *JMBRAS* 30, 2 (1957) 1-110. Malay civilization in Malacca and Acheh, and doctrinal development of Indionesian Islam; chapters one through three provide an illuminating historical framework of Sufism.

1092

Wake, Christopher. "Malacca's Early Kings and the Reception of Islam." *Journal, Southeast Asian History* 6, 2 (1964) 104-128. The early 15th century history of Malacca and its conversion to Islam.

Early European Contacts

1093

MacGregor, I. A. "Europe and the East," being chapter 20 (591-614) in the *New Cambridge Modern History.*

2. *The Reformation,* (ed.). G. R. Elton. Cambridge: Cambridge University Press, 1958. A summary outline of Portuguese activity and organization in Malacca and elsewhere in Southeast Asia during the 16th century.

1094

MacGregor, I. A. "Notes on the Portuguese in Malaya." *Journal, Malayan Branch, Royal Asiatic Society* 28, 2 (1955) 5-47. The Portuguese during their occupation of Malacca in the 16th and 17th centuries.

1095

Boxer, C. R. "The Achinese Attack on Malacca in 1629, as Described in Contemporary Portuguese Sources," in J. Bastin (ed.) *Malayan and Indonesian Studies.* Oxford: The Clarendon Press, (1964) 105-121.

1096

Gibson-Hill, C. A. "Johore Lama and other ancient sites on the Johore River," *JMBRAS,* 28, 2 (1955) 126-197. A modestly-worded title that conceals the fact that this is a history of Johore from the 16th to the 19th century.

1097

MacGregor, I. A. "Johore Lama in the Sixteenth Century." *Journal, Malayan Branch, Royal Asiatic Society* 28, 2 (1955) 48-125. The institutions and career of the capital of the Johore Empire in the 16th century.

1098

Gibson-Hill, C. A. *Singapore Old Strait and New Harbour, 1300–1870.* Memoir of the Raffles Museum No. 3. Singapore: Government Printer, 1956. A meticulous work of scholarship, concentrating largely on early historical references to the narrow Strait that became the modern harbor of the island.

Malacca

1099

Meilink-Roelofsz, M. A. P. *Asian Trade and European influence in the Indonesian Archipelago between 1500 and about 1630.* The Hague: M. Nijhoff, 1962. A most thorough work in which the great entrepôt, Malacca, receives considerable attention; so too the Asian trader.

1100

Glamann, K. *Dutch-Asiatic Trade, 1620–1740.* The Hague: M. Nijhoff, 1958. Dealing in sequence with commodity after commodity; Malacca figures throughout, as a major regional port, rather than the port of any Malay state.

1101

Van Leur, J. C. *Indonesian Trade and Society.* The Hague: W. van Hoeve, 1955. A collection and translation of some brilliant major essays, in which the role of Islam, the place of Malacca, and the position of Asians in their own history are emphasized.

1102

Brodrick, J. *Saint Francis Xavier, 1506–1552.* London: Burns Oates, 1952. A well-documented study which includes much about Malacca, from St. Francis's own correspondence.

1103

Irwin, G. "Malacca Fort." *Journal of Southeast Asian History* 3 (1962) 19-44. A study of the fort, from 1512 to 1807.

1104

Harrison, B. "Malacca in the Eighteenth Century: Two Dutch Governors' Reports," *JMBRAS,* 27, 1 (1954) 24-34. Interesting comments by two Dutchmen on the situation in Malacca.

1105

Birch, Walter de Gray (ed.). *The Commentaries of the Great Afonso Dalboquerque.* 4 vols. London: Hakluyt Society, 1875. The account of how the 16th century Portuguese leader attacked and captured Malacca, and a description of that post, is in vol. 3.

1106

Irwin, G. "Governor Couperus and the Surrender of Malacca, 1795," *JMBRAS* 29, 3 (1956) 86-133. The tame collapse of the Dutch to the British.

1107

Irwin, John. "Indian textile trade in the seventeenth century: (2) Coromandel Coast." *Journal of Indian Textile History* 2 (1956) 24-42. Outlines cotton trade with Malay Peninsula as standard article of barter.

1108

Cheng, T. T. *Sino-Portuguese Trade from 1514-1644*. Leyden: Brill, 1934. Deals briefly with Malacca.

1109

Sen, S. P. "The Role of Indian Textiles in Southeast Asian Trade in the Seventeenth Century." *Journal, Southeast Asian History* 3, 2 (1962) 92-110.

British

BEGINNING: 1786—1867

1110

Mills, Lennox, *British Malaya, 1824-1867*. Journal, Malayan Branch, Royal Asiatic Society 33, 3 (1960). Published originally in 1925, this pioneer but useful monograph is here reprinted, with revisions, and edited by C. M. Turnbull; very extensive bibliography.

1111

Tregonning, K. G. *The British in Malaya: The First Forty Years, 1786-1826*. Tucson: University of Arizona Press (for the Association of Asian Studies) 1965. A detailed study of the effect of the pull of China on the British in India; giving particular attention to Penang.

1112

Marks, Harry J. *The First Contest for Singapore, 1819-1824*. The Hague: M. Nijhoff, 1959. A study of the Anglo-Dutch rivalry which centered on the landing by Raffles on Singapore Island, and ended with a Treaty in 1824.

1113

Wurtzburg, C. E. *Raffles of the Eastern Isles*. London: Hodder and Stoughton, 1954. A huge reservoir of unassimilated material on all aspects of Raffles, the founder of Singapore.

1114

Hahn, Emily. *Raffles of Singapore*. New York: Doubleday, 1946. An accurate and provocative biography.

1115

Cowan, C. D. "Early Penang and the Rise of Singapore, 1805-1832." *JMBRAS* 23, 2 (1950). 1-210. The only published collection of official documents of the period taken from East India Company records.

1116

Hill, A. H. "The Hikayat Abdullah. An annotated translation." *JMBRAS* 28, 3 (1955) 1-345. The engaging autobiography of Abdullah, the observant Malay companion of Raffles; a Malay history that presents the early 19th century scene from the Malay point of view.

1117

Coope, A. E. *The Voyage of Adbullah. A translation from the Malay with notes and appendices*. Singapore: Malay Publishing House, 1949. Abdullah takes an observant and critical pen as he travels up the almost unknown east coast of the Malay Peninsula, in 1838.

1118

Wong Lin Ken. *The Trade of Singapore, 1819-1869*. *JMBRAS* 33, 4 (1960). A substantial and scholarly monograph on the British, Dutch, Indonesian, Malaysian, Siamese, Cambodian and Chinese trade, and the resultant growth of a free port in its first 50 years of existence.

1119

Bogaars, G. "The Effect of the Opening of the Suez Canal on the Trade and Development of Singapore," *JMBRAS* 29, 1 (1955) 99-143. A detailed study illustrating the rapid increase in number of vessels and quantity of trade, after the canal was cut.

1120

Parkinson, C. N. *British Intervention in Malaya, 1867-1877*. Singapore: University of Malaya Press, 1965. A detailed account of the crucial decade of intervention in the Malay Peninsula, written with charm and wit, and based on extensive use of original materials.

1121

Cowan, C. D. *Nineteenth-Century Malaya: The Origins of British Political Control*. London: Oxford University Press, 1961. Complementary to Parkinson; deals largely with the London scene, during the 1867-1877 period, emphasizing the economic aspect.

1122

Swettenham, F. *British Malaya*. London: Allen & Unwin, 1955. While the earlier chapters of this history have long been superseded, the 19th century is here narrated with power by one who will have you remember that he played a major role for 30 years in this British-controlled Malaya.

1123

Gullick, J. M. *Indigenous Political Systems of Western Malaya*. London: The Athlone Press, 1958. The British preserved much of the Malay way of life which they found when they intervened in the 1870's; the political element of this is outlined in a significant piece of research.

1124

Clodd, H. P. *Malaya's First British Pioneer. The Life of Francis Light*. London: Lujac, 1948. The men who established the first British settlement, on the island of Penang in 1786, and events subsequent to the establishment; one of the few biographies of major characters of this period.

1125

Middlebrook, S. M. and Gullick, J. M. *Yap Ah Loy*. *JMBRAS* 24, 2 (1951). The dynamic Chinese character who dominated Kuala Lumpur from 1862 until his death in 1885; an excellent monograph.

1126

Gullick, J. M. *Captain Speedy of Larut. JMBRAS* 26, 3 (1953). This monograph on an improbable giant of a man who was prominent on the Perak tin fields in the 1870's throws light on conditions immediately following British intervention there.

1127

Jackson, James C. "Chinese Agricultural Pioneering in Singapore and Johore, 1800–1917," *JMBRAS* 38, 1 (1965) 71-105. British intervention and Malay rule have been well described, but little attention has been given to the economic basis; to some extent this has been rectified here, in a detailed study of the *kangchu* system.

1128

Thio, E. "The Singapore Chinese Protectorate: Events and Conditions leading to its Establishment, 1823–1877." *Journal of the South Seas Society* (Singapore) 16 (1960) 40-80. Illustrates how the British, unaware of the problems of the major community on the island, the Chinese, gradually evolved an administration for this community.

1129

Wong, C. S. *A Gallery of Chinese Kapitans*. Singapore: Ministry of Culture, 1963. Interesting notes on the traditional Chinese community leaders in the Malay Peninsula.

1130

Simmonds, E. H. S. "Francis Light and the Ladies of Thalang." *Journal, Malayan Branch, Royal Asiatic Society*, 38, 2 (1965) 215-228. Late 18th century correspondence by various Thai women with Francis Light on Thalang or Junk Ceylon.

TRANSFORMATION: 1869—1941

Like Indonesia, and indeed the rest of Southeast Asia, the Suez Canal, opened in 1869, begins the modern age. It introduces at close range the industrialized, expanding maritime nations of Western Europe to an inert area far below them in standards of living and in political strength. The West overwhelms Southeast Asia, and effects a transformation.

Nowhere is this transformation more discernable than in Malaysia, and particularly in the Malay states. There are dramatic changes here, politically, economically, and socially. A static Malay agricultural society, unable to control a new element — Chinese tin miners — accepts the British, who then permit and encourage a modernizing process still continuing, but which, by 1941, had failed to create a nation. In the Borneo territories, a similar but separate process occurred.

1131

Emerson, R. Malaysia. *A Study in Direct and Indirect Rule.* Kuala Lumpur: University of Malaya Press, 1965. Published originally in New York in 1937, this classic is a brilliantly perceptive and detailed study of British rule in particular before the Pacific War.

1132

Palmer, J. Norman. *Colonial Labor Policy and Administration. A History of Labor in the Rubber Plantation Industry in Malaya, c. 1910–1941.* New York: J. J. Augustin (for the Association of Asian Studies) 1960. A comprehensive study of the economic background and the establishment of the rubber industry; the formation of the labor force from Indians, Chinese, and Javanese; labor administration and legislation, and wage policy; substantial bibliography.

1133

Mills, Lennox A. *British Rule in East Asia. A Study of Contemporary Government and Economic Development in British Malaya and Hong Kong.* London: Oxford University Press, 1942. A most detailed study of the governments and economics of 20th-century Malaya.

1134

Swettenham, F. *Footprints in Malaya.* London: Hutchinson, 1942. A fascinating biography of the last thirty years of the 19th century, by one who participated in nearly everything.

1135

Cant, R. G. "Pahang in 1888. The Eve of British Administration." *Journal of Tropical Geography* 19 (1964) 4-19. A reconstruction of the large, neglected East Coast Malay state.

1136

Thio, E. "The Extension of British Control to Pahang." *Journal, Malayan Branch, Royal Asiatic Society* 30, 1 (1957) 46-74. The part played by Weld and others in bringing this state under British control.

1137

Allen, J. De V. "Two Imperialists: A Study of Sir Frank Swettenham and Sir Hugh Clifford." *JMBRAS* 37, 1 (1964) 41-73. Through these two men, the dynamic of the whole imperialist movement is examined.

1138

Gullick, J. M. *Kuala Lumpur, 1880–1895. JMBRAS* 28, 4 (1955). The conversion of a rumbustious, immensely vital mining camp into the genteel federal capital of 1895 is handled well in this monograph.

1139

Roff, W. "Kaum Muda-Kaum Tua: Innovation and Reaction among the Malays, 1900–1941," in K. G. Tregonning (ed.) *Papers on Malayan History.* Singapore: Malaysia Publishing House, 1962. 162-192. The contrasting reaction of the conservative and radical wings of the Malay intelligentsia to the many changes crowding into the peninsula.

1140

Thio, Eunice. *British Policy in the Malay Peninsula, 1880–1910.* Vol. I. *The Southern and Central States.* Kuala Lumpur: University of Malaya Press, 1967. A detailed study of an eventful 30 years.

1141

Tarling, N. *Piracy and Politics in the Malay World: A Study of British Imperialism in Nineteenth Century South-East Asia.* London: University of London Press, 1963. Copious quotations from contemporary sources re: British efforts to eliminate armed attacks on peaceful movement in Malaysian waters.

1142

McIntyre, David. "Political History, 1896–1946," in Wang Gungwu (ed.) *Malaysia.* New York: Praeger, 1964. 138-148. The failure of Britain to create one unified administration embracing its entire region of control in Malaysia.

1143

Soenarno, Radin. "Malay Nationalism, 1896–1945." *Journal of Southeast Asian History* 1 (1960) 1-28. Based on primary material, a useful study of the communal awakening of the Malay.

1144

Sheppard, M. C. "A Short History of Trengganu." *JMBRAS* 22, 3 (1949). 1-74. The political history of an east coast state from earliest times to 1945.

1145

Chan Su-Ming. "Kelantan and Trengganu, 1909–1939." *JMBRAS,* 38 (1965) 159-198. The internal picture of Malay political, economic and social changes during a period of British-directed administration.

1146

Kiernan, V. G. "Britain, Siam, and Malaya, 1875–1885." *Journal of Modern History* 28 (1956) 1-20. British efforts to acquire more of north Malay States are negated by Britain's Foreign Office, anxious to keep Siam as a strong buffer between Burma and French Indo-China.

1147

Thio, E. "The British Forward Movement 1880–1889," in K. G. Tregonning (ed.) *Papers on Malayan History.* Singapore: Malaya Publishing House, (1962) 120-134. Due to Siam, and British interests in maintaining her, this forward movement was confined.

1148

Jamaluddin, Mon Bin. *A History of Port Swettenham.* Singapore: Malaysia Publishing House, 1963. The establishment and growth of a new port to service central Malaysia and, in particular, the new rubber industry.

1149

Jackson, R. N. *Immigrant Labour and the Development of Malaya, 1786–1920.* Kuala Lumpur: Government Printer, 1961. The Chinese and Indian immigrants who poured in during the latter part of the 19th and the early part of the 20th century are treated here. See the section, *"Economic Patterns"* for other references.

1150

Sandhu, Kernial Singh. "Indian Immigrants to Malaya, 1786–1957," in K. G. Tregonning (ed.) *Papers on Malayan History.* Singapore: Malaysia Publishing House, 1962. 40-72. The causes, types, and numbers of immigrants, brought to Malaya particularly for the rubber industry.

1151

Parkinson, C. N. "The Pre-1942 Singapore Naval Base," in *United States Naval Institute Proceedings,* 82, 9 (1956) 939-954. Published also as: *Britain in the Far East. The Singapore Naval Base.* Singapore: Donald More, 1955. An outline of the factors that decided Britain to withdraw from the China Sea, and build a defensive base on Singapore in the 1920's.

1152

Makepeace, W., Brooke, G. E. and Braddell, R. St. J. *One Hundred Years of Singapore.* London: Murray, 2 vols. 1921. The commercial firms, and much else of the 19th century Singapore.

1153

Thompson, V. *Postmortem on Malaya.* New York: Macmillan, 1943. A study of the colonial type of Malayan administration in the 1930's; shrewd anti-imperialist observations on economic arrangements with much material.

The Chinese

Because of their numbers and their influence, the inhabitants of Malaysia of Chinese origin merit considerable attention. There are two main themes; that they constitute a problem or that they can be regarded as an asset. Either way, they cannot be ignored, as they are in Malaysia to stay.

1154

Purcell, V. *The Chinese in Malaya.* London: Oxford University Press, 1948. A considerable portion of this unrivalled study concerns the 1867–1941 period.

1155

Tregonning, K. G. "The Chinese and the Plural Society in Malaya," in E. Szczepanik (ed.) *Symposium on Economic and Social Problems of the Far East:* Hong Kong University Press, 1962. 420-428. Outlines the impact of internal and external factors that separated the Chinese from the Malays during the 20th century, and which made each determined to preserve that separateness.

1156

Jackson, R. N. *Pickering, Protector of Chinese.* Kuala Lumpur: Oxford University Press, 1965. A biography of the first British-appointed officer charged with responsibilities concerning the Chinese.

1157

Wu Lien Teh. *Plague Fighter.* Cambridge: Cambridge University Press, 1959. The autobiography of a Malayan Chinese doctor, who gives an insight into life in a colonial society.

1158

Purcell, V. *The Memoirs of a Malayan Official.* London: Cassell, 1965. Another insight from a very different point of view; Purcell was associated with the Chinese in Singapore and elsewhere for a long time.

1159

Song Ong Siang. *One Hundred Years of the Chinese in Singapore.* Singapore: University of Malaya Press, 1967. A chronological account of the activities of a large number of Straits Chinese mainly from 1819 to 1919; a detailed, valuable and unique work originally published in 1923.

1160

Ng Siew Yoong. "The Chinese Protectorate in Singapore, 1877–1900." *Journal of Southeast Asian History* 2 (1961) 76-99. A study of the successes and tribulations in assisting the Chinese. See Thio for earlier work.

1161

Cheng U Wen. "Opium in the Straits Settlements, 1867–1910." *Journal, Southeast Asian History* 2 (1961) 52-75. The part played by this drug in the revenue of the Colony is brought out clearly.

1162

Ee, J. "Chinese Migration to Malaya, 1896–1941." *Journal of Southeast Asian History* 2 (1961) 33-51. A detailed study based on official records.

1163

Sandhu, Kernial Singh. "Chinese Colonization of Malacca; a study in population change, 1500 to 1957." *Journal of Tropical Geography,* 15 (1961) 1-26. Historical geography, applied by means of maps and text, to a long-established Malayan community.

1164

Wang, Gungwu. "Sun Yat Sen and Singapore." *Journal of the South Seas Society,* 15 (1959) 55-68. Outlines the period spent in the Straits Settlements by the Chinese leader, and his influence on the Chinese community.

1165

Png Poh Seng. "The Kuomintang in Malaya." *Journal of Southeast Asian History* 2 (1961) 1-32. From Chinese and official British sources, a detailed account of the activities in Malaya of this powerful Chinese organization. See also the author's "The Kuomintang in Malaya" in K. G. Tregonning (ed.) *Papers on Malayan History.* Singapore: Malaysia Publishing House, 1962. 214-225.

1166

Suyama, T. "Pang Society: The Economy of the Chinese Immigrants," in K. G. Tregonning (ed.) *Papers on Malayan History.* Singapore: Malaysia Publishing House, 1962, 193-213. The important role in economic endeavor of kinship guilds and their characteristics.

1167

Gosling, L. A. P. "Migration and Assimilation of Rural Chinese in Trengganu," in J. Bastin (ed.) *Malayan and Indonesian Studies.* Oxford: The Clarendon Press, 1964. 203-321. Eighteenth and 19th century Hokkien settlements in the interior indicate a history of assimilation by the Malay communities around them.

The Pacific War: 1941–1945

As it was in Indonesia, the defeat of the colonial power by the Japanese was a traumatic experience for the country. It stirred the lethargic political thinking of all concerned, British as well as Malay, Chinese, and Indian. It acted as a major factor in shaping the future, a major operation without the anesthetic.

1168

Kirby, S. Woodburn. *The War Against Japan.* Vol. 1. *The Loss of Singapore.* London: Her Majesty's Stationery Office, 1957. The official British War history volume which tells in great detail and very clearly, the disasters suffered by the British in Hong Kong, British Borneo, Malaya, Sumatra and Java, from 1941 to 1942.

1169

Wigmore, Lionel. *The Japanese Thrust. Australia in the War of 1939–1945.* Series One. The Army. Canberra: The Australian War Memorial 1957. The Australian role in the Malayan campaign and the collapse of Southeast Asia; part III includes a factual account of prisoners of war until 1945.

1170

Percival, A. E. *The War in Malaya.* London: Eyre and Spottiswoode, 1949. The defeated British general tells of his part in the unsuccessful campaign, in an unemotional account.

1171

Tsuji, Masonobu. *Singapore. The Japanese Version.* Sydney: Ure Smith, 1960. The chief of planning and operations on the Japanese side writes a fair and revealing account of his participation.

1172

Chapman, E. Spencer. *The Jungle is Neutral.* London: Chatto and Windus, 1954. A classic of nearly four incredible years of survival with the Chinese communists in the Malayan jungle during the Japanese occupation.

1173

Dol Ramli. "History of the Malay Regiment, 1933–1942." *Journal, Malayan Branch, Royal Asiatic Society* 38 (1965) 199-243. Its formation, and its heavy fighting against the Japanese, including its fiercest battle on Singapore Island; a piece of detailed research.

1174

Jones, F. C. *Japan's New Order in East Asia, 1937–1945.* London: Oxford University Press, 1954. Japanese policy in Malaya between 1942–45 is dealt with (on pp. 382-391) as part of a study of Japan's military rise and fall.

1175

Itagaki, Y. "The Japanese Policy for Malaya under the Occupation," in K. G. Tregonning (ed.) *Papers on Malayan History.* Singapore: Malaya Publishing House, 1962, 256-267. Administrative measures between 1942-1945 which tend to imply that, in fact, Japan had no policy for Malaya.

1176

Chin Kee Onn. *Malaya Upside Down*. Singapore: Chin Kee Onn, 1946. The trials and tribulations of the Chinese in Singapore during the occupation.

1177

Lee Ting Hui. "Singapore under the Japanese." *Journal of the South Seas Society*, 17 (1961) 31-70. A detailed study of life in the occupied port, based on contemporary material and interviews.

1178

Kathigasu, Sybil. *No Dram of Mercy*. London: Neville Spearman, 1954. Tortured to the point of paralysis, sentenced to death, reprieved; a moving book by a gallant Malayan-Indian woman.

1179

Glover, E. M. *In Seventy Days*. London: Muller, 1949. The managing editor of a Malayan newspaper group gives an illuminating account of pre-war journalism and opposition to the official colonialdom; and describes the Malayan campaign as it looked to his very critical eye.

1180

Hill, Anthony. *Diversion in Malaya*. London: Collins, 1948. A school teacher writes of education and other aspects of a peaceful pre-war life; then defends and escapes after the collapse of Singapore.

1181

Toye, Hugh. *The Springing Tiger. A Study of Subhas Chandra Bose*. London: Cassell, 1959. A study of the leader of the provisional government of Free India, his activities among the Malayan Indians, and the role played by the Indian National Army in Malaya.

1182

Donnison, F. S. V. *British Military Administration in the Far East, 1943–46*. London: Her Majesty's Stationery Office, 1956. The "banana colonels" of the returning British, and their valiant efforts to restore administrative efficiency, are dealt with here.

1183

Harrisson, T. *World Within. A Borneo Story*. London: Cresset Press, 1959. A description of the interior people and the anti-Japanese activities in which they assisted the author after he had parachuted down to them.

1184

Hall, Maxwell. *Kinabalu Guerrillas*. Kuching: Borneo Literature Bureau, 1962. The 1943 rising of the west coast against the Japanese, led by Albert Kwok; the only non-Chinese resistance in all Malaysia, and the fearful massacre that followed.

1185

Keith, Agnes. *Three Came Home*. London: M. Joseph, 1948. The experiences of an internee in Kuching camp, from 1942 to 45.

Toward Independence: 1945—1957

It is difficult to separate from political patterns the history of this period, which above all was a gallop towards independence. One element can be distinguished, however — the war which was fought by the British and the Malayan forces against the armed units of the Malayan Communist Party. They rose in revolt in 1948. The fighting lasted until 1960. Far more than mere military measures were taken, and any record of the "Emergency" must refer to the important political, social and economic measures that also were introduced at this time. They materially assisted in the quelling of the revolt, and the movement to independence.

1186

Hanrahan, Gene Z. *The Communist Struggle in Malaya*. New York: Institute of Pacific Relations, 1954. A well-documented study of the history of the Malayan Communist Party.

1187

Clutterbuck, R. L. *The Long, Long War*. New York: Praeger, 1966. A good general history of the "Emergency," written by a senior British officer with access to records of both sides.

1188

Miller, Harry. *Menace in Malaya*. London: Harrap, 1954. Given access to confidential papers, together with personal contacts and long experience, a Malayan journalist's account of the M.C.P. and the "Emergency."

1189

Pye, Lucien W. *Guerrilla Communism in Malaya. Its Social and Political Meaning*. Princeton: Princeton University Press, 1956. Investigates by means of personal interviews, the reasons that people in underdeveloped regions such as Malaya turn communist.

1190

Short, Anthony. "Communism and the Emergency," in Wang Gungwu (ed.) *Malaysia*. New York: Praeger, 1964. 149-160. Describes the history of the Malayan Communist Party in five phases, of which the "Emergency" (1948–1960) was phase four.

1191

Tilman, Robert O. "The Non-Lessons of the Malayan Emergency." *Asian Survey* 6 (1966) 407-419.

1192

Morrison, Ian. "Aspects of the Racial Problem in Malaya." *Pacific Affairs* 22 (1949) 239-253. The post-war developments that intensify the racial problem, with special reference to the outbreak of the "Emergency."

1193

Freedman, Maurice. "The Growth of a Plural Society in Malaya." *Pacific Affairs* 33 (1960) 158-168. A clear outline of the historical factors that produced Malays and Chinese, each determined to preserve their own markedly different cultures, and the resultant tensions.

1194

Renick, R. Dhu. "The Malayan Emergency: Causes and Effects." *Journal of Southeast Asian History* 6 (1965) 1-39. A study of the official emergency regulations, particularly those involving resettlement.

1195

Sandhu, Kernial Singh. "Emergency Resettlement in Malaya." *Journal of Tropical Geography* 18 (1964) 157-183. A study, complete with maps, illustrations and bibliography, of an important politico-socio economic result of the "Emergency." See also his "The Squatter in Malaya," in *Journal of Southeast Asian History* 5 (1964) 143-177.

1196

Dobby, E. H. G. "Resettlement Transforms Malaya: A Case History of Relocating the Population of an Asian Plural Society." *Economic Development and Cultural Change* 1 (1953) 163-189. An examination by an eminent geographer of the "New Villages" created by the "Emergency."

1197

Brimmell, J. H. *A Short History of the Malayan Communist Party*. Singapore: Donald Moore, 1956. A brief outline, most of which is incorporated in his *Communism in Southeast Asia*. London: Oxford University Press, 1959.

1198

Miers, R. *Shoot to Kill*. London: Faber & Faber, 1959. A vivid, dispassionate account of a British regiment involved in the "Emergency."

1199

Henniker, M. C. A. *Red Shadow over Malaya*. Edinburgh: Blackwood, 1955. A Brigade of Ghurkas against the communists, from 1952 to 1954.

1200

Purcell, V. *Malaya: Communist or Free?* London: Gollancz, 1954. A sharp criticism of General Templer and the handling of the "Emergency."

1201

Carnell, Francis G. "Communalism and Communism in Malaya." *Pacific Affairs* 26 (1953) 99-117. A survey of the socio-political problems created by communism and the racial antipathy between Chinese and Malays.

1202

Rees-Williams, David R., Tan Cheng Lock, Awberry, S. S. and Dalley, F. W. *Three Reports on the Malayan Problem.* New York: Institute of Pacific Relations, 1949. Here three dissimilar reports, by a British Colonial Minister, a Straits Chinese, and two British members of Parliament, emphasize different aspects of the Malayan "Emergency."

1203

Bartlett, V. *Report from Malaya.* London: Verschoyle, 1954. A short report of a happy country unhappily at war.

1204

Han Suyin. *And the Rain My Drink.* London: Jonathan Cape, 1956. A novel, but one which gives an unsurpassed account from first-hand knowledge of a Chinese "new village" during the "Emergency."

The Borneo States

It is possible to record only the modern history of the Borneo States that came into Sarawak, for no records of an earlier period have survived. The archaeological work in particular of the former curator of the Sarawak Museum, Mr. T. Harrisson, has disclosed that organized human life in what is now Sarawak stretches back to perhaps 40,000 B.C. Yet it is not until the 18th century that we find more than a brief comment on conditions there.

Islam spread across from Malacca, and there are a few accounts of Brunei as an important diffusion center for this religion in the 15th and 16th centuries, but the absence of good ports, such as Malacca, or powerful streams, or a homogeneous population, all mitigated against the growth of a state of any size. Brunei, prior to the 19th century, would appear to be the only state powerful enough to control more than a few rivers. We know little enough about it; far less about Sarawak and Sabah.

Sarawak and Sabah must be seen as two distinct and different legs. Their history scarcely overlaps, and rarely merges. In the 19th century both come under British influence, and a connected history begins. The first descriptions of the land and the peoples were written then; but even now, 150 years later, much still remains to be studied in both these areas. No doubt, as they gradually mesh with Malaysia, this will be done.

Modern History

SARAWAK

1205

Runciman, S. *The White Rajahs.* Cambridge: Cambridge University Press, 1960. The latest of the general histories. A clear and dispassionate study from the early 19th century; extensive bibliography.

1206

Irwin, G. *Nineteenth Century Borneo: A Study in Diplomatic Rivalry.* Singapore: Eastern Universities Press, 1965. Based on official Dutch and British sources, this gives a detailed account of the diplomacy and Borneo ambitions of Batavia, The Hague, and London which were activated by Raja James Brooke.

1207

Liang Kim Bang and Lee, E. *Sarawak 1941–1957; Sarawak in the Early Sixties.* Singapore: Malaysia Publishing House, 1964. Two brief research papers at the University of Singapore, fully documented.

1208

Longhurst, H. *The Borneo Story.* London: N. Neame, 1956. A brief history of the Borneo Company from 1856 to 1956, including its trade in Sarawak, where it began, and also in Siam and elsewhere.

1209

MacDonald, M. *Borneo People.* London: Jonathan Cape, 1956. The one-time British High Commissioner for Southeast Asia writes an observant book about the Ibans, Kayans, Kenyahs, Chinese and other people amongst whom he stayed in the 1950's.

1210

Hahn, Emily. *James Brooke of Sarawak.* London: Arthur Barker, 1953. A gifted writer tells clearly the life of the colorful 19th century adventurer and romantic who created Sarawak.

1211

Brooke, A. *The Facts About Sarawak.* London: Private Printing, 1946. A collection of letters and documents assembled by Antony Brooke at the time when Sarawak was ceded to the Crown; a cession which he opposed.

1212

Morrison, Ian. "Local Self Government in Sarawak." *Pacific Affairs* 22 (1949) 178-184. Outlines details of important beginnings initiated in 1948.

1213

Anon. *The Danger Within. A History of the Clandestine Communist Organization in Sarawak.* Kuching: Government Printer, 1963. An official report, based mainly on captured communist documents, describing the history, the objects and the achievements of the illegal, subversive and militant communist organization in Sarawak.

1214

Lee, Yong Leng. "Agriculture in Sarawak." *Journal of Tropical Geography* 21 (1965) 21-29. The commodities grown; with maps and diagrams.

1215

Sarawak Government. *Report on the Census of Population, 1960.* Kuching: Government Printer, 1962. A detailed population count, with numerous tables.

SABAH

1216

Tregonning, K. G. *A History of Modern Sabah, 1881–1963.* Singapore: University of Malaya Press, 1964. Originally published as *Under Chartered Company Rule, North Borneo 1881–1946.* Singapore: 1958, and based on the Chartered Company Records; a survey of Sabah's history, economic development, Chinese immigration and administration; with extensive bibliography.

1217

_____. *North Borneo.* London: Her Majesty's Stationery Office, 2nd imp. 1965. A three-month officially sponsored tour resulting in a comprehensive coverage of the State, interwoven with considerable economic, and historical data; includes a chapter on Brunei.

1218

Baker, M. *Sabah: The First Ten Years as a Colony, 1946–1956.* Singapore: Malaysia Publishing House, 1965. A study of the political, educational and economic development that occurred in what was North Borneo's first and last ten years under British Colonial administration.

1219

Keith, A. *Land Below the Wind*. Boston: Little, Brown & Co., 1939. Peaceful Sandakan before the Pacific War; a classic by an American on life at an east-coast port, reprinted many times.

1220

Rutter, O. *British North Borneo*. London: Constable, 1922. A most detailed work on the jungles, the agriculture, minerals, administration and native affairs of North Borneo. A comprehensive coverage of the state's activities.

1221

Tregonning, K. G. "William Pryer, the Founder of Sandakan." *Journal, Malayan Branch, Royal Asiatic Society* 27, (1954) 35-50. Based on contemporary diaries and dispatches, this describes the heroic efforts of the first European to be established on the east coast of Sabah, in 1878.

1222

_____. "North Borneo, 1957." *Pacific Affairs* 31 (1958) 65-74. A brief survey of labor, education, health and other aspects of the state.

1223

Lee, Yong Leng. "Some Factors in the Development and Planning of Land Use in British Borneo." *Journal of Tropical Geography* 15 (1961) 66-81. Changes in community life, land tenure, immigration, settlement schemes and other factors; with maps.

1224

Pope-Hennessy, James. *Verandah. Some Episodes in the Crown Colonies, 1867–1889*. London: George Allen & Unwin. 1964. Fascinating account of the author's Irish grandfather in Labuan from 1867 to 71; a most improbable Colonial officer.

BRUNEI

1225

Hughes-Hallett, H. R. "A Sketch of the History of Brunei." *Journal, Malayan Branch Royal Asiatic Society*, 18, 2 (1940) 23-42. A brief outline which has never been superseded, nor supplemented.

1226

Harrisson, T. *Background to the Brunei Rebellion*. Kuching: 1963. A series of articles inspired by the 1962 revolt, although not particularly concerned with it, originally published in the *Straits Times*.

1227

Tregonning, K. G. *"The Partition of Brunei." Journal of Tropical Geography* 11 (1959) 84-89. How the annexations by Sarawak and Sabah in the 19th century created the convoluted boundaries of Brunei.

1228

Brunei. *Annual Report, 1963–* . As with the other Borneo States, contains a comprehensive survey; with bibliography.

POLITICAL PATTERNS

One of the attractions of studying Southeast Asian politics is the variety of patterns presented. Within that area one can study and compare a wide range of political institutions. Most of the states of Southeast Asia at one time or another operated under the democratic parliamentary system. In some countries, this failed to take root, and the plant died. In Malaysia a parliamentary system modeled on the British pattern still prevails. It was introduced only in 1955, when Malaya's first national elections were held, and the role of a legally constituted opposition is still somewhat suspect, but several elections have been held since independence in 1957, and the poli-

tical pattern established would appear to be comparatively stable. It has been extended to the other component parts of Malaysia, while it operates also in the Republic of Singapore.

General Works

1229

Palmer, J. Norman. "Malaysia" in G. McT. Kahin (ed.) *Governments and Politics of Southeast Asia*. Ithaca: Cornell University Press, 1965. As with the other sections in this outstanding work, a major contribution is made here to our understanding of the political patterns of the country; with useful reading list for specialized study.

1230

Ratnam, K. J. *Communalism and the Political Process in Malaya*. Singapore: University of Malaya Press, 1965. A study of issues such as religion, citizenship, language, elections and independence, to illustrate the communal problem in Malaya since 1948.

1231

Sheridan, L. A. (ed.). *Malaya and Singapore. The Borneo Territories. Being Vol. 9 of The British Commonwealth: The Development of its Laws and Constitutions*. London: 1961. A detailed study by specialist authors, including R. H. Hickling, who drafted the 1957 Malayan constitution, on constitutional and legal developments in all the Malaysian territories prior to the formation of Malaysia.

1232

Mills, Lennox A. *Malaya: A Political and Economic Appraisal*. Minneapolis: University of Minnesota Press, 1958. The 1945-1957 political scene described fully, together with an outline of economic developments.

1233

Milne, R. S. "Politics and Government," in Wang (ed.) *Malaysia*, 323-335. An outline of, and commentary upon, the political systems prevailing in Malaya, Singapore, Sarawak, and Sabah immediately prior to Malaysia.

1234

Miller, Harry. *Prince and Premier*. London: Harrap, 1959. A biography of Tungku Abdul Rahman, leader of U.M.N.O. and Prime Minister of Malaya when it became independent in 1957; factual, yet somehow the charm and the steel of the father-figure it attempts to portray are lacking.

1235

Silcock, T. H. and Ungku Abdul Aziz. "Nationalism in Malaya" in W. L. Holland (ed.) *Asian Nationalism and the West*. New York: The MacMillian Co., 1953. 267-345. A detailed examination of anti-colonial developments prior to, during, and in the immediate years after the Pacific War.

1236

Carnell, Francis G. "Constitutional Reform and Elections in Malaya." *Pacific Affairs* 27 (1954) 216-235. An outline of constitutional developments and their political impact, prior to independence.

1237

Ratnam, K. J. "Political Parties and Pressure Groups," in Wang (ed.) *Malaysia*. New York: Praeger, 1964. 336-345. The structure, aims and membership of four main political parties, and a consideration of trade unions and other pressure groups.

1238

Groves, Harry E. *The Constitution of Malaysia*. Singapore: Malaysia Publications Ltd., 1964.

Specialized Studies

1239

Roff, Margaret. "The M.C.A. 1948–1965." *Journal of Southeast Asian History* 6 (1965) 40-53. The foundations and growth of the major Chinese political party, the Malayan Chinese Association, and its relations with the Malays.

1240

Soh Eng Lim. "Tan Cheng Lock: His Leadership of the Malayan Chinese" *Journal, Southeast Asian History* 1 (1960) 29-55. A Straits Chinese who became first president of the Malayan Chinese Association and a national political leader.

1241

Carnell, Francis G. "The Malayan Elections." *Pacific Affairs* 28 (1955) 315-330. The first general election of the country, in 1955.

1242

Gamba, Charles. "Labour and Labour Parties in Malaya." *Pacific Affairs* 31 (1958) 117-130. A survey of post-war, non-communist, left-wing political developments.

1243

Tregonning, K. G. "Malaya, 1955." *Australian Quarterly* 28, 2 (1956) 20-35. Comments on the Malayan and Singapore elections of that year.

1244

Groves, H. E. "Constitutional Problems," in Wang (ed.) *Malaysia*, 356-364. Gives constitutional measures that protect the dissentient political voice; how an effective opposition can legally exist.

1245

Vlieland, C. A. "The 1947 Census of Malaya." *Pacific Affairs* 22 (1949) 59-63. Attempts to dispel false ideas as to who were indigenous and who were immigrants to Malaya.

1246

Tilman, R. O. *Bureaucratic Transition in Malaya*. Durham: Duke University Press, 1964. The civil service when independence came in 1957 was largely British; this surveys how that came to be and what then happened. The bureaucracy is seen both as a factor of change and of continuity.

1247

Jones, S. W. *Public Administration in Malaya*. London: Royal Institute of International Affairs, 1953. The constitution and the administrative system are treated historically, along with the emergence of political problems and other developments, to 1951; a sound survey.

1248

Tilman, Robert O. "Public Service Commissions in the Federation of Malaya," in *Journal of Asian Studies* 20 (1960–61) 181-196. An analysis of the working of the institution that selects, promotes and disciplines the public services. See also his "Policy Formulation, Policy Execution and the Political Elite Structure of Contemporary Malaya," in Wang (ed.) *Malaysia*, 346-355, where an attempt to identify groups of political elites is made.

1249

McGee, T. G. "The Malayan Elections of 1959, A Study in Electoral Geography." *Journal of Tropical Geography* 16 (1962) 70-99. Election analysis as a means of studying national unity and the extent of integration of three main ethnic groups.

1250

Smith, T. E. *Elections in Developing Countries*. London: MacMillan, 1960. A study of electoral procedures in tropical Africa, the British Caribbean and Southeast Asia, in which the author refers constantly to his experience in organizing Malaya's first elections in 1955.

1251

_____. "The Malayan Elections of 1959." *Pacific Affairs* 33 (1960) 38-47. A commentary on events preceding, and the detailed results of, the first elections of an independent Malaya.

1252

Federation of Malaya. Official Year Book. Kuala Lumpur: Government Printer, 1962, et seq. Replacing, and better arranged than, the *Annual Reports* of the British days, this is a comprehensive official review of the activities of the nation.

1253

Ness, Gayl D. "Economic Development and the Goals of Government in Malaya," in Wang (ed.) *Malaysia* 307-320. Examines Malaya's acceptance of development as a political goal, and shows how politics affects this.

Malaysia

1254

Hanna, Willard A. *Sequel to Colonialism: The 1957–1960 Foundations for Malaysia*. New York: American Universities Field Service Press, 1965. A series of vivid field dispatches written between 1957–1960 on aspects of the immediate scene.

1255

_____. *The Formation of Malaysia: New Factor in World Politics*. New York: AUFS, 1964. A series of vivid despatches describing the contemporary political scene while in particular, politicians of various enthusiasms struggled to create a new state.

1256

Purcell, V. *Malaysia*. London: Thames & Hudson, 1965. A general history with a useful appendix, a "who's who" of Malaysian leaders.

1257

Tregonning, K. G. *Malaysia and Singapore*. Melbourne: Cheshires, 1966. A brief outline of the land, the peoples, the economy, the history and politics of Malaysia, including the stormy two-year period of Singapore participation, and its expulsion.

1258

Osborne, Milton E. *Singapore and Malaysia*. Ithaca: Data Paper, 53, Southwest Asia Program, Cornell University, 1964. The problems and controversies that arose between the two during and after the formation of Malaysia.

1259

Milne, R. S. "Singapore's Exit from Malaysia; the Consequences of Ambiguity." *Asian Survey* 6 (1966) 175-184. Could Singapore participate in Malaysian politics, or not?

Singapore

1260

Maddox, William P. "Singapore: Problem Child." *Foreign Affairs* 40 (1962) 479-488. Events that led to Singapore's entry into Malaysia, by the U. S. Consul General on the island.

1261

Lee Kuan Yew. *The Battle for Merger*. Singapore: Government Printer, 1961. A series of broadcasts by the Singapore Prime Minister on the history of the communist reaction to the Singapore move towards independence through merger with Malaya.

1262

Milne, R. S. "Singapore's Exit from Malaysia — The Consequences of Ambiguity." *Asian Survey* 6 (1966) 175-184. To what extent were politics in Malaya to be insulated from Singapore politicians? Could they participate or not?

1263

Bradley, C. Paul. "Leftist Fissures in Singapore Politics." *The Western Political Quarterly* 18 (1965) 292-308. A ten-year outline of the Peoples Action Party, from 1954 to 1964.

1264

Leifer, Michael. "Politics in Singapore." *Journal of Commonwealth Political Studies* 11 (1964) 107-19. Comments on the moves of the first term of government of the Peoples Action Party, 1959–1963.

1265

_____. "Singapore in Malaysia: The Politics of Federation." *Journal of Southeast Asian History* 6 (1965) 54-70. An acute study of the tensions created by Singapore joining Malaysia.

Malaysia and Borneo

1266

Tilman, Robert O. "Malaysia: The Problems of Federation." *The Western Political Quarterly* 16 (1963) 897-911. Four basic communal problems which have bedeviled politics in Malaysia are separated; with little hope that they will be resolved.

1267

_____. "The Alliance Pattern in Malaysian Politics: Bornean Variations on a Theme," in *South Atlantic Quarterly* 543 (1964) 60-74. The racial composition of "party" politics in Sarawak and the communal voting pattern in the 1963 election.

1268

_____. "The Sarawak Political Scene." *Pacific Affairs* 37 (1964–65) 412-425. A description of political parties and the Sarawak 1963 elections.

1269

Milne, R. S. "Political Parties in Sarawak and Sabah." *Journal of Southeast Asian History* 6 (1965) 104-117. Pungent comment on the quick formation of political parties from 1961 onwards, and a study of their development.

1270

Glick, Henry Robert. "Political Recruitment in Sarawak: A Case Study of Leadership in a New State." *The Journal of Politics* 28 (1966) 81-99. An analysis of elected and appointed officials, as an indicator of social change.

1271

Van Der Kroef, Justus M. "Communism and the Guerrilla War in Sarawak." *The World Today* 20 (1964) 50-60. A review of probable communist links with Sarawak political parties.

1272

_____. "Communism in Sarawak Today. A Survey." *Asian Survey* 6 (1966) 568-579. A comprehensive review of a major crisis.

Foreign Relations

1273

Taylor, Alastair M. "Malaysia, Indonesia and Maphilindo," in *International Journal* 19 (1964) 155-171. The causes and effects of confrontation, as seen from Canada.

1274

Winks, Robin W. "Malaysia and the Commonwealth," in Wang (ed.) *Malaysia*. New York: Praeger, 1964. 375-399. Examines Malaya's relations with, and underlying links with Britain, Australia and New Zealand in particular; and examines its acceptance of the concept of the Commonwealth.

1275

Brackman, Arnold C. *Southeast Asia's Second Front. The Power Struggle in the Malay Peninsula*. New York: Praeger, 1966. A substantial work dealing with the formation of Malaysia and the hostility towards it of Indonesia, in particular.

1276

Kahin, George McT. "Malaysia and Indonesia." *Pacific Affairs* 37 (1964) 253-270. The confrontation issue explained from the Indonesian angle; somehow the Malaysians are in the wrong.

1277

Zainal Abidin bin Abdul Wahid. "Malaysia, South-East Asia and World Politics," in Wang (ed.) *Malaysia*. New York: Praeger, 1964. 365-374. Refers to the communist threat in Singapore, and the opposition of Indonesia, the Philippines and Brunei to Malaysia.

1278

Tregonning, K. G. "The Claim for North Borneo by the Philippines." *Australian Outlook* (The Journal of the Australian Institute of International Affairs), 16, 3 (1962) 283-291. An examination of the historic basis to the claim by the Philippines that it was entitled to Sabah.

1279

Boyce, P. "Twenty-One Years of Australian Diplomacy in Malaya." *Journal, Southeast Asian History* 4, 2 (1963) 65-100. Studies the increasingly close relations between the two countries between 1941 and 1962.

ECONOMIC PATTERNS

The economic patterns of Malaysia are similar to those of the other parts of Southeast Asia. A weak agricultural base, where chronic indebtedness and inefficient production keep the whole structure weak, topped off by a plantation economy of rubber and tin; minor commodities such as oil palm, timber, coffee and copra, which figure prominently in West Malaysia, also are involved, but have been relatively little-studied. Singapore has its own pattern, a tight urban conglomeration, where numerous banks, insurance companies and shipping lines play an important role, and where industrialization is being attempted. Malaysian-Singaporean economic patterns are among the most flourishing of all Southeast Asia, with a healthy currency and considerable strength in the international monetary market. This has been achieved by the wide overseas sale of its rubber, tin and other products which have been worked and exported with efficiency in contrast to its home-based rice production.

General Works

1280

Silcock, T. H. and Fisk, E. K. (ed.). *The Political Economy of Independent Malaya*. Singapore: Eastern Universities Press, 1963. A series of valuable research papers by the two editors and others at the Australian National University, mainly on the economic patterns of contemporary Malaya.

1281

Wong Lin Ken. "The Economic History of Malaysia. A Bibliographic Essay." *The Journal of Economic History*, 25, 2 (1965) 244-262. Comments on numerous items dealing with trade, tin, rubber, population, immigration, labor, banks.

1282

Allen, G. C. and Donnithorne, Audrey G. *Western Enterprise in Indonesia and Malaya. A Study in Economic Development*. London: Allen & Unwin, 1957. The history and the current position of the banking, shipping, mining and agriculture attempted by the Europeans in Malaya and Indonesia.

1283

The Economic Development of Malaya. Being a Report of a Mission organized by the International Bank for Reconstruction and Development, at the request of the Governments of the Federation of Malaya, The Crown Colony of Singapore and the United Kingdom. Singapore: Government Printer, 1957. A detailed study of resources available for economic and social development.

1284

Wheelright, E. L. *Industrialisation in Malaya*. Melbourne: Melbourne University Press, 1965. An analysis of the industrialization of Malaya and Singapore from 1957 onwards, with a critical assessment of both policies and results.

1285

Silcock, T. H. *The Economy of Malaya*. Singapore: Donald Moore, 1959. A brief but stimulating introduction to Malaya's economy.

1286

Puthucheary, J. J. *Ownership and Control in the Malayan Economy*. Singapore: Eastern Universities Press, 1960. A study, undertaken mainly in Changi jail, of the structure and influence of European and Chinese control of primary and secondary industries; using 1953 as a base year of study.

1287

Silcock, T. H. (ed.). *Readings in Malayan Economics.* Singapore: Eastern Universities Press, 1961. Economic growth, rubber, tin, currency and credit in selected articles; useful introductory comments to each section.

1288

Li Dun-Jen. *British Malaya: An Economic Analysis.* New York: American Press, 1955.

1289

Zinkin, Maurice. *Asia and the West.* London: Chatto and Windus, 1951. A survey of Malaya's socio-economic problems of the 20th century, on pp. 152-160.

Rubber

1290

Bauer, P. T. *The Rubber Industry. A Study in Competition and Monopoly.* Cambridge: Harvard University Press, 1948. A detailed account of the Malaysian and Indonesian rubber industry before the Pacific War.

1291

Ooi Jin-Bee. "The Rubber Industry of the Federation of Malaya." *Journal of Tropical Geography* 15 (1961) 46-65. A historical and geographic summary, with maps.

1292

Fryer, D. W. "The Plantation Industries — The Estates," in Wang Gungwu (ed.) *Malaysia.* New York: Praeger, 1964. 227-245. A brief history, with details of distribution, size, ownership, replanting; with useful graphs and tables.

1293

Jackson, James C. "Smallholding Cultivation of Cash Crops," in Wang (ed.) *Malaysia.* 246-273. Their ownership in the Malay States is studied in detail, while replanting schemes, and expansion of production, and similar developments in Sabah and Sarawak are referred to.

1294

Greenwood, J. M. F. "Rubber Smallholdings in the Federation of Malaya." *Journal of Tropical Geography* 18 (1964) 81-100. A useful study of various aspects of 41.5% of the rubber of Malaya, the world's largest natural rubber producer.

1295

Palmer, J. Norman. *Colonial Labor Policy and Administration. A History of Labor in the Rubber Plantation Industry in Malaya, 1910–1941.* New York: J. J. Augustin, 1960. A detailed study of scrupulous scholarship involving many aspects of the rubber industry. Based on primary material no longer available.

1296

McHale, Thomas R. "Natural Rubber and Malaysian Economic Development." *Malayan Economic Review* 10 (1965). An analysis of natural-synthetic competition, and an outline of existing trends affecting production, consumption and trade of Malayan rubber.

1297

Wilson, Joan. *The Singapore Rubber Market.* Singapore: Eastern Universities Press, 1958. A clear account of how Singapore, with its links with the foreign exchange and banking resources of the city of London, plays a major part in the world's rubber trading.

1298

McHale, Thomas R. "Commodity Control Schemes for Rubber, Retrospective and Prospective." *Kajian Ekonomi Malaysia* 1, 2 (1964) 13-29. An analysis of previous control schemes, and a discussion of the changed social and economic context facing any new restrictive program.

1299

Chan, Kwong Wah, Francis. "A Preliminary Study of the Supply Response of Malayan Rubber Estates between 1948 and 1959." *Malayan Economic Review* 7 (1962) 77-94. This study of the effect of price changes on Malaya's major industry shows an inflexibility of supply.

1300

Gamba, Charles. *Synthetic Rubber and Malaya.* Singapore: Donald Moore, 1956. A brief study explaining the stabilizing, if depressing, role of synthetic rubber on Malaya's economy.

1301

Ungku Aziz. *Subdivision of Estates in Malaya.* 6 vols. Kuala Lumpur: Department of Economics, University of Malaya, 1962. Results of a survey to investigate why, how, by whom, and the results of, a post-war phenomenon — the breaking up and piecemeal sale of rubber estates.

1302

Joseph, K. T. "Problems of Agriculture," in Wang Gungwu (ed.) *Malaysia.* New York: Praeger, 1964. 274-292. The problems of increasing the production of coconut, oil palm. rice, sago, pineapple, and other crops are examined.

Tin

1303

Wong Lin Ken. *The Malayan Tin Industry to 1914.* Tucson: University of Arizona Press (for the Association of Asian Studies), 1965. A detailed historical introduction, demonstrating how the 19th-century Chinese miners came to be replaced by the dredges and limited-liability companies of the West.

1304

Ooi Jin-Bee. *Mining Landscapes of Kinta.* Journal of Tropical Geography, 4 (1955). A monograph on the geography of a fabulously tin-wealthy valley, and a detailed consideration of mining; with numerous maps and illustrations.

1305

Fermon, L. *Report Upon the Mining Industry of Malaya.* Kuala Lumpur: Government Printer, 1940. An officially sponsored study, a comprehensive review of the history and their current position of all production aspects of the mining industry.

1306

Ingham, F. T. and Bradford, E. F. *The Geology and Mineral Resources of the Kinta Valley, Perak;* being Federation of Malaya Geological Survey, District Memoir No. 9. Kuala Lumpur: Government Printer, 1960. Contains a mass of historical, geological, and statistical information concerning the world's greatest tin valley.

1307

Blythe, W. L. "Historical Sketch of Chinese Labor in Malaya." *Journal, Malayan Branch, Royal Asiatic Society* 20, 1 (1947) 64-114. An account of the recruitment and employment of Chinese labor, in particular, in the mines and estates, until the Pacific War.

1308

Yip Yat Hoony. "The Marketing of Tin Ore in Kampar." *Malayan Economic Review* 4 (1959) 45-55. Describes the role of the Chinese tin-ore dealers and their relations with the mines.

1309

Chee Siew Nim. "The International Tin Agreement, 1953." *Malayan Economic Review* 2 (1957) 35-53. A critical look at the problems connected with tin marketing by international agreements.

1310

————. *Labour and Tin Mining in Malaya.* Ithaca: Data Paper 7, Southeast Asia Program, Cornell University, 1953. The labor on thirty Chinese-owned tin mines are examined in 1950.

1311

Yip Yat Hoony. "Post War International Tin Control — with Special Reference to Malaysia." *Kajian Ekonomi Malaysia* 1, 2 (1964) 51-87. A detailed survey of international restriction plans and their implementation; with three tables.

1312

Tregonning, K. G. *Straits Tin. A brief account of the first seventy-five years of The Straits Trading Company Limited, 1887–1962.* Singapore: Straits Press, 1962. One of the world's great tin smelting companies has its history and operations outlined.

Singapore

1313

State of Singapore Development Plan, 1961–1964. Singapore: Government Printer, 1961. A comprehensive exposition of government expenditure and construction plans, together with forecast of revenue and finance, for its first four-year plan.

1314

Goh Keng Swee. "Entrepreneurship in a Plural Economy." *Malayan Economic Review* 3 (1958) 1-7. Singapore's Minister for Defense draws attention to the entrepreneur class in Singapore.

1315

Goh Keng Swee. "Social, Political and Institutional Aspects of Development Planning." *Malayan Economic Review* 10 (1965) 1-15. Some of the difficulties in planning for growth.

1316

The Straits Times Directory of Singapore and Malaysia. Singapore: Straits Press, 1966. A comprehensive annual directory of all official as well as business organizations within the area.

1317

Handbook: Handbook of Malaysian and Singapore stocks and shares. Singapore: Compiled and published by Lyall and Evatt, Stock, Share and Exchange Brokers, 1966. An annual, which gives seven-year details of industrial, tin, and rubber companies listed on the Singapore stock exchange.

1318

Stahl, K. *The Metropolitan Organization of British Colonial Trade.* London: Faber and Faber, 1951. A brief account (pp. 63-121) of four British commercial firms, together with an outline of rubber and tin concerns.

1319

Saw Swee Hock. "The Changing Population Structure in Singapore during 1824–1962." *Malayan Economic Review* 9 (1964) 90-101. The importance of immigration on race composition, abnormal age structure and ratio between the sexes; with graphs and tables.

1320

You Poh Seng. "Housing Survey of Singapore, 1955." *Malayan Economic Review* 2 (1957) 54-78. The results of a survey into characteristics of accommodation in a densely occupied slum area.

1321

Report of the Housing Committee, Singapore, 1947. Singapore: Government Printer, 1947. An outline of the slum problem, since tackled very effectively.

1322

Burdon, T. W. *The Fishing Industry of Singapore.* Singapore: Donald Moore, 1957. The men, the fish, the nets, the boats, the market, with recommendations for change.

1323

Benham, F. *The National Income of Singapore.* London: Royal Institute of International Affairs, 1959. A brief assessment of public and private expenditure, capital formation, and national income.

Malaya

1324

Ma, Ronald and You Poh Seng. "The Economic Characteristics of the Population of the Federation of Malaya, 1957." *Malayan Economic Review* 5 (1960) 10-45. A detailed and illuminating breakdown of the 1957 census.

1325

Gamba, Charles. "Poverty and Some Socio-Economic Aspects of Hoarding, Saving and Borrowing in Malaya," in *Malayan Economic Review* 3 (1958) 33-62. A detailed study of Malay, Indian and Chinese poverty in Malaya, and of their borrowing systems; with conclusions having Asia-wide relevance.

1326

Swift, M. G. "The Accumulation of Capital in a Peasant Society." *Economic Development and Cultural Change* 5 (1957) 325-337. Saving, property, and social assets in a Malay kampong are studied to show that productive investment in such a village is very low.

1327

Benham, F. *The National Income of Malaya, 1947–1949.* Singapore: Government Printer, 1951. An official report on the economic activities of Malaya and Singapore, supported by numerous tables.

1328

Bilas, Richard A. "Growth of Physical Output in the Federation of Malaya: 1930–1960." *Malayan Economic Review* 8 (1963) 81-90. Looks at changes in the output of primary industries.

1329

Sendut Hamzah. "Patterns of Urbanization in Malaya." *Journal of Tropical Geography* 16 (1962) 114-130. Factors affecting the development, composition, and location of towns; see also his "urbanization" in Wang Gungwu (ed.) *Malaysia* 82-96, for restatement of these characteristics.

1330

McGee, T. G. "The Cultural Role of Cities: A Case Study of Kuala Lumpur." *Journal of Tropical Geography* 17 (1963) 178-196. An analysis of a wide variety of statistical data from 1947.

1331

Kinloch, Robert T. "The Growth of Electric Power Production in Malaya." *Annals of the Association of American Geographers* 56 (1966) 220-235. New industrial demand replaces the tin industry as the major consumer.

Rural Industries

1332

Ungku A. Aziz. "Facts and Fallacies about the Malay Economy — Retrospect, with New Footnotes." *Ekonomi* 3, 1 (1962) 6-30. Written originally in 1957, and thereafter much discussed; author urges a new approach to the problems of the rural Malays, urges they be treated as agriculturalists, not as Malays.

1333

_____. "Poverty and Rural Development in Malaysia." *Kajian Ekonomi Malaysia* 1, 1 (1964) 70-105. A stimulating and provocative survey by the Malay professor of economics at the University of Malaya.

1334

_____. "Poverty, Proteins and Disguised Starvation." *Kajian Ekonomi Malaysia* 2, 1 (1965) 7-48. Outlines a dynamic relationship between protein and poverty.

1335

Ho, R. "Land Settlement Projects in Malaya: An Assessment of the role of the Federal Land Development Authority." *Journal of Tropical Geography* 20 (1965) 1-15. A critical examination of the government's role in rural land development since 1959.

1336

Grist, D. H. *An Outline of Malayan Agriculture.* Kuala Lumpur: Government Printer, 1936. A classic which gives details on every aspect of agriculture in Malaya. Currently being reprinted by the University of Malaya Press.

1337

Dobby, E. H. G. and others. *Padi Landscapes of Malaya. Journal of Tropical Geography* 10 (1957). A monograph on the land, the people, and the rice of selected areas of Malaya; maps, tables and graphs.

1338

Ding Eng Tan Soo Hai. *The Rice Industry in Malaya, 1920–1940.* Singapore: Malaysia Publishing House, 1963. A critical study of a government policy to grow more rice, and an examination of its cultivation during this period.

1339

Fisk, E. K. *The Economics of the Handloom Industry of the East Coast of Malaya.* Singapore: *Journal, Malayan Branch, Royal Asiatic Society* 32, 4 (1959). A survey by the government of the manufacture of sarongs almost entirely by women at Kuala Trengganu and Kota Bahru.

1340

Hill, A. H. "The Weaving Industry in Trengganu." *Journal, Malayan Branch, Royal Asiatic Society* 22, 3 (1949) 75-84. The technical processes involved, and the various types of cloth produced, in sarong manufacture.

1341

Burdon, T. W. and Parry, M. L. *Malayan Fishing Methods.* Singapore: Journal, Malayan Branch, Royal Asiatic Society, 27, 2 (1954). Malay fishing methods off Trengganu and Kelantan as compared with Singapore methods; in addition C. R. Gibson-Hill writes on small fishing boats.

1342

Lim Tay Boh. (ed.). *Problems of the Malayan Economy.* Singapore: Donald Moore, 1956. A series of radio broadcasts; provocative and informative.

Ports and Shipping

1343

Tregonning, K. G. *Home Port Singapore: The Straits Steamship Company, 1890-1965.* Singapore: Oxford University Press, 1967. A detailed study of the changes in the regional trading pattern of Singapore during the previous 75 years, as illustrated by the history of this coastal steamship company, operating from Singapore.

1344

Allen, D. F. *Report on the Major Ports of Malaya.* Kuala Lumpur: Government Printer, 1951. An official study of the history, administration, adequacy or otherwise, of Singapore, Penang, Port Swettenham and Malacca.

1345

Allen, D. F. *Report on the Minor Ports of Malaya.* Kuala Lumpur: Government Printer, 1953. A similar detailed study of the functions and prospects of some 54 small ports in Malaya; illustrated.

Banks and Finance

1346

King, Frank H. *Money in British East Asia.* London: Her Majesty's Stationery Office, 1957. Deals with the history of the monetary system in Malaya and Borneo, and outlines aspects of the currency position.

1347

Caine, Sydney. "Monetary Systems of the Colonies: Malaya." *The Banker, 1948–49.* Republished in T. H. Silcock (ed.) *Readings in Malayan Economics.* Singapore: Eastern Universities Press, (1961) 446-453. Outlines the form of currency in use.

1348

Tan Ee Leong. "The Chinese Banks Incorporated in Singapore and the Federation of Malaya," *Journal Malayan Branch Royal Asiatic Society* 26 (1953) 113-139. Fourteen Chinese banks, with much historical information, but very little on capital remittances or other germane topics.

1349

Swift, M. G. "Capital, Saving and Credit in a Malay Peasant Economy," in R. Firth (ed.) *Capital, Saving and Credit in Peasant Societies.* London: Allen and Unwin, 1964. 133-156. Postal savings banks, gold and cattle are methods of saving, while land-buying is the major use of capital; credit is not an essential part of the village economy, and a standard of living results which compares favorably with other Asian peasant economies.

1350

Sherwood, P. W. "The Watson-Caine Report on the Establishment of a Central Bank in Malaya." *Malayan Economic Review* 2 (1957).

Labor

1351

Gamba, Charles. *The Origins of Trade Unionism in Malaya.* Singapore: Eastern Universities Press, 1962. A large study of postwar (1945-1950) origins of trade unions; extensive bibliography.

1352

_____. *The National Union of Plantation Workers. The History of the Plantation Workers of Malaya, 1946-1958.* Singapore: Eastern Universities Press, 1962. The major union in Malaya and one of the largest non-urban unions in the world, has its early troubles and subsequent growth sympathetically described.

1353

_____. *Labour Law in Malaya.* Singapore: Donald Moore, 1955. A survey of labor and trade union legislation by a university lecturer who later became the first judge of the Industrial and Arbitration Court in Singapore.

1354

Nijhar, K. S. "Growth of Union Membership and Size of Trade Union Units in Malaya." *Kajian Ekonomi Malaysia,* 2, 2 (1965) 32-48. A survey from 1946 to 1965.

SOCIAL AND CULTURAL PATTERNS

No other country in Southeast Asia has such a diverse population, Chinese, Malays, Indians, Dayaks, Kedazans, Eurasians, and many other racial groups make up numerous social patterns. The rural pattern welcomed by the Malays is in contrast to that of the urban Chinese; but then Malays also live in the towns and Chinese are agriculturalists. The religions are even more numerous than the races. The sociologist has scarcely scratched the surface of the varying patterns. Possibly the Malay, with Islam the major factor in his way of life, has received the most attention, but in his case, as with the Chinese and others, much remains to be done.

General Works

1355

Ryan, N. J. *The Cultural Background of the Peoples of Malaya.* Kuala Lumpur: Longmans, 1963. The influences that have produced the contemporary social patterns of the Malays, Indians, and Chinese of West Malaysia.

1356

Slimming, John. *Temiar Jungle: A Malayan Journey.* London: John Murray, 1958. The assistant protector of aborigines describes the life of the Temiar people deep in the Kelantan jungle.

1357

Williams-Hunt, P. D. R. *An Introduction to the Malayan Aborigines.* Kuala Lumpur: Government Printer, 1952. A useful outline of the culture of the interior peoples.

1358

Skeat, W. W. and Blagden, C. O. *Pagan Races of the Malay Peninsula.* 2 vols. London: MacMillan, 1906. Still the standard work for the social patterns of the non-Muslim aborigine peoples.

1359

Evans, I. H. N. *Negritoes of Malaya.* Cambridge: Cambridge University Press, 1937. An attempt, based on 20 years' work, to correct and amplify Skeat and Blagden's comments on this section of the aborigine.

1360

Winstedt, R. *The Malays: A Cultural History.* London: Routledge & Kegan Paul. 4th Edition 1956. A study of the animistic, Hindu, and Islamic elements incorporated in the Malay social patterns.

1361

Firth, Rosemary. *Housekeeping among Malay Peasants.* 2nd ed. New York: Humanities Press, 1966. Published originally in 1943, revised and with two fresh chapters; conditions of housekeeping and all other aspects of a Malay peasant woman's life, with patterns of change in 23 years, in a Kelantan village.

1362

Wilkinson, R. J. *Malay Customs and Beliefs.* Journal, Malayan Branch, Royal Asiatic Society 30, 4 (1957). Written in 1906–08; deals with the traditional beliefs and the customs in the daily life of the Malay.

1363

Maxwell, George. *In Malay Forests.* Singapore: Eastern Universities Press, 1957. Written in 1907, a classic account of life in the Malay States at the turn of the century.

1364

Swift, M. G. *Malay Peasant Society in Jelebu.* London: The Athlone Press, 1965. A matrilinear people, different in this respect from other Malays, have their kinship system and economy studied in some detail by a social anthropologist.

1365

De Josselin de Jong, P. E. *Minangkabau and Negri Sembilan.* The Hague: M. Nijhoff, 1952. A comparative study of the socio-political systems of the matrilinear Minangkabau on Sumatra and in Malaya.

1366

De Moubray, G. A. de C. *Matriachy in the Malay Peninsula and Neighbouring Countries.* London: Routledge & Sons, 1931. The Minangkabau in Negri Sembilan, with their matrilineal rights of property despite their Moslem faith.

1367

Djamour, Judith. *Malay Kinship and Marriage in Singapore.* London: The Athlone Press, 1959. A sociological study of the structure of Singapore Malay society — kinship, marriage, divorce, and much else.

1368

Firth, R. *Malay Fishermen: Their Peasant Economy.* London: Kegan Paul, 1946. A classic study, which has never been surpassed, of the social patterns and life of an east-coast fishing *kampong.*

Specialized Studies

THE MALAYS

1369

Ali, S. Husin. *Social Stratification in Kampong Bagan: A Study of Class, Status, Conflict and Mobility in a Rural Malay Community.* Singapore: MBRAS Monograph No. 1. 1964. A case study of social differences in a Malay village.

1370

Lewis, Diane. "Inas: A Study of local History." *JMBRAS* 33 (1960) 65-94. Many aspects of a small Malay community in Negri Sembilan.

1371

Alwi bin Sheikh Alhady. *Malay Customs and Traditions.* Singapore: Eastern Universities Press, 1962. General Malay birth, marriage, funeral, and household cultural patterns, and royal customs in language, etiquette and in connection with the monarchy.

1372

Hill, A. H. "Wayang Kulit Stories from Trengganu." *JMBRAS* 22, 3 (1949) 85-105. Translated extracts from the repertoire of a Malay shadow-play performance.

1373

Sheppard, Mubin. "Pa Dogol and Wa' Long." *JMBRAS* 38 (1965) 1-5. Two comic characters in the Kelantan shadow play.

1374

Zainal Abidin bin Ahmad. "Malay Festivals: and some of Malay Religious Life," in *JMBRAS* 22, 1 (1949) 94-106. Malay religious and semi-religious observances.

1375

Gullick, J. M. *Indigenous Political Systems of Western Malaya.* London: The Athlone Press, 1958. Based on English and Malay sources, describes the political institutions operated by the Malays in the states of Perak, Selangor and Negri Sembilan immediately prior to the arrival of the British in 1874.

1376

Tjoa Soei Hock. *Institutional Background to Modern Economic and Social Development in Malaya: with special reference to the East Coast.* Kuala Lumpur: Liu and Liu, 1963. A Utrecht thesis, published there in 1963 by D. Elinkwijt as "Economic Aspects of Life in Malaya, with special references to the East Coast," this deals with the social and economic implications of "kendury" or Malay religious feast.

1377

Swift, M. G. "Rural Sociology in Malaya." *Current Sociology* 8 (1959).

1378

Kenelm, O. L. Burridge. "The Malay Composition of a village in Johore." *JMBRAS* 29, 3 (1956) 60-77. The inter-relationships of 41 households, with a migratory background.

THE CHINESE

1379

Purcell, Victor. *The Chinese in Malaya.* London: Oxford University Press, 1948. A historical background, together with chapters on Chinese religion, secret societies, social problems, labor and immigration, education, political parties and economics. Much of this is embodied in his *The Chinese in South-East Asia.* London: Oxford University Press. 2nd ed. (1965) 223-382.

1380

Kaye, Barrington. *Upper Nankin Street.* Singapore. The University of Malaya Press, 1960. A sociological study of a densely inhabited part of Chinatown, with considerable use of statistics, tables and appendices, some revealing photographs.

1381

Newell, William H. *Treacherous River: A Study of Rural Chinese in North Malaya.* Kuala Lumpur: University of Malaya Press, 1962. The social pattern of a Teochiu agricultural village in Province Wellesley; one of the few studies on non-urban Chinese in Southeast Asia.

1382

Freedman, Maurice. *Chinese Family and Marriage in Singapore.* London: Her Majesty's Stationery Office, 1957. An excellent study on the role of kinship in the ordering of social life among the Chinese in Singapore.

1383

Comber, Leon. *Chinese Secret Societies in Malaya: A Survey of the Triad Society from 1800 to 1900.* New York: J. J. Augustin, 1959. A useful account based almost entirely on documentary evidence collected by W. L. Wynne, and published as *Triad and Tabud,* for official use only, in 1941.

1384

Freedman, Maurice and Topley, Marjorie. "Religion and Social Re-alignment among the Chinese in Singapore." *Journal of Asian Studies* 21 (1961–62) 3-24. How the structure of Singapore society has affected and varied the religious pattern brought from China.

1385

Elliot, A. J. A. *Chinese Spirit Medium Cults in Singapore.* Singapore: Donald Moore, 1964. A scholarly monograph on a neglected aspect of Chinese culture in Southeast Asia.

1386

Jones, Russell. "Chinese Names. Notes on the use of surnames and personal names by the Chinese in Malaya." *Journal Malayan Branch Royal Asiatic Society* 32, 3 (1959) 1-84.

OTHER PEOPLES

1387

Harrisson, Tom. "The Malays of South-West Sarawak before Malaysia." *Sarawak Museum Journal* 11 (1964) 341-511. The land of southwest Sarawak, and in considerable detail, the cultural pattern of the Malay inhabitants.

1388

Freeman, J. D. *Iban Agriculture.* Colonial Research Studies 18. London: Her Majesty's Stationery Office, 1955. A careful account of Iban customary behavior and cultural patterns.

1389

Morris, H. S. *Report on a Melanau Sago-Producing Community in Sarawak. Colonial Research Studies* 9. London: Her Majesty's Stationery Office, 1953. An account of the Melanau community; customary behavior and way of life.

1390

Williams, Thomas Rhys. *The Dusun. A North Borneo Society.* New York: Holt, Rinehart and Winston, 1965. Cultural patterns are outlined here.

1391

Geddes, W. R. *Nine Dayak Nights.* London: Oxford University Press, 1961. A charming and intelligent account of the Dayaks by a British anthropologist who sketches in their cultural pattern with subtlety.

1392

Tien Ju-K'ang. *The Chinese of Sarawak.* London: Monograph on Social Anthropology 12, London School of Economics and Politics, 1954. The diverse social patterns of the Chinese in Sarawak, as well as their origins, relations with other races, education and much else.

1393

Evans, I. H. N. *The Religion of the Tempasuk Dusuns of North Borneo.* Cambridge: Cambridge University Press, 1954. A large collection of notes taken over many years by one who lived and died among them; covering many aspects of the social patterns, beliefs and behavior of one community in Sabah.

1394

_____. "Dusun Customary Law at Kadamaian." *Journal, Malayan Branch Royal Asiatic Society* 22, 1 (1949) 31-37. Dusun crimes and punishment.

1395

Alman, E. and Alman, J. *Handcraft in North Borneo.* Jesselton: Sabah Publishing House, 1963. A slim pioneer study of one aspect of the cultural life of Sabah.

Education

1396

Wong, R. H. F. "Education and Problems of Nationhood," in Wang Gungwu (ed.) *Malaysia.* New York: Praeger, 1964. 199-209. Outlines the problems where schools teach different loyalties in different languages and where trained teachers are in short supply.

1397

Mason, F. *The Schools of Malaya.* Singapore: Donald Moore, 3rd ed. 1959. A brief survey of the school system and government policy on education, by the former professor of education at the University of Singapore.

1398

Chelliah, D. D. *A History of the Educational Policy of the Straits Settlements, 1800 to 1925.* Singapore: G. Kiat, 1960. Published originally in 1947, a London Ph.D. study by a long-time mission teacher.

1399

Wijeysingha, E. *History of Raffles Institution, 1823–1963.* Singapore: University Education Press, 1963. A study of Singapore's leading school; the training ground of many of its political elite, who are singled out for attention.

1400

Lim Tay Boh. *Commission of Inquiry into Education, Singapore Report.* Cmd. 8 of 1964. Singapore: Government Printer, 1964. A detailed report on all aspects of education prevailing in Singapore, with numerous tables and statistics, and embodying numerous recommendations for the future.

1401

Wang Gungwu. *Nanyang University, Singapore. Curriculum Review Committee.* Singapore: Government Printer, 1965. A controversial report recommending various changes which led to communist-inspired student riots and boycotting of the University in 1965–66.

1402

Butwell, Richard. "A Chinese University for Malaya." *Pacific Affairs* 26 (1953) 344-348. Outlines the steps that led to the formation of Singapore's Nanyang University in 1953, the only Chinese-language university in Southeast Asia.

1403

Purcell, Victor. "The Crisis in Malayan Education." *Pacific Affairs* 26 (1953) 70-75. A brief comment on the crisis facing Chinese language education.

1404

Loh, Keng Aun. *Fifty Years of the Anglican Church in Singapore Island.* Singapore: Malaya Publishing House, 1963. A brief study based on Church records, of its educational, health and other activities.

1405

Ho Seng Omn. *Education for Unity in Malaya.* Penang: Ganesh, 1952. An argument for English as the means of educational instruction and for national unity.

Literature

1406

Taib bin Osman, Mohd. "Trends in Modern Malay Literature." in Wang Gungwu (ed.) *Malaysia.* New York: Praeger, 1964. 210-224. Traces the 20th century literature in Malay; short stories, poetry and books; with a great upsurge in creative activity after the Pacific War.

1407

Rice, Oliver. (ed. and trs.). *Modern Malay Verse: 1946–1961.* Kuala Lumpur: Oxford University Press, 1963. An anthology of recent poetry by the leading Malay writers of the post-war scene.

1408

Winstedt, R. *A History of Classical Malay Literature.* Journal, *Malayan Branch, Royal Asiatic Society* 31, 3 (1958). A monograph published originally in 1939, dealing with histories, laws, legends, folk literature, poetry, and other aspects of classical literature: contemporary works are ignored.

1409

Hochstadt, Herman. *The Compact.* Singapore: G. Kiat, 1959. A collection of Malayan short stories, published between 1953 and 1959 by contemporary writers.

INDONESIA

GENERAL

Indonesia is the largest country in Southeast Asia. Its myriad islands stretch over an area comparable to that of the United States. It has the largest population as well, a little over one hundred million, and it could be the wealthiest, with considerable natural resources. It has the longest connected history, with cultural roots stretching back for millennia. Currently it is the sick man of Southeast Asia, but its inherent qualifications, its past, present, and future possibilities suggest that should its illness be cured, it could become the leader, at least of island Southeast Asia.

Bibliographies

1410

Kennedy, Raymond. *Bibliography of Indonesian Peoples and Cultures*. New Haven: Southeast Asia Studies, Yale University, by arrangement with Human Relations Area Files, 2nd rev. ed. 1962. The main concentration is anthropological — including language, history, and archaeology — but items on geography, colonial administration, education, and economics are listed island by island; mainly Dutch language, not annotated.

1411

Feith, Herbert. "Indonesia," in G. McT. Kahin (ed.) *Governments and Politics of Southeast Asia*. 2nd ed. Ithaca: Cornell University Press, 1965. 270-278. A useful short annotated reading list of readily available works in the English language.

1412

Seodjatmoko, and others. *An Introduction to Indonesian Historiography*. Ithaca: Cornell University Press, 1965. A collection of extremely useful bibliographical essays by a number of outstanding scholars from various countries. Includes source materials on archaeological research, pre-17th century writings, Malay, Chinese, Javanese, Portuguese, Dutch, Japanese, and English language sources.

1413

Hall, D. G. E. *Historians of South East Asia*. London: Oxford University Press, 1961. Twelve scholarly bibliographical articles pertain to Indonesia in this collection. Periods covered range from pre-historic to modern times, with works in Malay, Bugis, Javanese, Dutch, Portuguese, and other languages.

1414

Echols, John M. "Notes on Materials for the Study of Atjeh in the Cornell University Library." *Indonesia* 1 (1966) 124-130. A brief bibliographic essay on the northernmost province in Sumatra.

1415

Coolhaas, W. P. *A Critical Survey of Studies on Dutch Colonial History*. Koninklijk Instituut Voor Taal-, Land- en Volkenkunde. Bibliographical Series 4. S'Gravenhage: M. Nijhoff, 1960. Whoever wants to become an expert on this subject will have to learn Dutch; this survey shows what he may expect to find. Other small monographs in this bibliographical series also are useful, particularly for those interested in languages.

1416

Teeuw, A. *A Critical Survey of Studies on Malay and Bahasa Indonesia*. Koninklijk, Instituut Voor Taal- Land- en Volkenkunde. Bibliographical Series 5, S'Gravenhage: M. Nijhoff, 1961. A bibliographical essay of relevance to both Indonesia and Malaysia by a recognized authority; virtually all publications wholly or partly devoted to the Malay or Bahasa Indonesia languages, or important

for the study of these languages are included: a 67-page bibliography is appended.

1417

Suzuki, Peter. *Critical Survey of Studies on the Anthropology of Nias, Mentawel and Enggano*. Bibliographical Series 3. S'Gravenhage: M. Nijhoff, 1958. Lists research published on these three island groups off the west coast of Sumatra.

1418

"Selected Documents Relating to the 'September 30 Movement' and Its Epilogue." *Indonesia* 1 (1966) 131-205. Statements by all concerned, from Colonel Untang who began it, to the PKI who suffered most, and Indonesian Army which ended it.

1419

Echols, John M. *Preliminary Checklist of Indonesian Imprints During the Japanese Period (March 1942 – August 1945) With Annotations*. Ithaca: Bibliography Series, Modern Indonesian Project, Cornell University, 1965. Books, almanacs and folders, newspapers and periodicals issued during the war in Indonesia are listed and annotated.

1420

Lev, Daniel S. *A Bibliography of Indonesian Government Documents and Selected Indonesian Writings on Government in the Cornell Library*. Ithaca: Data Paper 31, 1958. A 58-page listing of government holdings in what has become the major repository of Indonesian language publications in the U.S.A.

1421

Anderson, Benedict R. *Bibliography of Indonesian Publications. Newspapers, Non-Government Periodicals and Bulletins 1945–1958 at Cornell University*. Ithaca: Data Paper 33. Southeast Asia Program, Cornell University 1959.

1422

Boxer, C. R. "Some Sources for the history of Timor." *Far Eastern Quarterly* 9 (1949) 63-65.

Journals

1423

Bijragen Tot de Taal-, Land- en Volkenkunde. 1851–   . The leading Dutch journal on Indonesia which, since the war, has been publishing articles in English and Dutch; anthropological and historical bias.

1424

Indonesia. Established in 1966 by Cornell University as a bi-annual journal for all those interested in Indonesia; aims at the widest possible range of subject matter.

1425

Indonesie. Tweemaandelijks Tijdschrift Gewijd Aan Het Indonesisch Cultuusgebied. 'S-Gravenhage: N. V. Uitgeverij W. Van Hoeve. 1947–1957. A postwar journal which attracted an international collection of scholars, with articles in Dutch and English.

1426

Ekonomi dan Keuangan Indonesie. [Economics and Finance in Indonesia]. A scholarly Indonesian journal which publishes in English as well as Indonesian.

Land, People, and Language

1427

Pelzer, Karl J. "Physical and Human Resource Patterns," in Ruth T. McVey (ed.) *Indonesia*. New Haven: Southeast Asian Studies, Yale University, by arrangement with Human Relations Area Files, 1963. 1-23. An outline of the physical geography, the climate, and population distribution, with four tables, maps, and bibliography.

1428

————. "The Agricultural Foundation," in Ruth T. McVey (ed.) *Indonesia*. New Haven: Yale University by arrangement with HRAF, 1963. 118-154. The essentially agrarian economy of the archipelago outlined by a senior geographer.

1429

Netherlands East Indies. Vol. 1. London: Naval Intelligence Division, Admiralty, 1944. A 500-page survey of the land and the geography of Indonesia, prepared during the war, and released recently for general use.

1430

Pelzer, Karl J. "Land Utilization in the Humid Tropics: Agriculture," in *Proceedings of the Ninth Science Congress of the Pacific Sciences Association,* 1957. Bangkok: Secretariat, Ninth Pacific Science Congress, 1958. 124-143. Frequent references to Indonesia in an essay dealing with tropical agriculture.

1431

Atlas Nasional Tentang Indonesia dan Seluruh Duniah. Djakarta: Penerbit Ganaca, 1960. A useful atlas of Indonesia; maps in the Indonesian language.

1432

Ormeling, F. J. *The Timor Problem: A Geographical Interpretation of an Underdeveloped Island.* Groningen: J. B. Wolters, 1956. Unfavorable physical conditions, interrelated with a social setting that impedes progress; decline of trade, an alarming agrarian situation, soil erosion, and human malnutrition; with a 15-page bibliography on Timor.

1433

Bruner, Edward. "Kinship Organization among the Urban Batak of Sumatra." *Transactions of the New York Academy of Sciences,* 22 Series II (1959). Differing social structure between Batak agricultural villagers and Batak in Medan are compared.

1434

De Jong, J. P. B. de Josselin. *Oirata, A Timorese Settlement on Kisar.* Studies in Indonesian Culture No. 1. Amsterdam: Uitgave van de N. V. Noord-Hollandsche Uitgevers-Maatschappij, 1937. A linguistic and ethnological study of a village in the eastern part of Indonesia.

1435

Koentjaraningrat, R. M. "The Javanese of South Central Java," in George P. Murdock (ed.) *Social Structure in Southeast Asia.* Viking Fund Publications in Anthropology 29. Chicago: Quadrangle Books, 1960. 88-115. Social stratification, habits of childbirth, infancy through to adulthood, marriage and death, the family, kinship, and the community.

1436

Scharer, H. *Ngaju Religion: The Conception of God among a South Borneo People.* Rodney Needham (tr.), preface by P. E. de Josselin de Long. The Hague: M. Nijhoff, 1963.

1437

Freeman, J. D. "The Iban of Western Borneo," in George P. Murdock (ed.) *Social Structure in Southeast Asia.* Viking Fund Publication in Anthropology, 29. Chicago: Quadrangle Books, 1960. 65-87. Kinship and community structure of the Iban of Sarawak and Kalimantan.

1438

Downs, R. E. *The Religion of the Bare'e-Speaking Toradja of Central Celebes.* 'S-Gravenhage: Uitgeverji Excelsior, 1956. The ancestor worship and religious practices and rituals of this interior group.

1439

Cunningham, Clark E. "Order in the Atoni House," in *Bijdragen* 120 (1964) 34-68. The house as the ritual and economic unit of the illiterate mountain slope Atoni of Timor.

1440

Tobing, Ph. L. *The Structure of the Toba-Batak Belief in the High God.* Amsterdam: J. van Campen, 1956. The myths, rituals and ceremonies of the Toba-Batak, and a description of these people beside the high lake in Sumatra.

1441

Kunst, Jaap. *The Peoples of the Indian Archipelago.* Leiden: E. J. Brill, 1946. A nine-page outline of the Indonesian Malays, with 32 photographs.

1442

Hurgronje, C. Snouck. *The Achehnese.* 2 Vols. Leyden: E. J. Brill, 1906. The government, domestic life, agriculture, fishing, literature, and education and religion; a classic study.

1443

Echols, John M. and Hassan Schadily. *An Indonesian-English Dictionary.* Ithaca: Cornell University Press, 2nd Ed., 1963. A practical, comprehensive and substantial dictionary of modern Indonesian terms with English equivalents, of use particularly to those who deal with contemporary Indonesian. Illustrative phrases and sentences are used to explain words and idioms in modern usage.

HISTORY

Thanks largely to the fine work of many Dutch scholars, the history of Indonesia has been unfolded. For over 100 years, the earlier pioneer research of even earlier enthusiasts has been enlarged, modified, and developed to the extent that in the Dutch language there is a corpus of knowledge that excels that of all other countries of Southeast Asia. In archaeological, ethnological, and other research too, the Dutch have studied their former territory with skill and perseverance. Much of this has become available to the English-speaking world, and is now supplemented and enriched by studies made elsewhere.

Indonesia's long past can be traced to the stone age, and to the ancient States of the first millennia A.D. when an Indianized influence shaped the culture of much of the archipelago. The coming of the European at first was of little moment, for he was but one of many foreigners and traders, and the rulers of the islands found him at times only slightly more persistent. But as Portuguese gave place to Dutch, and as the centuries advanced, the European presence became a dominating one, until in the late 19th century, Indonesia, like nearly all of Southeast Asia, came under colonial rule.

Its turbulent efforts to end that colonialism and to shape again its own destiny is the history of the contemporary scene, a history that has not ended, and which presents us with political and social patterns of great interest.

General Works

1444

Vlekke, B. H. M. *Nusantara: A History of Indonesia.* The Hague: W. van Hoeve, 1959. A comprehensive, well-written general history of Indonesia, covering the last two millennia, giving perhaps the best general introduction in the English language to the history of Indonesia.

1445

McVey, Ruth T. (ed.). *Indonesia.* New Haven: Southeast Asia Studies, Yale University, by arrangement with Human Relations Area Files, 1963. Ten authorities contribute on the politics, economics, geography, history, social structure and culture of Indonesia; provides an excellent introduction to the major facets of the nation today; useful chapter bibliographies.

1446

Robequain, Charles. *Malaya, Indonesia, Borneo, and the Philippines. A Geographical, Economic and Political description of Malaya, the East Indies and the Philippines.*

Robequain, Charles (con't.)
2 ed. New York: Longmans, 1959. Indonesia receives the major attention in this detailed work; the physical and climatic geography, the economic system created by the colonialists, and their other achievements are treated in over 440 pages.

1447

Legge, J. D. *Indonesia*. New York: Prentice Hall, 1964. A brief but stimulating general history of seven chapters, from earliest times, with the emphasis on events after 1870. Gives fresh insight into many problems.

1448

Vandenbosch, Amry. *The Dutch East Indies: Its Government, Problems and Politics*. 3rd ed. Berkeley: University of California Press, 1942. An important and detailed study of government, economic problems and politics in Indonesia, of particular use for the 19th and 20th centuries, to the Pacific War.

1449

Wertheim, W. F. *Indonesian Society in Transition: A Study of Social Change*. 2nd rev. ed. The Hague: van Hoeve, 1959. The class struggle in Indonesian society, and the exploitation of the West receive attention in this survey of the development of Indonesia's economic and social revolution through the past centuries to the present.

1450

Furnivall, J. S. *Netherlands India. A Study of Plural Economy*. New York: MacMillan, 1944. The major portion of this survey is devoted to the 19th and 20th centuries, where the application of the various economic policies, the social economy, administrative and political measures are seen in detail through the eyes of a British scholar and Burma administrator.

1451

Hall, D. G. E. *A History of South East Asia*. 2nd ed. New York: St. Martins Press, 1964. As most of the other regional works of note, this gives major attention to Indonesia, and provides in many chapters its history from earliest times.

1452

Dekker, Niels A. Douwes. *Tanah Air Kita*. The Hague: van Hoever, 1950. Photographs of singular beauty provide an excellent introduction to Indonesia's richly varied culture.

1453

Mintz, Jeanne S. *Indonesia. A Profile*. New York: D. van Nostrand, 1961. A useful brief introduction, written for the non-specialist.

1454

Graaf, H. J. De. *Geschiedenis van Indonesie*. [*History of Indonesia*]. The Hague: van Hoeve, 1949. A standard work on Indonesia, embodying much research, and including the fruits of sustained Dutch scholarship; particularly valuable for the 15th and 16th centuries.

1455

Encyclopaedie van Nederlandsch-Indie. [Encyclopaedie of the Netherlands Indies]. 4 Vols. The Hague: M. Nijhoff, 1917–21, with 5 supplements, 1927–1940. A basic reference work, a veritable treasure trove of historical, cultural, anthropological, economic, and geographical articles, relating to all aspects of Indonesia.

Surveys of Colonial History

1456

Klerck, E. S. de. *History of the Netherlands Indies*. 2 vols. Rotterdam: W. L. & J Brusse, 1938. A factual account from the arrival of the Dutch in the late 16th century to the 1930's; dry colonial history.

1457

Angelino, A. D. Kat. *Colonial Policy*. Abridged and trans. by C. J. Renier and the author. 2 vols. The Hague: M. Nijhoff, 1931. Vol. 1 deals with general principles in colonial administration and the structure of Eastern societies, Vol. 2 is a rich study of the Dutch in Indonesia. This is an abridgement of the standard work on Dutch colonial policy, *Staatkundig belied en bestuurszorg in Nederlandsch-Indie,* published the previous year.

1458

Hyma, Albert. *The Dutch in the Far East: A History of the Dutch commercial and colonial Empire*. Ann Arbor: George Wahs, 1942. A general survey in eight chapters, dealing with the trading and commercial aspects of the Dutch in Indonesia, from the 17th to the 20th century.

1459

Klaveren, J. J. van. *The Dutch Colonial System in the East Indies*. Rotterdam: D. Benedictus, 1953.

Historiography

1460

Smail, John. "On the Possibility of an Autonomous History of Modern Southeast Asia," *Journal, Southeast Asian History* 2 (July 1961) 72-102. A brilliant rejection of the previous concepts of Europocentric and Asiacentric histories, with an affirmation of the need, with particular relevance to Indonesia, of a "loco-centric" view, a stand in Indonesia itself.

1461

Benda, H. "The Structure of South-East Asian History." *Journal, Southeast Asian History* 3, 1 (March 1962) 106-139. The historiographical problems raised by Smail and others, and the need for Indonesian society itself to be the center of attention, are examined carefully.

1462

Van der Kroef, Justus M. "On the Writing of Indonesian History," *Pacific Affairs* 31 (1958) 352-371. A critical discussion of the writings of Van Leur, C. C. Berg and C. J. Resink in particular, and the historiographical challenges they present.

1463

Alatas, Syed Hussein. "On the Need for an Historical Study of Malaysian Islamization." *Journal, Southeast Asian History* 4, 1 (1963) 62-74. Attempts to formulate a new methodology and periodization, particularly from the 13th to the 16th centuries in Indonesian history.

1464

Johns, Anthony H. "The Role of Structural Organizations and Myth in Javanese Historiography." *Journal of Asian Studies* 24 (1964) 91-99. A discussion of the cultural factors in some early Javanese sources.

Pre-history

1465

Heekeren, H. R. van. *The Stone Age of Indonesia*. The Hague: M. Nijhoff, 1956. Summarizes in three main chapters the known data on Indonesian paleolithic, mesolithic and neolithic history.

1466

_____. *The Bronze-Iron Age of Indonesia*. 'S-Gravenhage: M. Nijhoff, 1958. A tentative and incomplete picture of the post-neolithic period, stray finds from all over the archipelago are commented on, as are megalithic cultures, urn cemeteries and the bronze Dong-s'on culture.

1467

Bosch, F. D. K. *Selected Studies in Indonesian Archaeology*. The Hague: M. Nijhoff, 1961. A selection of articles by the former director of archaeology in the Netherlands East Indies, including an outstanding piece on "the problem of the Hindu colonization of Indonesia."

Pre-Islam

1468

Stutterheim, W. F. *Studies in Indonesian Archaeology*. The Hague: M. Nijhoff, 1956. Five articles are collected here, including a major study on the Borobudor; in addition an ancient Javanese cult is described along with a comparison between present Javanese copper drawings and those of a millennium or more ago.

1469

Wales, H. G. Quaritch. *Ancient South-East Asian Warfare*. London: B. Quaritch, 1952. The Indianization of a permanent pastime of man is stressed in relation to Sri-vijaya and Java from the 7th century A.D.

1470

Coedes, G. *Les états hindouises d'Indochine et d'Indonesie.* Paris: E. de Boccard, 1948. A classic study by the eminent French scholar, broad yet detailed, on the centuries of Indonesian history before Islam.

1471

Kempers, A. J. Bernet. *Ancient Indonesian Art.* Amsterdam: van der Peet, 1959. A scholarly survey of the ancient arts of Java, based on archaeological research; numerous illustrations.

1472

Schnitger, F. M. *Forgotten Kingdoms in Sumatra.* Leyden: E. J. Brill, 1964. Originally published in 1939, the Palembang museum conservator writes of the antiquities of Sumatra; with a series of dramatic plates. See also his *The Archaeology of Hindoo Sumatra.* Leiden: E. J. Brill, 1937.

1473

Pigeaud, Th. G. *Java in the Fourteenth Century: The Nagara-Kertagama.* 5 vols. The Hague: M. Nijhoff, 1931. An English translation, together with commentary, of a rare and important Javanese chronicle.

1474

Krom, N. J. *Hindoe-Javaansche geschiedenis.* [Hindu-Javanese History]. 2nd rev. ed. The Hague: M. Nijhoff, 1931. A meticulous work of detailed scholarship on the pre-Islamic centuries of Indonesian history, which although now challenged on points of interpretation, has remained as an essential reference to scholars of this period; Krom remains as a towering figure.

1475

Coedes, G. "The Empire of the South Seas (Srivijaya from the 7th to the 13th centuries)." *Journal, Siam Society,* 35, 1 (1944) 1-16. A clear outline of Sri-vijayan contacts with China, and its possessions on the Malay peninsula and elsewhere.

1476

Wolters, O. W. "The Po-ssu Pine Trees." *Bulletin of the School of Oriental and African Studies* (University of London) 23 (1960) 323-350. Uses four Chinese texts written between the 4th and 6th centuries A.D. to discuss early Sumatran trade in resin.

Early Islam

1477

Schrieke, Bertram J. O. *Indonesian Sociological Studies.* 2 vols. The Hague: van Hoeve, 1955-57. Vol. 1 contains penetrating studies on the historico-sociological aspects of Indonesian trade 1300–1500 A.D., as well as the 16th and 17th centuries.

1478

Van Leur, J. C. *Indonesian Trade and Society.* The Hague: Van Hoeve, 1955. Three brilliant chapters in one of his essays (157-246) deals with "The World of Southeast Asia: 1500–1650."

1479

Hill, A. H. "The Coming of Islam to North Sumatra." *Journal, Southeast Asian History,* 4 (1963) 6-21. Fourteenth-century records are used to identify when and where Islam arrived in north Sumatra, while other sources are consulted to show that it came from India.

1480

Johns, A. H. "Malay Sufism; as illustrated in an anonymous collection of 17th century tracts." *Journal, Malayan Branch, Royal Asiatic Society,* 30, 2 (1957) 1-110. A collection of Sufi tracts composed at Acheh, which, with Malacca, was one of the key areas in the dissemination of Moslem learning, and a center of Moslem trade, accompanied by an able introduction.

1481

Cortesao, Armando. (ed. and trs.). *The Suma Oriental of Tome Pires.* 2 vols. London: Hakluyt Society, 1944. Vol. 1 contains a lengthy description of the Indonesian islands, written in Malacca in 1512–1515.

1482

Johns, A. H. "Sufism as a Category in Indonesian Literature and History." *Journal, Southeast Asian History* 2, 2 (1961) 10-23. An Islamic movement, particularly important from the 13th to the 18th century, is described as one major element in Indonesian history.

1483

Graaf, H. J. De. "The Origin of the Javanese Mosque." *Journal, Southeast Asian History* 4, 1 (1963) 1-5. Reproductions of early prints illustrate his contention that the mosque style came from western India in the 14th century.

1484

Hill, A. H. "Hikayat Raja-Raja Pasai." *Journal, Malayan Branch, Royal Asiatic Society* 33, 2 (1960) 1-215. A revised romanized version together with an English translation of the oldest Malay text known, the chronicles of the Kings of Pasai, dealing with the late 13th and early 14th centuries in Sumatra.

1485

Purbatjaraka, Purnadi. "Shahbandars in the Archipelago." *Journal, Southeast Asian History* 2, 2 (1961) 1-9. A brief outline of the origins and role of this Indonesian wide port authority.

Early Asian Travelers

1486

Gibb, H. A. R. (ed. and trs.). *Ibn Battuta: Travels in Asia and Africa, 1325–54.* London: Routledge, 1953. The celebrated 14th century traveler describes Sumatra and Java (or perhaps the Malay Peninsula) in X, pp. 272-281.

1487

Willetts, William. "The Maritime Adventures of Grand Eunuch Ho." *Journal, Southeast Asian History* 5, 2 (1964) 25-42. Chinese naval activity in the southern seas between 1405–1433, with references to Java, Palembang, and Acheh.

1488

Mills, J. V. "Notes on Early Chinese Voyages," in *Journal, Royal Asiatic Society* (1951) 3-24. Deals with Chinese voyages into Southeast Asia from the 7th century onwards, in four main periods; with particular reference to Cheng Ho.

1489

Lo Jung-Pang. "The Decline of the Early Ming Navy." *Oriens Extremus* 5 (1958) 149-168. The southern voyages of the early 15th century are discussed here.

1490

Duyvendak, J. J. "The True Dates of the Chinese Maritime Expeditions in the Early Fifteenth Century." *T'oung Pao* 34 (1939) 341-312. A brilliant study of the Chinese sources narrating the voyages of Cheng Ho.

1491

Tregonning, K. G. "Kublai Khan and South-East Asia." *History Today* 7 (1957) 163-170. The 13th century Chinese invasion which helped initiate the Madjapahit empire.

1492

Buhler, Alfred. "Patola Influence in Southeast Asia." *Journal of Indian Textile History* 4 (1959) 4-46. The patola are the famous silk wedding saris from Gujerat; accounts of them as highly valued imports in Indonesia date from the 14th century.

The Portuguese

1493

Lach, Donald F. *Asia in the Making of Europe.* Vol. I. *The Century of Discovery.* Books 1 and 2. Chicago: University of Chicago Press, 1965. As part of a six-volume work, the two books of volume I examine closely the arrival of the Portuguese, their early 16th century impact on Asia and vice versa.

1494

Boxer, C. R. "The Portuguese in the East 1500–1800," in H. V. Livermore (ed.) *Portugal and Brazil, an introduction.* London: Oxford University Press, 1953. 185-247. A general outline.

1495

_____. "Portuguese and Dutch Colonial Rivalry, 1641–1661. "*Studia Revista Semestral* (July 1958) 7-42. Close economic links in Europe contrasted with battles on three continents and on seven seas; Southeast Asian rivalry, particularly in Indonesian-Malaysian waters, figures throughout.

1496

_____. *Fidalgos in the Far East, 1550–1770*. The Hague: M. Nijhoff, 1948. Although dealing largely with Macao, there are frequent references to the Portuguese on Timor. *See also* his "Joao Pereira Corte-Real and the construction of Portuguese East-Indiamen in the 17th century," in *Mariners Mirror* XXVI (1940) 388-406.

The Early Dutch

1497

Masselman, G. *The Cradle of Colonialism*. New Haven: Yale University Press, 1963. A full-scale study with a detailed bibliography of the first fifty years or so when the Dutch established themselves in Indonesia. Book one deals with the initial voyages of the late 16th century; book two with the Indonesian scene of the early 17th century, and the early decades of the Dutch settlements; and book three is concerned with the British competition, and their almost total withdrawal from Java and elsewhere by 1623.

1498

Boxer, C. R. *The Dutch Sea borne Empire, 1600–1800*. London: Hutchinson, 1965. This stimulating work shows the Indonesian activities of the Dutch during this period as a major, but not overwhelming part of Dutch history as a whole.

1499

Van Leur, J. C. *Indonesian Trade and Society. Essays in Asian Social and Economic History*. The Hague: van Hoeve, 1955. The author would be horrified to find himself classified in this section, as he insisted that Indonesia itself, and not the Dutch on Indonesia should be the subject of study. This work is divided into three sections: on early Asian trade; the world of Southeast Asia, 1500–1650: on the 18th century; with other essays and long reviews. It has had a marked historiographical impact on all Southeast Asian scholars, and has a significance far beyond the narrow confines of Indonesian history.

1500

Schrieke, Bertram J. O. *Indonesian Sociological Studies. Selected Writings*. Vol. 2. *Ruler and Realm in early Java*. The Hague: van Hoeve, 1957. A detailed account of Javanese history from the 13th to the 18th century, in which the Dutch appear as only one of many participants.

1501

Meilink-Roelofsz, M. A. P. *Asian Trade and European Influence in the Indonesian Archipelago between 1500 and about 1630*. The Hague: M. Nijhoff, 1962. The influence of the Portuguese and more particularly the Dutch on Asian trade, with particular reference to Malacca and other trading ports in Java, Sumatra and elsewhere; the emphasis is on Asia, rather than the European; a valuable study of both the Dutch and Indonesia generally in the sixteenth century.

1502

Glamann, Kristof. *Dutch-Asiatic Trade, 1620–1740*. The Hague: M. Nijhoff, 1958. The basic role of the Dutch in Indonesia in these early centuries was trade; here eight important commodities: pepper, spices, piecegoods, silk, copper, sugar, coffee, tea, are separately examined.

1503

Boxer, C. R. "Cornelius Speelman, and the Growth of Dutch Power in Indonesia, 1666–1684." *History Today* 8 (March 1958) 145-154. One of Holland's outstanding imperialists, and his Indonesian conquests.

1504

Leupe, P. A. "Seige and Capture of Malacca from the Portuguese in 1640–1641," *Malayan Branch, Royal Asiatic Society*. 14 (1936) 1-178. Dutch documents, translated by MacHacobian, dealing with the Dutch occupa-

tion of the Straits of Malacca between 1636 and 1639, and the siege and capture of the port, together with various reports submitted shortly after.

1505

Boxer, C. R. "The Dutch East-Indiamen: their Sailors, their Navigators, and Life on Board, 1602–1795." *Mariners Mirror* 49 (1963) 81-104. A scholarly and lively essay dealing with many aspects of the Dutch ships that sailed to Indonesia.

1506

Skinner, C. (ed. and trs.). *Sja'ir Perang Mengkasar* [A Rhymed Chronicle of the Macassar War] by Entji Amin. The Hague: N. Nijhoff, 1963. A well-edited presentation of a classical Malay poem written before 1700, dealing with the bitter fighting between the Dutch and the Macassarese between 1666 and 1669, and the capture of Macassar.

1507

Coolhaas, W. P. (ed.). *Generale Missiven der V.O.C.* 2 Vols. The Hague: M. Nijhoff, 1964. Batavia in the 17th century; official correspondence relating mainly to Dutch commercial activity.

1508

Colenbrander, H. T. (ed.). *Jan Pietersz Coen: Bescheiden omtrentzijn bedriff in Indie*. [Jan Pietersz Coen: Documents concerning his activities in the Indies]. 7 Vols. The Hague: M. Nijhoff, 1919–1952. The editor collected everything that even remotely touched on the wide-reaching activities of the famous Dutch governor-general.

1509

Valentijn, Francois. *Ond en nieuw Oost-Indien*. [The Old and New East Indies]. 5 Vols. Dordrecht and Amsterdam: van Braam and de Linden, 1724–26. A famous collection by a Dutch church minister of contemporary records of all types, with numerous maps and illustrations.

1510

Sen, S. P. "The Role of Indian Textiles in Southeast Asian Trade in the Seventeenth Century," *Journal, Southeast Asian History*, 3, 2 (1962) 92-110. Their destination usually was Indonesia.

The Early British

1511

Foster, Sir William (ed.). *The Voyages of Sir James Lancaster to Brazil and the East Indies, 1591–1603*. London: The Hakluyt Society, 1940. The East India Company's first voyages are described here from contemporary accounts, with characteristics of Acheh and Java early in the 17th century.

1512

_____. (ed.). *The Voyage of Sir Henry Middleton to the Moluccas, 1604–1606*. London: The Hakluyt Society, 1943. This contains eye-witness descriptions of Jakarta, Bantam, the Celebes, and Moluccas and other Indonesian islands.

1513

Bassett, D. K. "The Amboyna Massacre." *Journal, Southeast Asian History* 1, 2 (1960) 1-19. The facts behind the execution of ten Englishmen by the Dutch on Amboyna Island in 1623.

1514

_____. "The English East India Company in the Far East 1623–1684." *Journal, Royal Asiatic Society,* April and October 1960, 32-47, 145-157. Bantam, the British outpost on Java, was the precarious base for trade with Japan and China.

1515

_____. "English Trade in the Celebes 1613–1667." *Journal, Malayan Branch, Royal Asiatic Society* 31, 1 (1958) 1-39. The opposition of the Dutch, the Spaniards in Manila and the Moluccas and the Sultan of Macassar gradually made trade impossible; by 1667 the Dutch had won.

1516

Suntharalingam, R. "The British in Banjermassin: An Abortive Attempt at Settlement 1700–1707." *Journal, Southeast Asian History* 4, 2 (1963) 33-64. As part of an effort to trade with China, Borneo was chosen as a place where goods could be obtained; the Sultan of Banjermassin, however, had other ideas.

Late 18th and Early 19th Centuries: Dutch and British

1517

Tarling, N. *Anglo-Dutch Rivalry in the Malay World, 1780– 1824.* Cambridge: Cambridge University Press, 1962. The rivalry studied here is a diplomatic one; five different sets of negotiations during this 44-year period settled the spheres of interest of the two parties.

1518

Wurtzburg, C. E. *Raffles of the Eastern Isles.* London: Hodder & Stoughton, 1954. A large biography complete with bibliography in which the affairs of Raffles on Java between 1811 and 16, and later on Sumatra take up over 300 pages.

1519

Van Welderen Rengers, Daniel W. *The Failure of a Liberal Colonial Policy: Netherlands East Indies, 1816–1830.* The Hague: M. Nijhoff, 1947. A ten-chapter study, in detail, on the administration of van der Capellan (1819–26) and du Bois (1826–30); both failed in their different ways to encourage the agricultural production necessary for a satisfactory revenue, and their failure led to the compulsory cultivation system.

1520

Wright, H. R. C. *Free Trade and Protection in the Netherlands 1816–1830.* Cambridge: Cambridge University Press, 1955. Contains one chapter, entitled "Free Trade and Mercantilism in the Dutch East Indies," which outlines the reluctant liberalism of 1819–1826, and the mercantilist policies which followed.

1521

Bassett, D. K. "British Trade and Policy in Indonesia, 1760– 1772." *Bijdragen Tot de Taal-, Land-, En Volkenkunde,* 120 (1964) 197-223. The failure of British expansionist schemes from Bencoolen.

1522

_____. "Thomas Forrest, an eighteenth century mariner." *Journal, Malayan Branch, Royal Asiatic Society.* 34, 2 (1961) 106-121. An Indian-based "country trader," who came repeatedly into Indonesian waters in the late 18th century.

1523

Ahmat, Sharom. "Some Problems of the Rhode Island Traders in Java 1799–1836." *Journal, Southeast Asian History* 6, 1 (1965) 94-106. Brown and Ives of Providence found pirates, British blockade and confiscation, lack of agents, and tropical diseases almost overwhelming problems in maintaining a coffee trade with Java.

1524

Bastin, J. "Palembang in 1811 and 1812." *Bijdragen Tot de Taal-, Land-, En Volkenkunde,* 119 (1963) 161-188. The great Calcutta business house of John Palmer & Co. which was agent for the Dutch Indonesian government, arranged a number of loans for it, and in other ways as well, played some part in Indonesian affairs in the 1820's.

1525

Bassett, D. K. "The Surrender of Dutch Malacca, 1795." *Bijdragen tot de tall- land- en Volkenkunde* 117 (1961) 344-359. The weak resistance of the garrison suggested treason. The episode is examined.

1526

Wright, H. R. C. *East-Indian Economic Problems of the Age of Cornwallis and Raffles.* London: Luzac, 1961. A careful appraisal of the policies of Raffles in Java and Sumatra, in which coffee cultivation, land and labor utilization, the opium trade, the tin industry, textiles and other economic aspects of 1805–11 Java are considered.

1527

Bastin, J. *Raffles Ideas on the Land Rent System in Java and the MacKenzie Land Tenure System.* 'S-Gravenhage: M. Nijhoff, 1954. A study of the pattern of land ownership in Java, and the efforts of Raffles to change it, during his governorship in 1811–13.

1528

_____. "Palembang in 1811 and 1812." *Bijdragen Tot de Taal-, Land- en Volkenkunde,* 109 and 110 (1953 and 1954) 300-320, 64-88. Deals in detail with the massacre of the Dutch garrison there in 1811, and whether Raffles was responsible or not.

1529

Suntharalingam, R. and Puvanarajah, T. "The Acheh Treaty of 1819." *Journal, Southeast Asian History* 2, 3 (1961) 36-46. Outlines the factors which influenced the British on Penang and in India to seek a treaty with the Sultanate of Acheh, leading to the mission of Raffles in 1819.

1530

Renier, G. J. *Great Britain and the Establishment of the Kingdom of the Netherlands, 1813–1815.* London: Allen & Unwin, 1930. The return of Indonesia after the Napoleonic wars is dealt with in the final chapter.

1531

Bastin, John. *The Native Policies of Sir Stamford Raffles in Java and Sumatra. An Economic Interpretation.* Oxford: Clarendon, 1957. Raffles governed Java from 1811–16, and then Bencoolen on Sumatra, 1818–24; this is a study of what he accomplished.

1532

Wright, H. R. C. "The Moluccan Spice Monopoly, 1770– 1824." *Journal, Malayan Branch, Royal Asiatic Society* 31, 4 (1958) 1-127. A monograph on the two British periods of occupation of the Moluccas in 1793–1803 and 1810–17.

1533

Gibson-Hill, C. A. (ed.). "Documents relating to John Clunies Ross, Alexander Hare and the establishment of the Colony on the Cocos-Keeling Islands." *Journal, Malayan Branch, Royal Asiatic Society* 25, 4 and 5 (1952). A lengthy and exquisite introduction deals with Raffles, British settlement on Borneo and another proposed on Sumatra, and much pertaining to the Dutch in the early 19th century.

1534

Bastin, John. *The British in West Sumatra 1685–1825. A Selection of Documents with an Introduction.* Kuala Lumpur: University of Malaya Press, 1965. Correspondence from Bencoolen taken from the East India Company's records in London.

Indigenous Relations

1535

Van der Kroef, Justus M. "Prince Diponegoro: Progenitor of Indonesian Nationalism." *Far Eastern Quarterly* 8 (1949), 424-450. The hero of the Java War (1825–30) is included in this study of Dipa Negara (1785–1855).

1536

Muhammad Yamin. *Sedjarah peperangan Dipanegara, Pahlawan Kemerdekaan Indonesia.* [History of the war of Dipanegara, Hero of Indonesian Freedom]. Djakarta: Jajasin Pembangunan, 1952. An elaboration of the concept now generally accepted, that the Java War of 1825–30 was a nationalistic movement involving all the people.

1537

Muhamad Radjab. *Perang Paderi di Sumatera Barat 1803– 1838.* [The Padri War in West Sumatra, 1830–1838]. Djakarta: Perpustakaan Perguruan Kementerian P. P. dan K., 1954.

1538

Van der Kroef, J. M. "Two Forerunners of Modern Indonesian Independence: Iman Bondjol and Thomas Matulesia." *The Australian Journal of Politics and History* 8 (1962) 148-163. Nationalist opposition to the Dutch on their return in 1815, on Sumatra and the Moluccas.

Modern Period

1539

Emerson, Rupert. *Malaysia: A Study in Indirect Rule*. Kuala Lumpur: University of Malaya Press, 1964. Written and published originally before the Pacific War, this Harvard study has remained as a valuable detailed examination of colonial rule in Indonesia and Malaya during the late 19th and 20th century period.

1540

Van Niel, Robert. *The Emergence of the Modern Indonesian Elite*. The Hague: van Hoeve, 1960. A scholarly interpretation of Indonesian history during the first 25 years of the 20th century, a period that witnessed an unprecedented social change among the Indonesian leader group; the transformation of Javanese society is here examined.

1541

Benda, Harry J. "The Pattern of Administrative Reforms in the Closing Years of Dutch Rule in Indonesia." *Journal of Asian Studies* 25 (1966) 589-605. Establishes that the absence of any official preoccupation with nationalism did not imply an absence of a colonial policy; this was to provide sound administration. Four decades of 20th century reforms were part of this policy.

1542

Zinkin, Maurice. *Asia and the West*. London: Chatto & Windus, 1951. Indonesia's 20th century socioeconomic problems figure throughout this critical study of imperialism.

1543

Kennedy, R. "The Colonial Crisis and the Future," in R. Linton (ed.) *The Science of Man in the World Crises*. New York: Columbia University Press, 1945; 306–346. Outlines Dutch policy designed to preserve indigenous institutions.

1544

Van Helsdingen, W. H. and Hoogenberk, H. (eds.). *Mission Interrupted. The Dutch in the East Indies and Their Work in the Twentieth Century*. A Symposium. Amsterdam: Elsevier, 1945. Sixteen articles on various aspects of Indonesia during the first 40 years of the 20th century, including western economic development, governments, welfare, relations between Islam and the government.

1545

Wallace, Alfred Russel. *The Malay Archipelago: The Land of the Orangutan and the Bird of Paradise; a Narrative of Travel, with Studies of Man and Native*. New York: Dover Publications, 1962. Originally published in 1869, and listed here for reasons of its new availability, an eminent naturalist describes much of the natural and human life of Indonesia as the modern age was dawning.

1546

Kartini, Raden A. *Letters of a Javanese Princess*. Edited with an introduction by Hildred Geertz. Preface by Eleanor Roosevelt. New York: Norton, 1964. Published originally shortly after her death in 1911, and reprinted several times, these letters had a great impact on awakening Indonesia, and are now of historic interest.

1547

Schrieke, Bertram J. (ed.). *The Effect of Western Influence on Native Civilizations in the Malay Archipelago*. Batavia: G. Kolff, 1929. A collection of articles by Dutch scholars including B. Schrieke, G. W. J. Drewes and W. Middenendorp.

Culture System

1548

Van Niel, Robert. "The Function of Landrent under the Cultivation System in Java." *Journal of Asian Studies* 23 (1964) 357-375. A most scholarly examination of a major colonial policy which profoundly affected the socioeconomics of Java.

1549

Day, Clive. *The Policy and Administration of the Dutch in Java*. Kuala Lumpur: Oxford University Press, 1966. Published originally by Yale in 1904, this work is still a useful assessment in particular of the 19th century culture system, and the more liberal policies which replaced it.

1550

Van Deventer, S. *Bijdragen tot de kennis van het landelijk stelsel op Java*. [Contributions to an Understanding of the Agriculture System in Java]. 3 Vols. Zaltbommel: J. Norman, 1865–1866. This remains the major source for any examination in depth of the land-rent system in the 19th century.

1551

Caldwell, J. A. M. "Indonesian Export and Production from the Decline of the Culture System to the First World War," in C. D. Cowan (ed.) *Economic development of South-East Asia*. London: Allen & Unwin, 1964. 72-101. A useful study.

Outer Islands

1552

Bone, Robert C. "The International Status of West New Guinea Until 1884." *Journal, Southeast Asian History* 5, 2 (1964) 150-183. Traces the legal occupation of New Guinea from 1545 to 1814, when Dutch possession began; a tripartite partition in 1884 with Germany and Britain left it the owner of West Irian.

1553

Gould, James W. *Americans in Sumatra*. The Hague: Nijhoff, 1961. Americans have participated since before 1873 in trade with Sumatra, and after that date in oil and rubber; missionary activity from 1839 also is outlined.

1554

Pelzer, Karl J. "Western Impact on East Sumatra and North Tapanuli: the Roles of the Planter and the Missionary." *Journal, Southeast Asian History* 2, 2 (1961) 66-7. Two different occupations produced two different results.

1555

Cabaton, A. *Java, Sumatra and The Other Islands of The Dutch East Indies*. London: Fisher Unwin, 1911. Translated by Bernard Miall, a comprehensive survey, giving almost disproportionate weight to the early 20th century conditions of the outer islands, as well as Java.

Modern Islam

1556

Drewes, G. W. J. "Indonesia: Mysticism and Activism," in G. E. Von Grunebaum (ed) *Unity and Variety in Muslim Civilization*. Chicago: University of Chicago Press, 1955. 284-307. A study of Sumatran Islamic history from the 17th century shows why Islam in Indonesia is inconspicuous, and why non-Islamic factors remain; Javanese Islamic trends also are referred to, particularly the Islamic nationalist movements of the 20th century.

1557

Berg, C. C. "Indonesia," in H. A. R. Gibb. (ed.) *Whither Islam? A Survey of Modern Movements in the Moslem World*. London: Victor Gollancz, 1932. 237-312. A lengthy essay of relevance equally to the earlier period as to the 19th and 20th centuries, when modernizing influences such as western education are referred to, and the part played by Islam in the origin and growth of nationalism are discussed.

1558

Benda, Harry J. "Christian Snouck Hurgronje and the Foundations of Dutch Islamic Policy in Indonesia." *Journal of Modern History* 30 (1958) 338-347. Outlines the new, accommodating policy brought in 1889 by the Dutch Islamologist and statesman, Hurgronje, used successfully to end the Achehnese war; his larger concept of a healthy development of Indonesian society also is considered.

1559

Bousquet, G. H. *A French View of the Netherlands Indies*. London: Oxford University Press, 1940. Dutch attitudes and policy, in particular towards Islam in Indonesia, are viewed in a critical and provocative way by a French colonial expert on Islam.

1560

Roff, W. R. "The Malayo-Muslim World of Singapore at the close of the Nineteenth Century." *Journal of Asian Studies* 24 (1964) 75-90. Traces the development of Singapore as a Moslem center of learning and publishing, particularly for Indonesian scholars, during the late 19th century.

1561

Benda, Harry J. "Indonesian Islam under the Japanese Occupation 1942–1945." *Pacific Affairs* 28 (1955) 350-362. The emergence of Indonesian Islam as a political factor in the Masjumi party, formed by the Japanese, is discussed here. Further studies of this are referred to in the section dealing with the occupation period.

1562

Pijper, G. F. *Islam and the Netherlands.* Leiden: E. J. Brill, 1934.

1563

Bousquet, G-H, and J. Schacht (ed. & trs). *Selected Works of C. Snouck Hurgronje.* Leiden. Brill, 1957.

The Chinese

1564

Purcell, V. *The Chinese in Southeast Asia.* 2 ed. London: Oxford University Press, 1965. A substantial work, in which part VII (383-492) deals with the demography and history, the education and economics of the Chinese in Indonesia; a substantial bibliography of secondary sources.

1565

Williams, Lea E. *Overseas Chinese Nationalism: The Genesis of the Pan-Chinese Movement in Indonesia, 1900–1916.* Glencoe: The Free Press, 1960. A study of the two sections in the Chinese community, those newly arrived and those long in Indonesia, and their divergent reaction to the Chinese revolution of 1911.

1566

Cator, W. J. *The Economic Position of the Chinese in the Netherlands Indies.* Chicago: University of Chicago Press, 1936. Based on Dutch sources, gives a survey of the historical, economic, demographical, educational, and political position of the Chinese in Java, Sumatra, Borneo, Bangka, and Billiton.

1567

Lasker, Bruno. "The Role of the Chinese in the Netherlands Indies." *Far Eastern Quarterly* 5 (1946) 162-171. An introductory essay listing three pre-war functions: trade with China, inter-island trade and small power-using business.

1568

Fromberg, P. H. *Verspreide geschriften.* Leiden: Leidsche Uitgevers-maatschappij, 1926. The bulk of these writings concern the Chinese, particularly valuable being the author's 1911 study of the Chinese Movement on Java; the volume remains an invaluable source for any historical treatment of the Chinese in Indonesia.

Nationalist Beginnings

1569

Van Der Kroef, Justus M. "Economic Origins of Indonesian nationalism," in P. Talbot (ed.) *South Asia in the World Today.* Chicago: University of Chicago, 2 imp. 1951. The pattern of occupational differentiation in the colonial period followed lines of color-caste cleavage, producing a marked distaste for the Dutch.

1570

Vishal, Singh. "The Rise of the Indonesian Political Parties." *Journal, Southeast Asian History* 2, 2 (1961) 43-65. The formation of Budi Otomo, Sarekat Islam and other parties in the first quarter of the century.

1571

Thompson, Virginia. "Nationalism and Nationalist Movements in Southeast Asia," in Rupert Emerson. (ed.) *Government and Nationalism in Southeast Asia.* New

York: Institute of Pacific Relations, 1942. The Indonesian pre-war nationalist movement, and the colonial government, are dealt with on 97-106, 182-197.

Communism: Early Period

1572

McVey, Ruth T. *The Rise of Indonesian Communism.* Ithaca: Cornell University Press, 1965. Envisaged as the first volume in a general history of the Indonesian communist party, this work, based on Indonesian, Russian, Dutch, and German sources, traces the complex story up to the failure of the 1926–27 revolt; an exceptional work.

1573

Schrieke, B. *Indonesian Sociological Studies.* 2 Vols. The Hague: van Hoeve, 1955–57. Vol. One, in addition to other papers, contains an outstanding study on the causes and effects of communism on the west coast of Sumatra.

1574

McVey, Ruth T. "An Early Account of the Independence Movement." *Indonesia.* 1 (1966) 46-75. A translation of an influential report by Semaoen to the November 1921 Irkutsk Congress of the Toilers of the Far East, in which details are given of the activities of his party and its association with the labor organizations and other branches of the quarrel-ridden national movement.

1575

Benda, Harry J. and McVey, Ruth T. (ed.). *The Communist Uprisings of 1926–1927 in Indonesia. Key Documents.* Ithaca: Translation Series, Modern Indonesia Project, Department of Far Eastern Studies, Cornell University, 1960. Three basic documents: the Dutch governor-general's 1927 report; the report of the commission of inquiry which investigated the Bantam disturbances; and that of the commission which looked into Sumatra.

1576

Stromquist, H. Shelton. "The Communist Uprisings of 1926–27 in Indonesia: A Re-interpretation." *Journal, Southeast Asian History* 9, 2 (1967). The revolts are attributed to national feelings, not to international conspiracy, nor to rising hopes.

1577

Van Der Veur, Paul W. "E. F. E. Douwes Dekker: Evangelist for Indonesian Political Nationalism." *Journal Asian Studies* 17 (1958) 551-566. The career of the radical founder of the Party of the Indies in 1912.

The Japanese Occupation

1578

Kirby, S. Woodburn. *History of the Second World War. The War Against Japan.* Vol. 1. *The Loss of Singapore.* London: Her Majesty's Stationery Office, 1957. The Southeast Asian campaign of the Japanese, which climaxed in the capture of Java and included the occupation of all of the Dutch possessions: detailed and official war history.

1579

Benda, H. with James K. Irikura & Koichi Kishi. *Japanese Military Administration in Indonesia: Selected Documents.* New Haven: Translation Series 6, Southeast Asia Studies, Yale University, 1965. A translation of 83 official Japanese documents providing a gold mine on the Indonesian nationalist movement in particular during this period; with a scholarly introduction.

1580

Morrison, Samuel Eliot. *History of United States Naval Operations in World War II,* Vol. 3. *The Rising Sun in the Pacific, 1931–April 1942.* Boston: Little, Brown, 1950. Outlines the why and how of Japanese entry into the war, and in Part IV, deals with the naval and military moves against Indonesia, January–March 1942.

1581

Pluvier, J. M. "Dutch Indonesian Relations, 1940–1941." *Journal of Southeast Asian History* 6, 1 (1965) 33-47. The complete rejection by the Dutch of requests for minimal political concessions led to a hardening against them of even the moderate Indonesians, and resulted in an almost complete lack of opposition to the Japanese.

1582

Soetan Sjahrir. *Out of Exile.* New York: John Day, 1949. Letters while in internment to his Dutch wife written between 1934 and 1938 form part one; the second and major section written in 1947 recounts wartime sequence of events in Indonesia, when he organized the underground nationalist movement and helped precipitate the announcement in 1945 of his country's independence.

1583

Benda, Harry J. *The Crescent and the Rising Sun: Indonesian Islam under the Japanese Occupation, 1942–1945.* The Hague: van Hoeve, 1958. After discussing the origins of Islam in Indonesia, and the part it had played until then in the 20th century nationalist movement, the bulk of the book deals with the occupation years, and in particular, in the rise of the Masjumi movement from 1943 onwards, and the climacteric period of late 1944 to August 1945.

1584

Elsbree, Willard H. *Japan's Role in Southeast Asian Nationalist Movements, 1940–1945* Cambridge: Harvard University Press, 1953. The changing attitudes of the Japanese in Indonesia receive major attention in this study, based on Tokyo war-crimes material.

1585

Aziz, M. A. *Japan's Colonialism and Indonesia.* The Hague: M. Nijhoff, 1955. Japan's plans and preparation for conquest and the introduction of its occupation policy.

1586

Anderson, Benedict R. O'G. *Some Aspects of Indonesian Politics under the Japanese Occupation: 1944–1945.* Ithaca: Interim Report Series, Modern Indonesia Project, Cornell University, 1961. The belated fostering by the Japanese of a nationalist movement helped produce a new Indonesian state, as authoritarian as the Japanese or Dutch, and with ideas of racial expansionism; Japanese and Indonesian political movements in a tumultuous and character-forming period are discussed here.

1587

Benda, Harry J. "The Beginnings of the Japanese Occupation of Java." *Far Eastern Quarterly* 15 (1956) 541-560. Outlines the short-lived hopes of the nationalists when the Japanese arrived, and the ruthless occupation policy which silenced Indonesian aspirations by mid-1942.

1588

Gandasubrata, R. A. A. S. M. *An Account of the Japanese Occupation of Banjumas Residency, Java, March 1942 to August 1945.* trs. L. H. Palmer, Ithaca: Data Paper 10, Southeast Asia Program, Cornell University, 1953.

1589

Jones, F. C. *Japan's New Order in East Asia 1937–1945.* London: Oxford University Press, 1954. Japanese policy in Indonesia during the occupation period receives attention in this scholarly study.

1590

Silberman, Bernard S. *Japan and Korea. A critical bibliography.* Tucson: University of Arizona Press, 1962. For further references to Japan in the Pacific War, see pp. 26-8.

POLITICAL PATTERNS

The political patterns for almost all the life of independent Indonesia have been dominated by one man, President Sukarno. From the beginning, when a defiant announcement of independence was shouted over a radio station secured from Japanese control, until the end of 1965, for 20 years the political scene had as its main actor, director, and producer, President Sukarno. Democracy made a tardy appearance, political parties attempted to rule, but failed to secure the indigenous support such an institution demands for survival; while Sukarno kept the final strings of power in his hands. The slow step-back of the Dutch and the bitter, arid relations also made the political pattern more complicated, while the system of government, and the ideals that animated it, became more and more the personalization of Sukarno. Other major elements in the political pattern, particularly the communist party and the Indonesian army, were never able to establish fully their independence of the President; but he found in turn that he too could not be independent of them.

General Works

1591

Woodman, Dorothy. *The Republic of Indonesia.* London: The Cresset Press, 1955. The country, the people and the immediate past are briefly outlined, and numerous aspects of the politics, economics, and culture of the Republic of Indonesia are described.

1592

Fischer, Louis. *The Story of Indonesia.* New York: Harper, 1959. Indonesian history to the recent past is outlined, followed by a major examination of near-contemporary personalities, events, and problems.

1593

Grant, Bruce. *Indonesia.* Melbourne: Melbourne University Press, 1964. An excellent survey, with penetrating chapters on the Leader, the Communists, the Military and the Nation, and much else which helps to clarify the complex political patterns.

1594

Werthheim, W. F. *East-West Parallels. Sociological Approaches to Modern Asia.* The Hague: van Hoeve, 1964. A stimulating and wide-ranging collection of articles, mainly on Indonesia, in which topics such as nationalism, religious reform, social change, corruption, and the trading minorities in Southeast Asia are examined by a sociologist.

1595

Romein, J. and Wertheim, W. F. *A World on the Move. A History of Colonialism and Nationalism in Asia and North Africa from the Turn of the Century to the Bandung Conference.* Amsterdam: Djambatan, 1956. In the six chapters of this large, profusely illustrated book, Indonesia 1900–1955 figures prominently; vivid contemporary photos carry a message of hate and liberty.

1596

Bro, Margueritte Harmon. *Indonesia: Land of Challenge.* London: Victor Gollancz, 1955. A year and one-half in Indonesia produce a survey of contemporary conditions

Beginnings of the Republic

1597

Kahin, G. McT. *Nationalism and Revolution in Indonesia.* Ithaca: Cornell University Press, 1962. A classic account of the emergence of a nation; the outstanding work for the revolutionary 1945–50 period.

1598

Wehl, David. *The Birth of Indonesia*. London: Allen & Unwin, 1948. Describes in detail the events from August 1945, when Japan surrendered, until August 1947, when Dutch military action against the Republic ended as a result of U.N. intervention.

1599

Wolf, Charles Jr. *The Indonesian Story, The Birth, Growth and Structure of the Indonesian Republic*. New York: John Day, 1948. The opposing political and social forces that struggled in Indonesia between 1945 and 1947 are outlined here in this Institute of Pacific Relations study.

1600

Smail, John R. W. *Bandung in the Early Revolution 1945– 1946; A Study in the Social History of the Indonesian Revolution*. Ithaca: Monograph Series, Modern Indonesia Project, Cornell University, 1964. A detailed account of events which took place between August 1945 and March 1946. The revolutionary turbulence and excitement, the rapid-moving internal developments in which the Dutch play merely a peripheral part, is brilliantly evoked.

1601

Gerbrandy, P. S. *Indonesia*. London: Hutchinson, 1950. The wartime Dutch premier gives a detailed study of the chaos in Indonesia to 1949; an outspoken criticism of Dutch withdrawal.

1602

Taylor, Alastair M. *Indonesian Independence and the United Nations*. London: Stevens, 1960. An assessment of the contributions of the U.N. to the successful Indonesian struggle for independence between 1945 and 1949; both the Indonesian and Dutch scenes are sketched in, but major attention is given to the constant U.N. involvement.

1603

Collins, J. Foster. "The United Nations and Indonesia." *International Conciliation* 459 (1950) 115-200. With a different viewpoint than Taylor, this outlines the role of the U.N. in the Indonesian dispute from February 1946 until the Hague Conference.

1604

Abdul Haris Nasution. *Fundamentals of Guerrilla Warfare*. New York: Praeger, 1965. Written in 1953, General Nasution draws on his campaign experiences against the Dutch to write on guerrilla war; includes long extracts of instructions issued by him in 1948–49 to his guerrillas.

1605

Djajadiningrat, Indrus Nasir. *The Beginnings of the Indonesian-Dutch Negotiations and the Hoge Veluwe Talks*. Ithaca: Monograph Series, Modern Indonesia Project, Southeast Asia Program, Cornell University, 1958. This monograph covers the late 1945 until mid-1946 period, culminating in the little-known Hoge Veluwe Conference between the Indonesian nationalists and the Dutch.

1606

Graaf, H. J. "The Indonesian Declaration of Independence, 17 August, 1945." *Bijdragen Tot De Taal-, Land- En Volkenkunde* 115 (1959) 305-327. Details of the events and the movements of those directly concerned, such as Sukarno, Hatta, Maeda, and others, in the few days of August immediately prior to, and including the 16 and 17 of August.

1607

Schiller, A. Arthur. *The Formation of Federal Indonesia 1945–1949*. The Hague: van Hoeve, 1955. A description of the constitutional and legal steps taken to create a federal Indonesia.

1608

Coast, John. *Recruit to Revolution. Adventure and Politics in Indonesia*. London: Christophers, 1952. An exciting and revealing account of the activities of a young sympathizer of the Indonesian-nationalist struggle, who became the associate of Sukarno.

1609

Tantri K'ut. *Revolt in Paradise*. New York: Harper & Brothers, 1960. An American woman who came to be known as Surabaya Sue, writes of her pre-war life in Indonesia, her capture by the Japanese, her underground participation against the Dutch with the republicans.

1610

Sutter, John O. *Indonesienisasi: Politics in a Changing Economy, 1940–1955*. 4 Vols. Ithaca: Southeast Asia Program, Cornell University, 1959. A wealth of information on Indonesian modern economic history, and the effect of violent politics and nationalism on patterns of ownership and western enterprise.

1611

Kahin, G. McT. "Indonesian Politics and Nationalism," in W. L. Holland (ed.) *Asian Nationalism and the West*. New York: MacMillan, 1953, 65-196. An early statement of his research later embodied in his classic *Nationalism and Revolution*.

1612

Van Der Kroef, Justus M. *The Dialect of Colonial Indonesian History*, Amsterdam: du Peet, 1963. Emphasizes the identity of interests between the Dutch and the Indonesians on the one hand, and on the other, the social and economic differentiation.

1613

Palmier, Leslie H. "Indonesian-Dutch Relations." *Journal, Southeast Asian History* 2, 2 (1961) 24-34. Feels that much of the 1945–60 Indonesian animosity to the Dutch was due to internal factors in Indonesian politics.

1614

Anderson, Ben. "The Language of Indonesian Politics." *Indonesia* 1 (1966) 89-116. Modern Indonesian is evolving as a synthesis of a new politico-cultural intelligence and perspective.

PKI (*Partai Kommunist Indonesia*)

1615

Mintz, Jeanne S. *Mohammed, Marx and Marhaen: The Roots of Indonesian Socialism*. London: Pall Mall, 1965. Reviews the history of nationalism, and the interconnections with communism, up to the transfer of authority from the Dutch; then deals with the events and rationale up to the near result.

1616

Hindley, Donald. *The Communist Party of Indonesia 1951– 63*. Berkeley: University of California Press, 1964. Traces the rise of the party, particularly in Java, under the direction of Aidit; with a detailed section on the technique of mass agrarian support.

1617

McVey, Ruth T. "Indonesian Communism and the Transition to Guided Democracy," in A. Doak Barnett (ed.) *Communist Strategies in Asia*. New York: Praeger, 1963. 148-195. Examines the growth of the PKI from 1951, Indonesia's rejection of pariamentary government and political parties, the influence exerted on Sukarno by the PKI and its "nationalist" communist attitude.

1618

Van der Kroef, Justus M. *The Communist Party of Indonesia: Its History, Program and Tactics*. Vancouver: University of British Columbia, 1965. From the foundation of the Party in 1920 to the near present, with particular emphasis given to the last 20 years; a detailed account.

1619

Brackman, Arnold C. *Indonesian Communism: A History*. New York: Praeger, 1963. The growth and impact of the Communist Party of Indonesia (PKI) and its indigenous characteristics are examined in this full-length study.

1620

Van der Kroef, Justus M. "Peasant and Land Reform in Indonesian Communism." *Journal, Southeast Asian History* 4, 1 (1963) 30-61. The importance attached by the PKI to its peasant base, and the increasing attention it gave to agrarian questions after an ineffectual and indifferent beginning.

1621

Aidit, D. N. *The Selected Works of D. N. Aidit.* Vol. 1. *Indonesia.* Washington: Joint Publications Research Service, U. S. Department of Commerce. No date. A translation of the first volume of the *Selected Works of D. N. Aidit* published by Jajasan Pembaruan, Djakarta, in 1959. Material written by the PKI leader between 1951 and 1955 is included; each section has an editorial preface. A comprehensive picture of PKI policies on all major issues during this period.

1622

Van der Kroef, Justus M. "The Sino-Indonesian Partnership." *Orbis* 8 (1964) 332-356. Relations with China from 1962, and extensive treatment of PKI attitudes.

Regional Disturbances

1623

Mossman, James. *Rebels in Paradise: Indonesia's Civil War.* London: Jonathan Cape, 1961. An intimate and revealing account of the regionalist rebellion of 1958.

1624

Bouman, J. C. & others. *The South Moluccas: Rebellious Province or Occupied State.* Leyden: A. W. Sythoff, 1960. A collection of ten papers outlining various aspects of the struggle for, and the inherent righteousness of, an independent state of the South Moluccas.

1625

Bone, Robert C. *The Dynamics of the Western New Guinea (Irian Barat) Problem.* Ithaca: Monograph Series, Modern Indonesian Project, Cornell University, 1958. Examines the background and development of the Irian issue, 1946 to 1958.

1626

Van der Kroef, Justus M. "The West New Guinea Settlement: Its Origins and Implications: *Orbis* 7 (1963) 120-149. The ten-year background to the 1962 settlement of Indonesia's claim for the territory.

Regional Authority

1627

Legge, J. D. *Central Authority and Regional Autonomy in Indonesia: A Study in Local Administration 1950-1960.* Ithaca: Cornell University Press, 1961. A study of the problem of regional government from the inception of the republic, treating in detail various laws designed to develop a system of autonomy but which after 1959 came to be neglected and abandoned.

1628

Maryanov, Gerald S. *Decentralization in Indonesia as a Political Problem.* Ithaca: Interim Report Series, Modern Indonesia Project, Cornell University, 1958. A brief study of the use of decentralization and the political implications of the symbols used and the regional conflict of the republican period.

Local Government

1629

Goethals, Peter R. *Aspects of Local Government in a Sumbawan Village.* Ithaca: Monograph Series, Modern Indonesia Project, Cornell University, 1961. Based on two years field work in a Moslem village on Sumabawa Island, this outlines various aspects of the community life, such as village government, religious authority and kinship structure, and reveals not altogether surprisingly some post-colonial social and political changes.

1630

Jay, Robert R. "Local Government in Rural Central Java." *Far Eastern Quarterly* 15 (1956) 215-228. The administration of the *desa,* a collection of a few villages, is outlined here.

Bandung Conference

1631

Kahin, George McT. *The Asian-African Conference, Bandung, Indonesia,* April 1955. Ithaca: Cornell University Press, 1956. A succinct outline of the objects of the sponsors and the participants, and the proceedings of the Conference itself, by an experienced political scientist in attendance.

1632

Rowan, Carl T. *The Pitiful and the Proud.* New York: Random House, 1956. An American Negro gives an eye-witness report on Asia, including the Bandung Conference, 381-414.

1633

Hatta, Mohammed. "Indonesia's Foreign Policy." *Foreign Affairs* 31 (1953) 441-452. Although written prior to Bandung and by a politician by then under house arrest, these sentiments on non-alignment are relevant to the mood of the Conference.

The Chinese in Politics

1634

Somers, Mary F. *Peranakan Chinese Politics in Indonesia.* Ithaca: Interim Report Series, Modern Indonesia Project, Cornell University, 1964. A modest study of local-born Chinese and their role in the post-war politics of Indonesia.

1635

Willmott, Donald E. *The National Status of the Chinese in Indonesia, 1900–1958.* Ithaca: Modern Indonesia Project, Cornell University, 1961. A historical background is provided to a study of the Sino-Indonesian Treaty on Dual Nationality, and a consideration of the position in Indonesia in 1958 of both alien Chinese and Indonesian Chinese.

1636

Mozingo, David. "The Sino-Indonesian Dual Nationality Treaty." *Asian Survey* 1, 10 (1961) 25-31. A brief consideration of the compromise results of the Treaty, ratified in January 1960.

1637

Williams, Lea E. "Sino-Indonesia Diplomacy: A Study of Revolutionary International Politics." *China Quarterly* (1962) 184-199. Sino-Indonesian relations from 1949 to 1961, with an Indonesia uncowed by threats, and believing Chinese to be safely distant and basically good.

1638

Fried, Morton H. (ed.). *Colloquism on Overseas Chinese.* New York: Institute of Pacific Relations, 1958.

Modern Islam in Politics

1639

Van Nieuwenhuijze, C. A. O. *Aspects of Islam in Post-Colonial Indonesia.* The Hague: van Hoeve, 1958. Five essays: background to Islam; Islam in transition; Japanese Islam policy; the Dar-ul-Islam movement to 1949; the Indonesian State and Moslem concepts.

1640

Jay, Robert R. *Religion and Politics in Rural Central Java.* Ann Arbor: Cultural Report Series 12, Southeast Asia Studies, Yale University, 1963. An analysis of the historical development and more recent exacerbation of two opposed communities in Java, the *santris* (devout Moslems) and the *abangans* (Javanese Moslems with a syncretic system of beliefs). Attention is focused on a single village, rent by hostility.

1641

Von Der Mehden, Fred. *Religion and Nationalism in Southeast Asia.* Wisconsin: Wisconsin University Press, 1963. The changing role of Islam in the Indonesian nationalist movement of the 20th century is considered.

1642

Palmier, Leslie H. "Modern Islam in Indonesia: the Muhammadiyah after Independence." *Pacific Affairs* 27 (1954) 255-263.

1643

Natsir, Mohammad. *Some Observations concerning the role of Islam in National and International Affairs.* Ithaca:

Data Paper 16, Southeast Asia Program, Cornell University, 1954. The former chairman of Masjumi expresses here his ideas on the role of Islam.

1644

Van Nieuwenhuijze, C. A. O. "The Darul-Islam Movement in Western Java." *Pacific Affairs* 23 (1950) 169-183. This movement, working for the establishment of a strictly Moslem state, has its history outlined from 1945, when it was led by Kartosuwiryo; its non-conformity to the nationalist pattern set in Jakarta is shown clearly.

Sukarno

1645

Hanna, Willard A. *Eight Nation Makers. Southeast Asia's Characteristic Statesmen*. New York: St. Martins Press, 1964. The career of Sukarno, with a wealth of detail concerning his early life, occupies the first 100 pages of this 300-page book.

1646

Adams, Cindy. *Sukarno, An Autobiography, as told to Cindy Adams*. New York: Bobbs-Merrill, 1965. A superficial but interesting life story, with a series of revealing photos.

1647

Palmier, Leslie H. "Sukarno, the Nationalist." *Pacific Affairs* 30 (1957) 101-119. A mystic nationalism and an astute sense of political balance animated his activities reviewed here.

1648

Williams, Maslyn. *Five Journeys from Jakarta: Inside Sukarno's Indonesia*. New York: Morrow, 1966. A series of visits out of Jakarta in 1964, to West Irian, Sumatra, Sulawesi, and various parts of Java; a penetrating study of part of Indonesia as seen through the eyes of its inhabitants; an enlightening experience which helps to explain Sukarno's magic.

1649

Lewis, Reba. *Indonesia. Troubled Paradise*. New York: David McKay, 1962. The wife of a W.H.O. doctor, who arrived with guided democracy, gives here an intelligent account of Indonesia in 1957, with Sukarno everpresent.

1650

Hanna, Willard A. *Bung Karno's Indonesia: A Collection of 25 Reports Written for the American Universities Field Staff*. New York: American Universities Field Staff, 1960. A collection of on-the-spot surveys, so critical and candid on Sukarno and his regime, and so well documented by specific facts and figures, that it was banned in Indonesia.

Towards Guided Democracy (1950-1960)

1651

Feith, Herbert. *The Decline of Constitutional Democracy in Indonesia*. Ithaca: Cornell University Press, 1962. The failure of a parliamentary system between 1949 and 1957 due to a lack of leaders committed to making it work; a thorough analysis of background conditions, the immediate circumstances and the complex series of decisions and events which shaped the republic in this critical period.

1652

—————. *The Wilopo Cabinet, 1952–1953; A Turning Point in Post-Revolutionary Indonesia*. Ithaca: Monograph Series, Modern Indonesia Project, Cornell University, 1958. During the 14 months of this government's existence, basic changes occurred in the positions of power by the President, the army and the political parties. These changes are well described here.

1653

—————. "Dynamics of Guided Democracy," in Ruth T. McVey, (ed.) *Indonesia*. New Haven: Center for Southeast Asian Studies, Yale University, by arrangement with Human Relations Area Files, 1963. 309-409. An outline of political developments 1949 to 1962; with clear indications of a Sukarno at the end fighting for his political life amid widespread discontent.

1654

Kahin, G. McT. "Indonesia," in G. McT. Kahin (ed.) *Major Governments of Asia*. Ithaca: Cornell University Press, 1963. 535-700. A five-section study by the director of the modern Indonesia project at Cornell, in which the pre-1942 history is sketched in, followed by major emphasis on political development from 1945, together with an assessment of major problems, as of 1963, which are listed as the army, regionalism, economic issues, and foreign affairs. The political leadership escapes lightly.

1655

Palmier, Leslie H. *Indonesia and the Dutch*. London: Oxford University Press, 1962. Attributes the deterioration of relations with the Dutch in the 1957–1960 period as part of a basic conflict between Javanese and non-Javanese; a provocative study.

1656

Pauker, Guy J. "The Role of the Military in Indonesia," in J. J. Johnson (ed.) *The Military in the Underdeveloped Areas*. Princeton: Princeton University Press, 1962. A useful historical background on the army in Indonesia, together with a consideration of the role of the military in the more important current political issues.

1657

Soelaeman Soemardi. "Some Aspects of the Social Origin of Indonesian Political Decision-Makers," in *Transactions of the Third World Congress of Sociology*. London: International Sociological Association, 1956. Biographical data on cabinet ministers, parliamentarians and senior civil servants.

1658

Benda H. "Decolonization in Indonesia: The Problem of Continuity and Change." *The American Historical Review*. LLXX (1965) 1058-1073.

1659

Mackie, J. A. C. "Indonesian Politics under Guided Democracy." *Australian Outlook* 15 (1961) 260-279. Guided Democracy institutions in their general political context.

1660

Soedjatmoko. "The Role of Political Parties in Indonesia," in Philip W. Thayer (ed.) *Nationalism and Progress in Free Asia*. Baltimore: Johns Hopkins, 1956. 128-140. Places political parties of 1952 Indonesia in three groups; religious, nationalist and marxist, and describes their characteristics and limitations.

Confrontation

1661

Feith, Herbert. "Indonesia," in G. McT. Kahin (ed.) *Government and Politics of Southeast Asia*. 2 ed. Ithaca: Cornell University Press, 1965. 183-278. This stimulating and thoughtful study ends at the beginning of confrontation, but its examination of the political process in Indonesia, as well as the historical background, and the manner in which its major contemporary problems were approached, in particular, West Irian, make this an invaluable guide to the Indonesia of today, and help to explain its attitude over Malaysia.

1662

Brackman, Arnold C. *Southeast Asia's Second Front: the power struggle in the Malay Archipelago*. New York: Praeger, 1966. Contemporary history in the Malaysian-Indonesian world, in which the Indonesian opposition to Malaysia, the racial concept of Maphilindo, and other Indonesian-Malaysian developments of recent years are treated.

1663

Hindley, David. "Indonesia's Confrontation with Malaysia: A Search for Motives." *Asian Survey* 4 (1964) 904-914.

1664

Gordon, Bernard K. "The Potential for Indonesian Expansionism." *Pacific Affairs* 36, 4 (1963-64) 378-393. Outlines what he feels is a long-established and continuing expansionist sentiment in Indonesia aimed at recovering its "lost" territories of racial and cultural affinity.

1665

Sutter, John O. "Two Faces of Keonfrontasi: Crush Malaysia and the Gestapu." *Asian Survey* 6 (1966) 523-546. A comprehensive outline of the tangled and differing motives and attitudes in Indonesia towards Malaysia.

1666

Kahin, G. McT. "Malaysia and Indonesia." *Pacific Affairs* 37 (1964) 253-270. Supports the Indonesian stand.

1667

Indonesian Intentions Towards Malaysia. Kuala Lumpur: Government Printer, 1964. An official White Paper issued by the Malaysian Government, which reviews 19 years of Indonesian relations, including espionage and expansionist aspirations, and with details of confrontation. See also the more detailed *Indonesian Involvement in Eastern Malaya.* Kuala Lumpur: Department of Information, 1964, with details of the military incidents of 1963–65.

1668

Malaya-Indonesia Relations, 31 August 1957 to 15 September 1963. Kuala Lumpur: Government Printer, 1964. An official White Paper, outlining the diplomatic relations between the two countries until the sacking of the Malayan embassy in Djakarta, and the removal by the Indonesian government of all status from the Malayan ambassador, in September 1963.

1669

Dommer, Arthur J. "The attempted coup in Indonesia." *China Quarterly* 25 (1966) 144-170. A detailed eye-witness account of September 30, 1965, and developments which followed immediately thereafter.

1670

"Selected Documents Relating to 'the September 30 Movement' and Its Epilogue." *Indonesia* 1 (1966) 131-205. Published statements on the day, or immediately following the attempted coup and military reprisal of September 1965, by all those closely involved.

ECONOMIC PATTERNS

Indonesia's economy, although basically agricultural, has attracted several brilliant scholars to its study, by reason of its complicated pattern and its challenging problems. It possesses, particularly on Java, a soil of great fertility. Elsewhere, its economy is enriched by oils and minerals such as tin. Its economic wealth was never utilized by the indigenous inhabitants, for by the time that modern man sought gain as the goal in life, the area was controlled by the European, and although the Indonesian made batik or grew rubber in small quantities, innumerable psychological, political and educational barriers shut him off from the exploitation of his own lands. To a very great extent, that was done by foreigners. As a result, the economic pattern is a confused one.

General Works

1671

Paauw, Douglas S. "From Colonial to Guided Economy" in Ruth T. McVey (ed.) *Indonesia.* New Haven: Center of Southeast Asian Studies, Yale University, by arrangement with Human Relations Area Files, 1963. 155-247. A comprehensive survey, with 23 tables, of the post-Pacific War economic history of Indonesia.

1672

Geertz, Clifford. *Agricultural Involution. The Processes of Ecological Change in Indonesia.* Berkeley: University of California Press, 1963. A brilliant analyst, Dr. Geertz defies tidy bibliographical placing as his many-sided genius refuses to be confined. Here the socio-economic sickness in Indonesia is diagnosed by an anthropologist. He clarifies, in this piece of economic and social history, the main processes of change in rural Indonesia, and brings out sharply the contrast between Java and the Outer Islands in this process.

1673

Higgins, Benjamin & Jean. *Indonesia: The Crisis of the Millstones.* New York: Van Nostrand, 1963. The diversity of the economic problems and development plans, and its political problems, which could be tackled if evolution and not revolution were the motto. A wide-ranging outline.

1674

Boeke, J. H. and others. *Indonesian Economics. The Concept of Dualism in Theory and Practice.* The Hague: van Hoeve, 1961. A collection of papers by Dutch scholars, including J. H. Boeke, J. van Gelderen and others, dealing in part one with the theory of dualism, and various practical examples of it in the 20th-century Indonesian economy in Part II. Three papers on the village comprise the core of this section.

1675

_____. *Economics and Economic Policy of Dual Societies as exemplified by Indonesia.* Haarlem: H. D. Tjeenk Willink & Zoon N. V., 1953. An amalgamation of his two earlier works published in 1942 and 1946, on the structure, and the evolution, of the Indonesian Economy. He elaborates here his controversial ideas on the dualism of a western-style capitalist economy alongside an eastern non-capitalist peasant economy, with analytical detail.

1676

Higgins, Benjamin. "The Dualistic Theory of Underdeveloped Areas." *Economic Development and Cultural Change* 4 (1956) 99-115. Dr. Boeke's dualistic theory is examined critically and substantially answered.

1677

Allen, G. C. & Donnithorne, Audrey G. *Western Enterprise in Indonesia and Malaya.* London: Allen & Unwin, 1957. A survey of the Javanese sugar and other agricultural industries: mining, banking, shipping, public utilities, and other economic developments of the 19th and 20th centuries.

1678

Wertheim, W. F. (ed.). *Selected Studies on Indonesia. The Indonesian Town. Studies in Urban Sociology.* The Hague: van Hoeve, 1958. Four pre-war papers; the editor writes on the social problems of town development in Indonesia; the 1937 report on the living conditions in Batavia of laborers is translated in full; the disturbing examination by W. Brand of the markedly different death rates of various races in Bandung; and a paper on the revered remnants of ancient Mataram.

1679

Lasker, Bruno. *Human Bondage in Southeast Asia.* Chapel Hill: University of North Carolina, 1950. Indonesia appears repeatedly in this examination of slavery, serfdom, debt bondage, compulsory public services and labor relations in a colonial setting, from secondary sources.

1680

Boeke, J. H. *The Evolution of the Netherlands Indies Economy.* New York: Institute of Pacific Relations, 1946. Outlines measures taken by the Dutch to regulate production and trading in the principal export items of the islands.

1681

_____. *The Structure of Netherlands Indian Economy.* New York: Institute of Pacific Relations, 1942.

1682

Jacoby, Erich H. *Agrarian Unrest in Southeast Asia.* New York: Columbia University Press, 1949. Java is treated in chapter two, where the colonial economic development is outlined, as is the population pressure, land utilization, the failure of public credit institutions and the contrasting social development of the foreign and indigenous community.

1683

Boeke, J. H. *The Interests of The Voiceless Far East. Introduction to Oriental Economics.* Leiden: Institute of Pacific Relations, 1948. The battle between aggressive western capitalism and the pre-capitalist traditions of Indonesia creates a lack of balance.

1684

Polak, J. J. *The National Income of the Netherlands Indies, 1921–1939.* New York: Institute of Pacific Relations, 1942. Food crops, export crops, livestock and poultry, fisheries, forestry, mines and plantations, industrial production, trade and communications, government, and other sectors of the economy; with numerous graphs and tables.

1685

Gotz, J. F. F. "Railways in the Netherlands Indies, with special reference to the island of Java." *Bulletin of the Colonial Institute,* Amsterdam (1939). 267-290.

1686

Burkenroad, Martin D. "The Development of Marine Resources in Indonesia." *Far Eastern Quarterly* 5 (1946) 189-199.

1687

Langhout, John. *The Economic Conquest of Acheen by the Dutch.* The Hague: van Stockum, 1924. A historical outline from the Acheh War, then a consideration of the petroleum, lumbering, plantation, ship and other western-established industries in Acheh.

1688

Van Gelderen, J. *The Recent Development of Economic Foreign Policy in the Netherlands East Indies.* London: Longmans, Green, 1939. A slim volume dealing with post-world war economic development, and the government controls, by means of international regulations, of export and production.

1689

Collins, G. E. P. *East Monsoon.* London: Jonathan Cape, 1936. Sails with, illustrates, and describes the Macassarese sailing vessels that trade with Singapore on the Southeast monsoon.

Agriculture

1690

Bauer, P. T. *The Rubber Industry: A Study in Competition and Monopoly.* Cambridge: Harvard University Press, 1948. A detailed study of the pre-war industry in Indonesia and Malaya, from the time of the world depression and the establishment of international regulations over production; with the treatment of the small holders in Indonesia contrasting sharply with those in Malaya.

1691

Paauw, Douglas S. (ed.). *Prospects for East Sumatran Plantation Industries. A Symposium.* New Haven: Southeast Asia Studies, Yale University, 1962. Three studies on major plantation crops; rubber, tobacco and palm oil, by graduates of Nommensen University in Medan.

1692

Metcalf, John E. *The Agricultural Economy of Indonesia.* Washington: Agriculture Monograph 15, Department of Agriculture, Office of Foreign Agricultural Relations, 1952. A comparison of the immediate post-war and pre-war agricultural scene.

1693

Mackie, J. A. C. "Indonesia's Government Estates and Their Masters." *Pacific Affairs* 34 (1961) 337-360. Although previously the resource basis for economic development, the estates of Indonesia are seen here, under government control, as a declining factor in the future. The takeover period, 1957–1958, and the sag in production is examined.

1694

Pelzer, Karl J. "The Agrarian Conflict in East Sumatra." *Pacific Affairs* 30 (1957) 151-159. Conflict between foreign planters and Sumatran peasants.

1695

Van der Kolff, G. H. "An Economic Case Study: Sugar and Welfare in Java," in Phillips Ruopp (ed.) *Approaches to Community Development.* The Hague: van Hoeve, 1953. 188-206. The retarding influence exerted by the sugar industry of Java on peasant agriculture, and the possibility of cooperatives to improve conditions.

1696

Terra, G. J. A. "Some sociological aspects of agriculture in South East Asia." *Indonesie* 6 (1952–53) 297-316, 439-463. An outline of the history of agriculture in Indonesia and related areas, with observations on the social structure of the inhabitants and their relationship to agriculture.

1697

Dankes, W. H. *The "P" and "T" Lands. An Agricultural romance of Anglo-Dutch enterprise.* London: Eden Fisher, 1943. A large area of land sold in 1813 near two villages in Java, Pamanoekan and Tjiasemlanden, was developed as outstanding estates; to become the Anglo-Dutch Plantations of Java; a 114-page history of those estates.

1698

Van Hall, C. J. J. and Van de Koppel, C. (eds.). *De landbouw in de Indische archipel.* 3 vols. in 4 parts. The Hague: van Hoeve, 1946–50. The standard Dutch work on Indonesian agriculture, a comprehensive study by specialists. Each article is followed by a bibliography.

Marketing

1699

Dewey, Alice. *Peasant Marketing in Java.* New York: Free Press, 1962. The character of the internal market system in Java, the pattern of exchange, types of traders, small scale and large scale trade, finance and credit, and other aspects of the economic exchange of goods in a Javanese village.

1700

Mears, Leon A. *Rice Marketing in the Republic of Indonesia.* Djakarta: P. T. Pembangunan, 1961. A detailed survey of marketing organization and operation, consumption, of this industry; based on a 1957 survey. See also his articles in *Ekonomi dan Kenangan Indonesia* 11 (1958) 45-59, and 530-570.

1701

Mulia, Wanda. "The Processes of Changes in the Marketing Structure Since the Implementation of Guided Economy." *Ekonomi dan Kenangan Indonesia* 14 (1961) 58-70. Outlines the changes that resulted from the nationalization of Dutch commercial enterprises in 1958, the direct supervision of the government, and an Indonesianization of the commercial structure.

Labor

1702

Hawkins, Everett D. "Labor in Transition." in Ruth T. McVey (ed.) *Indonesia.* New Haven: Center for Southeast Asian Studies, Yale University, by arrangement with Human Relations Area Files, 1963. 248-271. A study of post-Pacific War labor organization and the labor force in Indonesia; useful bibliography.

1703

_____. "Indonesia," in Walter Galenson (ed.) *Labor in Developing Economies.* Berkeley: University of California Press, 1962. 71-137. The emergence of an Indonesian labor force, the development of trade unions, the problems of management, and the increasing role of government in labor relations are considered.

1704

Tedjasukmana, Iskander. *The Political Character of the Indonesian Trade Union Movement.* Ithaca: Modern Indonesia Project, Cornell University, 1959. Written by a former Indonesian minister of labor, this discusses the impact on labor unions in both colonial and republican periods of various political parties and their ideologies.

1705

Blake, Donald J. "The Role and Functions of Labor Organizations in Socialist Economic Development," in Rossall J. Johnson, Mohammad Sadli, and Subroto, (eds.) *Readings in Business Administration and Economics.* Djakarta: Facultas Ekonomi, Universiti Indonesia, 1961. 64-82. An analysis on how labor organizations, including trade unions, can work in non-western ways to improve the position of their members in a developing state, such as Indonesia.

1706

Coolie Budget Commission. Living Conditions of Plantation Workers and Peasants on Java in 1939–1940. Trs. by Robert Van Niel. Ithaca: Translation Series, Modern Indonesia Project, Cornell University, 1956. A revealing survey, undertaken by the Dutch colonial government, but never made public by them.

1707

Thompson, Virginia. *Labor Problems in Southeast Asia.* New Haven: Yale University Press, 1947. Labor conditions in Indonesia, essentially of the colonial period, are given in chapter four, pp. 117-166.

1708

Schiller, A. Arthur. "Labor Law and Legislation in the Netherlands Indies." *Far Eastern Quarterly* 5 (1946) 176-188. Traces the origins of labor laws from 1879; the modern labor code was introduced in 1926 and is commented on.

1709

Willner, Ann Ruth. "The Adaptation of Peasants to Conditions of Factory Labor: A Case Study in Java." *Asian Survey* 3 (1963) 560-571. Describes the social and cultural change from agrarian peasant to textile-mill worker in East Java.

1710

Blake, Donald J. "Labour Shortage and Unemployment in North East Sumatra." *Malayan Economic Review* 7 (1962) 106-118. The conditions under which a labor shortage in east Sumatran plantations has existed since 1958, alongside considerable urban unemployment in Medan are outlined, and (in the subsequent issue, 7, pp. 98-110) suggests a program to remedy this.

Labor Migration

1711

Sandra. *Sedjarah Pergerakan Buruh Indonesia.* Djakarta: P. T. Pustaka Rakjat, 1961. A detailed official history of the Indonesian Labor Movement, in two parts; before and after 1945.

1712

Wertheim, W. F. "Sociological Aspects of Inter-Island Migration in Indonesia." *Population Studies* 12 (1959) 184-201. Utilizes data gathered in a 1956 visit to the pioneer settlement districts of Sumatra, and discusses the problems of inter-island migration.

1713

Cunningham, Clark E. *The Postwar Migration of the Toba-Bataks to East Sumatra.* New Haven: Southeast Asia Studies, Yale University, 1958. A highland Batak village and a mixed community village on a former estate are studied in this account of the pre-war and post-war agrarian migration of the Batak.

1714

Pelzer, Karl J. "Tanah Sabrang and Java's Population Problem." *Far Eastern Quarterly* 5 (1946) 133-142. All signs indicate that the sparse population of the other islands will remain in contrast to the dense population of Java.

1715

Thompson, Warren S. *Population and Progress in the Far East.* Chicago: University of Chicago, 1959. The unprecedented population explosion in Indonesia and the lack of economic resources to sustain this growth indefinitely, are examined on pp. 345-359, as part of a general survey.

Banking and Exchange

1716

Charlesworth, Harold C. *A Banking System in Transition: The Origin, Concept and Growth of the Indonesian Banking System.* Djakarta: New Nusantara, 1959. A historical outline of the growth and development of the Indonesian banking system established by the Indonesian government since independence.

1717

Corden, W. M. & Mackie, J. A. C. "The Development of the Indonesian Exchange Rate System." *Malayan Economic Review* 7 (1962) 37-60. An outline of the development of the system since 1950, including related policies affecting trade, such as import tariffs, export subsidies, and taxes of various kinds.

1718

Schmitt, Hans O. "Foreign Capital and Social Conflict in Indonesia 1950–1958." *Economic Development and Cultural Change* 10 (1962) 284-293. A discussion of the exchange rate by one who regards it as of central importance for political alignments.

1719

Paauw, Douglas S. *Financing Economic Development: The Indonesian Case.* New York: Glencoe Free Press, 2nd printing 1961. A detailed examination of the capital required to implement the 1956 five-year plan, together with an assessment of savings, investment, inflation, the tax system and economic incentives, the role of local finance and other aspects of the economic debility of 1951–1957 Indonesia.

Batik and Other Industries

1720

Higgins, Benjamin H. *Entrepreneurship and Labor Skills in Indonesian Economic Development. A Symposium.* New Haven: Monograph 1, Southeast Asian Studies, Yale University, 1961. An introduction from Higgins precedes three excellent studies; by L. Palmier on Batik manufacture in a Chinese community; by E. D. Hawkins on Javanese entrepreneurs in the Batik industry; and by H. W. Guthrie on a skilled labor force.

1721

Kertanegara. "The Batik Industry in Central Java." *Ekonomi dan Kenangan Indonesia* 11 (1958) 345-401. A study undertaken by the Bureau of Economic Research at Gadjah Mada University, with the assistance of M.I.T.; a detailed analysis of production and sales of this home-based, labor-intensive industry.

1722

Lasker, Bruno. *Human Bondage in Southeast Asia.* Chapel Hill: University of North Carolina, 1950. An appendix, pp. 292-311, on "Bondage through worker indebtedness in the Batik industry of Java" has valuable information.

1723

Rao, Nagaraja K. "Small Scale Industry and Economic Development in Indonesia." *Economic Development and Cultural Change* 4 (1956) 159-170. One of a number of articles in this issue on Indonesia, it outlines the network of small village industries of Indonesia, on which the author feels an industrial complex can be developed.

1724

Aten, A. "Some remarks on rural industry in Indonesia." *Indonesie* 6 (1952-53) 536-564. The blacksmiths of Java, with maps and tables; a similar study, on pp. 411-422, on the umbrella industry.

1725

Geertz, Clifford. "Religious Belief and Economic Behaviour in a Central Javanese Town: Some Preliminary Considerations." *Economic Development and Cultural Change* 2 (1956) 134-158.

Mining

1726

Gerretson, C. *History of the Royal Dutch.* 4 vols. Leiden: E. J. Brill, 1953-57. A detailed history of oil in Indonesia, from the opening of the outer islands to private enterprise in 1850 and the discovery and working of oil in Sumatra in the 1880's, to 1914; involving many countries and covering many concerns, this, as with all oil histories, is a wide-ranging history.

1727

Braake, Alex L. Ter. *Mining in the Netherlands East Indies.* New York: Bulletin 4, Netherlands & Netherlands Indies Council, Institute of Pacific Relations, 1944. An outline history of the economically-worked minerals; tin, oil, coal, nickel and minor ores.

Development: National and International Efforts

1728

Geertz, Clifford. *Peddlers and Princes. Social Change and Economic Modernization in Two Indonesian Towns.* Chicago: University of Chicago Press, 1963. A Javanese market town and a Balinese court town are contrasted; economic revolution is producing a new middle class in one, and an upper revolution is occurring in the other; each have their problems. His six conclusions on the dynamics of development apply not merely to Indonesia, but to all Southeast Asia.

1729

_____. "Social Change and Economic Modernization in Two Indonesian Towns: A Case in Point," in Everett E. Hagen (ed.) *On The Theory of Social Change. How Economic Growth Begins.* Homewood, Ill.: Dorsey, 1962. A sharp, clear exposition of the contrast and conclusions ennunciated at length in *Peddlers and Princes.*

1730

Soemardjan, Selo. *The Dynamics of Community Development in Rural Central and West Java. A Comparative Report.* Ithaca: Modern Indonesia Project, Cornell University, 1963. A brief monograph on the different concepts of community development held by the three Indonesian ministries involved.

1731

Mears, Leon A. "Indonesia" in A Pepelasis, L. A. Mears & I. Adelman (eds.) *Economic Development: Analysis and Case Studies.* New York: Harper & Brothers, 1961. 418-467. A survey of the Indonesian economic scene, with an assessment of development prospects; useful bibliography.

1732

Higgins, Benjamin. *Indonesia's Economic Stabilization and Development.* New York: Institute of Pacific Relations, 1957. From the chaotic conditions of December 1949, when sovereignty was transferred, to 1956, when the struggle to establish economic stability and to initiate development remained unsuccessful; an excellent general study.

1733

Glassburner, Bruce. "Economic Policy-Making in Indonesia, 1950–1957." *Economic Development and Cultural Change* 10 (1962) 113-133. The political changes and conflicts made economic policy making fluctuate and vary.

1734

Mears, Leon A. "Economic Development in Indonesia through 1958." *Ekonomi dan Kenangan Indonesia* 14 (1961) 15-57. A review of conditions before independence, and a discussion of the economic difficulties thereafter.

1735

Indonesia. Perspective and Proposals for United States Economic Aid. A Report to the President of the United States. New Haven: Southeast Asia Studies, Yale University, 1963. A report on the eight-year development plan of Indonesia, containing recommendations on how the U.S.A. could help to implement that plan.

1736

Sutjatkoko, S. "Point four and Southeast Asia." *Indonesie* 4 (1950–51) 1-11. On Indonesia's colonial burden and the need for a new society if peace and prosperity are to be realized.

1737

Soedjatmoko. *Economic Development as a Cultural Problem.* Cornell: Translation Series, Modern Indonesia Project, Cornell University, 1958. Provocative ideas on the problem created within a traditional society by economic development. See also his brilliant inquiring comments on this in Robert N. Bellah (ed.) *Religion and Progress in Modern Asia.* New York: Free Press, 1965. v-xiv.

1738

Biro Pusat Statistik [Central Bureau of Statistics]. *Statistical Pocket book of Indonesia.* Djakarta: Biro Pusat Statistik, 1962. Along with ECAFE publications, and the London *Economist Three Monthly* Economic Review, this compendium, produced annually since 1957, is one of the few sources of demographic, economic, educational and other statistics published in English.

SOCIAL AND CULTURAL PATTERNS

The common faith of nearly all Indonesia is Islam. It came centuries ago, to an archipelago that had lived for a millennia with Hinduism or Buddhism, or some of both. Today the cultural synthesis is complex and varied, for one hundred years of the European has added its marks as well, and in different parts of the state one or another of these elements predominates. Thus, the modernizing ideas and faith that come originally from the West, the attitudes of Islam, the lingering social patterns of Hinduism, as well as the even older indigenous customs that have survived for perhaps 2,000 years, all mix and swirl in Indonesia today, to produce different patterns and different balances of society.

General Works

1739

Geertz, Hildred. "Indonesian Cutures and Communities," in Ruth T. McVey (ed.) *Indonesia.* New Haven: Center for Southeast Asian Studies, Yale University, by arrangement with HRAF (1963) 24-96. Describes three dissimilar Indonesian societies; Hinduized inland areas, trade oriented deeply Islamic coastal peoples, pagan tribal groups. The national network of institutions holds this diversity together; useful bibliography.

1740

Geertz, Clifford. *The Religion of Java.* New York: Free Press, 1959. The intricate complex of beliefs comprising the Javanese religious tradition is studied in a typical town, and contrasted to the less adulterated Islam also practiced there; the political, cultural, and artistic implications, and the social conflict and integration resulting, are penetrated in depth.

1741

Geertz, Hildred. *The Javanese Family — A Study of Kinship and Socialization.* New York: Free Press, 1961. The structure of the kinship system in part one, and the functioning in part two, where customs of pregnancy, child birth, infant care, social relations in childhood, adolescence and adulthood, and "Javanese Values and the Javanese Family" are described.

1742

Soemardjan, Selo. *Social Changes in Jogjakarta.* Ithaca: Cornell University Press, 1962. An interpretive survey of social change from the mid-18th century until the late 1950's.

1743

Palmier, L. H. *Social Status and Power in Java.* London: The Athlone Press, 1960. Javanese Society during the first stages of Indonesia's independence, with particular emphasis on the ways whereby the existing social system was being adapted to the new situation created by the revolution, and the emergence of new elite groups.

1744

Van der Kroef, Justus M. *Indonesian Social Evolution: Some Psychological Considerations.* Amsterdam: C. P. J. van der Peet, 1958. A theoretical exploration of the psychological and psycho-analytical factors underlying Indonesian community and social development, adhering to the Jungian methodology.

1745

Skinner, G. William (ed.). *Local, Ethnic and National Loyalties in Village Indonesia. A Symposium.* New Haven: Cultural Report Series, Southeast Asia Studies, Yale University, 1959. Six reports on social and political values, based on field research in widely separate and dissimilar villages in Indonesia.

1746

Soemardjan, Selo. "Some Social and Cultural Implications of Indonesia's Unplanned and Planned Development." *Review of Politics* 25 (1963) 64-90.

1747

De Josselin, de Jong, P. E. "An Interpretation of Agricultural Rites in Southeast Asia with a Demonstration of Use of Data from both Continental and Insular Areas." *Journal of Asian Studies* 24 (1965) 283-291. Indonesian myths and ceremonies dealing with rice are seen to be very similar to other rites elsewhere in Southeast Asia; a plea for comparative studies.

1748

Van der Kroef, Justus M. *Indonesia in the Modern World.* 2 vols. Bandung: Masa Baru, 1954-56. Eighteen essays, often stimulating and informative, on social changes in a rural society, problems of Chinese assimilation, entrepreneurs and the middle class, the Indonesian city, nationalism, and other aspects of independent Indonesia.

1749

Kennedy, Raymond. "Contours of Culture in Indonesia." *Far Eastern Quarterly* 2 (1942) 5-14.

Law

1750

Lev, Daniel S. "The Supreme Court and Adat Inheritance Law in Indonesia." *American Journal of Comparative Law,* 11, 2 (1962) 205-224. A rare account in English of the contemporary judicial system, with a study of an important role of the supreme court.

1751

————. "The Politics of Judicial Development in Indonesia." *Comparative Studies in Society and History* 7 (1964–65) 173-199. Conflict between judge, prosecutor, and police over questions of prestige and power.

1752

Ter Haar, B. *Adat Law in Indonesia.* New York: Institute of Pacific Relations, 1948. Published in Dutch in 1939, this is an authoritative study of the indigenous law, and the social organizations that sustain it in 17 defined areas of Indonesia; landrights in particular are studied here in the light of this customary law.

1753

Vreede-de Stuers, Cora. *The Indonesian Woman: Struggles and Achievements.* The Hague: Monton, 1960. The emancipation of the Indonesian woman is linked to national awakening; elements of contemporary social patterns reacting adversely against the efforts of women to achieve equality are emphasized.

Education

1754

Van Der Wal, S. L. *Some Information on Education in Indonesia up to 1942.* The Hague: Nuffic, 1961. Numerous tables and statistics support a brief factual outline.

1755

Hutasoit, M. *Compulsory Education in Indonesia.* Paris: UNESCO, 1954. Summarizes the history of education during the colonial period, then details aspects of contemporary Indonesian education. Author was secretary-general for ten years, Indonesia's ministry of education.

1756

Neff, Kenneth L. *National Higher Technical Education in Indonesia: Recent Trends.* Washington: Department of Health, Education and Welfare, 1960. Describes details of Gadjah Mada and Bandung Institute of Technology.

1757

Fagan, Edward R. "Extending the Roots of Indonesian Teacher Education." *International Review of Education* 9, 3 (1963-64) 278-287.

Specific Culture Groups

GENERAL WORKS

1758

De Josselin, de Jong, P. E. *Minangkabau and Negri Sembilan: socio-political structure in Indonesia.* Leiden: E. Ijdo, 1951. The Minangkabau with their matrilineal characteristics are studied in both Sumatra and the Malay Peninsula.

1759

Junus, Umar. "Some Remarks on Minangkabau Social Structure." *Bijdragen* 120 (1964) 293-325. A study of marriage, lines of relationship and kinship, in three associated villages.

1760

Bruner, Edward. "Urbanization and Ethnic Identity in North Sumatra." *American Anthropologist* 63 (1961) 508-521. The adverse effects of town life on the traditional social patterns of the Toba-Batak.

1761

Geertz, Clifford. "Tihingan: A Balinese Village." *Bijdragen* 120 (1964) 1-33. A Balinese gong-making village, with emphasis on its social, economic and political structure.

1762

————. "Form and Variation in Balinese Village Structure." *American Anthropologist* 61 (1959) 991-1012. Although extremely varied, the small scale social systems of Bali are related; seven common factors are discussed, and three villages.

1763

Bateson, Gregory. "Bali. The Value of a Steady State," in Meyer Fortes (ed.) *Social Structure: Studies Presented to A. R. Radcliffe-Brown.* London: Oxford University Press, 1949. The relaxed character of the Balinese is here sketched, with an emphasis on the lack of climax in music, drama and personal relationships, or acquisitiveness in economic matters.

1764

Wertheim, W. F. (ed.). *Selected Studies on Indonesia.* Vol. 5, by selected Dutch Scholars. *Bali: Studies in Life, Thought and Ritual.* The Hague: van Hoeve, 1960. Aspects of Balinese social patterns by a number of Dutch scholars.

1765

Belo, Jane. *Trance in Bali.* New York: Columbia University Press, 1960. An examination of the social and cultural implications of trance, studied in all its manifestations.

1766

————. *Bali: Rangda and Barong.* Seattle: Monograph 16, American Ethnological Society, University of Washington Press, 1949. A brief monograph on two mythological figures popular at village festivals.

1767

Du Bois, Cora. *The People of Alor. A Social-Psychological Study of an East Indian Island.* Minneapolis: University of Minnesota Press, 1944. Customs of infancy, childhood, adolescence and adulthood on the Timorese island of Alor; village institutions, religion, personality determinants; together with eight autobiographies.

1768

Suzuki, Peter. *The Religious System and Culture of Nias, Indonesia.* 'S-Gravenhage: Uitgeverij Excelsior, 1959. A study of the numerous aspects of life and death, on the island of Nias off the west coast of Sumatra.

1769

Koentjaraningrat. *Some Social-Anthropological Observations on Gotong Rojong Practises in Two Villages of Central Java.* Ithaca: Southeast Asia Program, Cornell University, 1961. The mutual help system of Java illustrated by a careful study of its application in different village situations.

1770

Anderson, Benedict. *Mythology and the Tolerance of the Javanese.* Ithaca: Monograph Series, Modern Indonesia Project, Cornell University, 1965.

1771

Palmier, Leslie H. "Changing Outposts: The Western Communities in Southeast Asia." *Yale Review* 57 (1958) 405-415.

THE CHINESE

1772

Willmott, Donald E. *The Chinese of Semarang, a changing minority community in Indonesia.* Ithaca: Cornell University Press, 1960. Five major factors are studied in influencing this immigrant community: new environment, Indonesian economy, Javanese culture, contact with the Dutch, communications with a changing China; the effect of all this on the way of life and social structure of the community is drawn out.

1773

Skinner, G. William. "The Chinese Minority," in Ruth T. McVey (ed.) *Indonesia.* New Haven: Center for Southeast Asian Studies, Yale University, by arrangement with Human Relations Area Files, 1963. 97-117. There are approximately 2.5 million South Chinese in Indonesia, overwhelmingly urban; many are locally rooted, others maintain their "Chinese-ness." Origin, location and other characteristics of both groups are discussed.

1774

————. "Change and Persistence in Chinese Culture Overseas: A Comparison of Thailand and Java." *Journal, South Seas Society* 6 (1960) 86-100. Chinese in Thailand are rapidly assimilated but in Java they remain Chinese for generations. The implications of this are discussed.

1775

Tan, Giok-Lan. *The Chinese of Sukarbumi: A Study in Social and Cultural Accommodation.* Ithaca: Monograph Series, Modern Indonesia Project, Cornell University, 1963. A detailed study of a West Javanese town, with the historical background of the Chinese inhabitants sketched in, then the ethnic divisions in the economy studied, as well as the perenakan (1st generation Chinese) subsistence patterns, and the family, religions and general way of life of the Chinese among the Javanese.

Modernization and Mobility

1776

Burger, D. H. *Structural Changes in Javanese Society: The Village Sphere and the Supra-Village Sphere.* Ithaca: Translation Series, Modern Indonesia Project, Cornell University, 1957. The western impact on Indonesia, particularly of the 19th century, examined by a sociologist, with a stimulating consideration of the aristocratic culture of Central and East Java.

1777

Jaspan, M. A. *Social Stratification and Social Mobility in Indonesia. A trend report and annotated bibliography.* 2nd ed. Djakarta: Gunong Agung, 1961. A brief 20-page essay on stratification and mobility followed by a useful 139-item annotated bibliography.

1778

Geertz, C. "Modernization in a Muslim Society: The Indonesian Case," in Robert N. Bellah (ed.) *Religion and Progress in Modern Asia.* New York: The Free Press, 1965. 93-108. Examines the religious school system of Indonesia as the master institution in the perpetuation of Islamic tradition, and as the focus of the current efforts to modernize Islamic society.

1779

Wertheim, W. F. "Changes in Indonesia's Social Stratification." *Pacific Affairs* 27 (1953) 41-52. The colonial social system based on color and the Moslem system based on religion have changed to a new stratification based on individual achievement in the State.

1780

————. "The Changing Structure of Eastern Society," in *Eastern and Western World.* The Hague: van Hoeve, 1953. 39-53. The influence of capitalism on the structure of traditional Javanese society.

1781

Palmier, Leslie H. "The Javanese Nobility under the Dutch." *Comparative Studies in Society and History* 11 (1960) 197-227.

The Arts

ARTS AND CRAFTS, MUSIC, DRAMA AND DANCE

1782

Wagner, Frits A. *Indonesia. The Art of an Island Group.* New York: McGraw-Hill, 1959. Comprehensive coverage of the prehistoric, Hindu, Buddhist and Moslem arts and crafts of the archipelago, with an historical outline in an excellently produced and illustrated volume; useful bibliography.

1783

Kunst, Jaap. *Music in Java.* 2 vols. 3rd rev. ed. The Hague: M. Nijhoff, 1949. The standard work on the history, theory and techniques of Javanese music; a classic with which only Colin McPhee's *Music of Bali* (New Haven: Yale University Press, 1963) can be compared.

1784

Hood, Mantle. "The Enduring Tradition: Music and Theatre in Java and Bali," in Ruth T. McVey (ed.) *Indonesia.* New Haven: Center for Southeast Asian Studies, Yale University, by arrangement with HRAF, 1963. 438-471. The wayang kulit, the gamelon and the classical dances are clearly explained.

1785

McPhee, Colin. *A House in Bali.* New York: John Day, 1946. An appreciative study of Balinese music by a discerning American composer.

1786

Covarrubias, Miguel. *Island of Bali.* New York: Knopf, 1937. A great artist and cultural anthropologist skillfully describes in a beautifully illustrated volume: the arts, the dances, the music and the drama of this unique island.

1787

De Zoete, Beryl and Spies, Walter. *Dance and Drama in Bali.* New York: Harper & Brothers, 1939. Still accepted as the most complete study of the many forms of dance and drama in Bali, which are outlined with sensitivity and appreciation.

1788

Mangkunegra VII of Surakarta, K. G. P. A. A. *On the Wajang Kulit (Purwa) and its Symbolic and Mystical Elements.* trs. by Claire Holt. Ithaca: Southeast Asia Program, Modern Indonesia Project, Cornell University, 1957. A talk given by the Sultan on the mystical and philosophical implications of the wayang kulit.

1789

Rassers, W. H. *Panji, The Culture Hero. A Structural Study of Religion in Java.* The Hague: M. Nijhoff, 1959. Translation of Dutch language writings of an eminent anthropologist; Javanese drama, on the origin of Javanese theatre, and on the Javanese kris; the divine hero Panji created the Javanese theatre and the gamelon orchestra and was also the first kris-smith.

1790

Forster, Harold. *Flowering Lotus: A View of Java.* New York: Longmans, Green, 1959. Javanese music, dance, theatre, and other arts described by an English professor who taught in Java.

1791

Lentz, Donald A. *The Gamelon Music of Java and Bali.* Lincoln: University of Nebraska Press, 1965. Concludes that the music is indigenous, and free from outside influence; of interest mainly to musicologists.

1792

Bowers, Faubion. *Theatre in the East; a survey of Asian dance and drama.* New York: T. Nelson, 1956. Contains a survey chapter on Indonesia, pp. 191-248.

LITERATURE

1793

Johns, Anthony H. "Genesis of a Modern Literature" in Ruth T. MvVey (ed.) *Indonesia.* New Haven: Center of Southeast Asian Studies, Yale University, by arrangement with HRAF, 1963. 410-437. An outline in particular of modern Indonesian novels from 1922, and poetry from 1920, with Chairil Anwar and Mochtar Lubis emerging as major contributors.

1794

Echols, John M. (ed.). *Indonesian Writing in Translation.* Ithaca: Monograph Series, Modern Indonesia Project, Cornell University, 1956. An anthology of modern Indonesian short stories, essays, chapters from some major works and poetry, with brief biographical notes on the authors, including Takdir Alisjabhana and others.

1795

Johns, Anthony H. "Chairil Anwar: An Interpretation." *Bjidragen* 120 (1964) 393-408. A poet who was hailed after the Japanese surrender as the creator of a new Indonesian poetry; he died in 1949.

1796

Lubis, Mochtar. *Twilight in Djakarta.* New York: Vanguard, 1964. A novel centered on the social and political conditions of Djakarta in the mid-1950's, written by a liberal critic who subsequently was placed under house arrest.

1797

Johns, A. H. "Amir Hamzah: Malay Prince, Indonesian Poet," in J. Bastin (ed.) *Essays in Honor of Sir Richard Winstedt.* London: Oxford University Press, 1963. The work and attitude of an outstanding modern Indonesian writer.

1798

————. "The Novel as a Guide to Indonesian Social History." *Bijdragen* 115 (1959) 232-248. Three Indonesian novels, published in 1922, 1938 and 1949, illustrate changing social values and elements of social tension.

1799

Jassin, H. B. *Kesusasteraan Indonesia Modern dalam Kritik dan Esei.* [Modern Indonesian Literature in Critiques and Essays]. 2 vols. Djakarta: Gunung Agung, 1962. A compilation of essays and reviews since 1946 from the pen of a well-known Indonesian writer.

1800

Raffel, Burton, (ed.). *Anthology of Modern Indonesian Poetry.* Berkeley: University of California, 1964. Represents all major contemporary Indonesian poets.

1801

Jaspan, M. A. *"Folk Literature" in Sumatra. Redjang Ka-Ga-Nga Texts.* Canberra: Australian National University, 1964. An indigenous non-Arabic script.

1802

Johns, Anthony H. *Rantjak Dilabueh. A Minangkabau Kaba.* Ithaca: Southeast Asia Program, Cornell University, 1958. A traditional poem of the Sumatran Minangkabau, which illustrates the value system and ethics of these people; with a valuable introduction.

THE PHILIPPINES

GENERAL

The Philippines once suffered the ignominy of being omitted from the standard historical text on Southeast Asia, as it was not thought to be part of that region. For a time it was linked to the U.S.A. so firmly, and isolated so completely from Asia, that indeed it had the appearance of being separate and distinct. Its largely English-speaking, Christian people added to this impression. Nevertheless, geographically, ethnologically and historically, the Philippines is a part of Southeast Asia. Its peoples have migrated in from the mongoloid heartlands and have developed a tropical culture similar to other parts of the region. As with them, it has received its modern Chinese people, and has gone through its colonial age; first under the Spanish and then under the more benign rule of the Americans. As with the rest of Southeast Asia, it is now endeavoring, in the face of many socioeconomic problems, to develop its economy, while maintaining political stability.

Bibliographies

1803

Eggan, Fred and others. *Selected Bibliography Of The Philippines Tropically Arranged and Annotated.* New Haven: Human Relations Area Files, 1956. Prepared by the Philippine Studies Program of the University of Chicago, a useful 138 page collection, almost entirely in the English language, covering numerous aspects of Philippine life.

1804

Houston, Charles O. *Philippine Bibliography. An Annotated Preliminary Bibliography of Philippine Bibliographies (Since 1900).* Manila: University of Manila, 1960. One-hundred and fifty-five bibliographies, secured from books, reports and journals, listed alphabetically and commented on.

1805

Hart, Donn V. and Eala, Quinton A. *An Annotated Guide to Current Philippine Periodicals.* New Haven: Bibliography Series, Southeast Asia Studies, Yale University, 1957. A careful introduction, illuminating the distinctive and unusual features of Philippine periodical publishing, supports a comprehensive guide to 312 periodicals published in the Philippines.

1806

Lietz, Paul S. *Calendar of Philippine Documents in the Ayer Collection of the Newberry Library.* Chicago: Newberry Library, 1956. 370 documents are listed, with contents summary; in addition, a list of transcripts from Philippine documents in Spanish archives.

1807

Robertson, James Alexander. *Bibliography of the Philippine Islands*. Cleveland: Arthur H. Clark, 1908. (Being Vol. 53 of *Blair and Robertson*). The basic bibliography of published material for the 300 years of Spanish occupation.

1808

Lopez, Cecilio. *Annotated Bibliography of the Philippine Social Sciences*. Quezon City: Social Science Research Council. University of the Philippines, 1956–1960. A series of volumes based on the extensive holdings at the University of the Philippines. Vol: Economies; 2: 3: Political Sciences.

1809

Hart, Donn V. "Philippine Publications: Available Materials and Sources of Acquisition." *Journal, Southeast Asian History* 8, 2 (1967). An account of materials being published in the Philippines, and specific descriptions of where and how to secure them.

1810

Boxer, C. R. "Some Aspects of Spanish Historical Writings on the Philippines," in D. G. E. Hall (ed.) *Historians of South-East Asia*. London: Oxford University Press, 1961. 200-212. Outlines the work between 1565 and 1887, mainly by members of the religious orders.

1811

Wickberg, E. B. "Spanish Records in the Philippine National Archives," in *Hispanic American Historical Review* 35 (1955) 77-89. A summary outline of the unused wealth in the Manila archives.

1812

Manuel, E. Arsenio. *Philippine Folklore Bibliography*. Quezon City: Philippine Folklore Society, 1965. A 125-page bibliography dealing with customs, beliefs, myths, archaeology, pre-history and the culture of any group in the Philippines.

Journals

1813

Philippine Studies (1953–   ). A quarterly, produced by the private University, the Ateneo de Manila, with a broad intellectual coverage.

1814

Asian Studies (1962–   ). Published by the Institute of Asian Studies, University of the Philippines, with concentration on historical material relating in particular to the Philippines.

1815

Philippine Journal of Public Administration (1957–   ). A quarterly, published by the Graduate School of Public Administration, University of the Philippines.

Land, People, and Language

PHYSICAL AND CULTURAL GEOGRAPHY

1816

Spencer, J. E. *Land and People in the Philippines: Geographic Problems in Rural Economy*. Los Angeles: University of California Press, 1954. Sponsored by the IPR, provides useful geographic data on land ownership, population growth, rural health, rural economy and other aspects of the rural Philippines in particular.

1817

Cutshall, Alden. *The Philippines*. New York: Van Nostrand, 1964. A survey of the Republic written by a geographer with extensive field experience in the archipelago.

1818

Dobby, E. H. G. *Southeast Asia*. London: University of London Press, 1960. Deals with the physiography, climate, soils, land utilization, population pattern and other aspects of its geography.

1819

Hainsworth, Reginald G. and Moyer, Raymond T. *Agricultural Geography of the Philippine Islands*. Washington: U. S. Department of Agriculture, Office of Foreign Agricultural Relations, 1945. Numerous maps, graphs and tables accompany a concise text on most phases of agriculture and geography.

1820

Huke, Robert and others. *Shadows on the Land; an Economic Geography of the Philippines*. Manila: Bookmark, 1963. Among the few published pieces, although poorly edited, this has useful information on the material development of the Philippine economy; in particular, rice, corn, coconut, sugar, abaca, tobacco, fishing and manufacture.

1821

Pendleton, Robert L. "Land Utilization and Agriculture of Mindanao, Philippine Islands." *The Geographical Review* 32, 2 (1942) 180-210. Two maps, 53 photos illustrate a study of climate, plant and animal life, soils and types of agriculture.

1822

Cole, Fay-Cooper. "Central Mindanao — the Country and its People." *Far Eastern Quarterly* 4, 2 (1945) 109-118. Pagans on a highland plateau.

1823

Pelzer, Karl J. *Pioneer Settlement in the Asiatic Tropics*. New York: Institute of Pacific Relations, 1945. The landless Filipinos, the density and distribution of population, land policy, the opening of Mindanao to settlement, and other agricultural aspects of geography are treated on pp. 81-159.

1824

Hendry, Robert S., (ed.). *Atlas of the Philippines*. Manila: Phil-Asian Publishers, 1959. Not very detailed, but the best available atlas on the Philippines.

PEOPLES

1825

Pavon, José Maria. *The Robertson Translations of the Pavon Manuscripts of 1838–39*. 4 vols. Chicago: Philippine Studies Program, Department of Anthropology, University of Chicago, 1957. An English translation of legends and folk tales collected on the Bisayan Island of Negros from 1838 to 39, together with an account of that date of the customs of the people.

1826

Ravenholt, Albert. *The Philippines. A Young Republic on the Move*. New York: Van Nostrand, 1962. Chapter 1, "The Islands and the People," is a useful introduction for the non-specialist.

1827

Robequain, Charles. *Malaya, Indonesia, Borneo and the Philippines*. London: Longmans, Green, 2 ed. 1959. The Philippine people and their land are dealt with in chapter 13, pp. 258-296.

1828

Cole, Fay-Cooper. *The Peoples of Malaysia*. New York: Van Nostrand, 1945. A clear outline of the Ifugao, Igorot, Tuguian, Ilocano, Bagobo and the Moro, in chapter VII, 126-197.

LANGUAGES

1829

Frei, Ernest J. *The Historical Development of the Philippine National Language*. Manila: Bureau of Printing, 1959. A survey of the literature dealing with Tagalog; also discusses the language problems during the Spanish regime, and those likely to result in any change-over from English as the official language to Tagalog.

1830

Chretien, Douglas. "A Classification of Twenty-One Philippine Languages." *The Philippine Journal of Science* 91, 4 (1962) 485-506. A paper based on *A Composite Vocabulary of Philippine Languages*. Manila: Institute of National Languages, 1953.

1831

Cabreros, Laya, Juan and Laya, Silvina C. *Basic Tagalog vocabulary; Tagalog-English, English-Tagalog*. Manila: Inang Wika Publishing Co., 1950. The main indigenous tongue.

1832

Carro, Andres. *Iloko-English dictionary*. Translated, augmented and revised by Morice Vanoverbugh. Baguio: Catholic School Press, 1957.

HISTORY

An almost complete absence of records makes any compilation of pre-16th century history most difficult. It is ignominious for any nation to admit that it had no history before it was conquered, and the beginning of Spanish rule in the 16th century is certainly not the beginning of Filipino history. A very considerable effort is necessary, however, to unravel that history. Meanwhile, the recorded history of the Philippines indicates a periodization that would establish one broad period from the 16th to the late 18th century; then the 19th century leading to the Revolution; the 20th century dominated by American influences leading to the independent state of today.

Throughout this time, the southern islands stand as a virtually separate unit. Moslem when to be a Filipino was to be Christian; never speaking Spanish and never conquered nor converted by them, yet never independent enough not to be under their control to the extent that other powers could not move in. Never really brought within the democratic Philippine state organized by the Americans, and still Moslem, separate and different, yet part of the independent state of today.

General Works

1833

Corpuz, Onofore D. *The Philippines.* New York: Prentice-Hall, 1965. A useful general history, with emphasis on political developments: accentuates the admixture of Spanish and American cultural traits with her indigenous background, discusses the historical roots of many contemporary elements and explains the socially conservative nature of her nationalism. A valuable bibliographical essay is included.

1834

Agoncillo, Teodoro A. and Alfonso, Oscar M. *A Short History Of The Philippine People.* Manila: University of the Philippines, 1961. Feels that before 1872 the Filipino scarcely had a history, as only the Spaniards participated; looks at events after that date in an aggressively nationalistic way and as the title implies, provides a basically anti-establishment interpretation of late 19th and 20th century development.

1835

Molina, Antonio M. *The Philippines Through The Centuries.* 2 Vols. Manila: U. S. T. Co-operative, 1960. A general historical text book from 1521 A.D. to independence, based to some extent on archival material.

1836

Bentez, Conrado. *History of the Philippines.* rev. ed. New York: Ginn, 1954. A reliable text which covers the entire Spanish period as well as the 20th century.

1837

De La Costa, H. (ed.). *Readings In Philippine History.* Manila: Bookmark, 1965. Selections from an extraordinarily wide range of materials, most of them primary sources, written by men close to the events they describe; from the first description of the Philippines and its people to contemporary times.

1838

Zaide, Gregorio F. *The Political and Cultural History of the Philippines.* rev. ed. 2 Vols. Manila: Philippine Educational Company, 1957. A clear and popular college text used throughout the Philippines.

1839

De La Costa, H. "History and Philippine Culture." *Philippine Studies* 9 (1961) 346-354. A plea for a rational historiographical base.

1840

Corpuz, O. D. "Western Colonization and the Filipino Response." *Journal, Southeast Asia History* 3, 1 (1962) 1-23. Discusses the carry-over of values and indigenous behavior patterns and their adaptation to contemporary life.

Pre-history

1841

Solheim, Wilhelm G. *The Archaeology of Central Philippines, A Study chiefly of the Iron Age and its relationships.* Manila: Monograph 10, the National Institute of Science and Technology, 1964. A detailed technical account of the Katanay cave site and its iron-age pottery and an assessment of the Philippine iron age.

1842

Beyer, H. Otley. "Outline Review of Philippine Archaeology by Islands and Provinces." *Philippine Journal of Science* 77 (1947) 205-374. A comprehensive survey of the archaeological position, by islands and provinces. A great amount of data.

1843

Solheim, Wilhelm G. "The Kulanay Pottery Complex in the Philippines." *Artibus Asiae* 4 (1957). Pottery excavated in the Visayan Islands that date perhaps from A.D. third century, and which share design elements with the Dong-s'on bronzes.

History: 16th to 19th Centuries

The Spanish administration reached a watershed of sorts in the late 18th century. For 300 years the Spanish maintained and developed their rule. Their monks converted and acquired land, while their lay administrators established a tenuous contact with Mexico; otherwise they made little impact on the islands, which remained isolated and little visited or known. As in Japan, however, outside forces gradually made an impression. In 1762 British troops captured Manila and in 1785 the Royal Philippine Company was formed. Both were pointers to a gradual challenge to the isolation of the islands, and to the long colonial subjection of its peoples.

GENERAL WORKS

1844

Blair, Emma Helen and Robertson, James Alexander (eds.). *The Philippine Islands 1493–1898: Explorations by Early Navigators, Descriptions of the Islands and Their Peoples, Their History and Records of the Catholic Missions, as Related in Contemporaneous Books and Manuscripts, Showing the Political, Economic, Commercial and Religious Conditions of These Islands From their Earliest Relations With European Nations to the Close of the Nineteenth Century.* 55 Vols. Cleveland: Arthur H. Clark, 1909. English translations covering an even wider range of works than expressed in the subtitle; an indispensable source for the 400 years. Although published over 50 years ago, an offset reproduction of the series was undertaken in Taiwan in 1962, and is available in Manila.

1845

Quirino, Carlos. *Philippine Cartography, 1320–1899.* 2nd ed. rev. Israel, 1963. A historical survey of maps of the Philippines, with a very useful essay by R. A. Skelton on the collection in the British Museum, and a 60-page bibliography of maps.

1846

Shurz, W. L. *The Manila Galleon.* New York: E. P. Dutton, 1959. First published in 1939, an account of the annual voyages of the Spanish galleon between Manila and Acapulco, the life line of the colony, from 1565 to 1815; because of the trading and commercial ramifications, including much that is relevant to events elsewhere in East Asia; a useful 30-page bibliography.

1847

Cunningham, Charles H. *The Audiencia in the Spanish Colonies, as Illustrated by the Audiencia of Manila*. Berkeley: University of California, 1919. A most detailed account, if difficult to secure, of Spanish colonial government in the Philippines.

1848

Madigan, Francis C. "The Early History of Cagayan de Oro." *Philippine Studies* 11 (1963) 76-130. Cagayan, a city on the north Mindanao coast, is on the cultural frontier between Islam and Christianity; its history from 1480.

1849

Parry, J. H. *The Spanish Seaborne Empire*. London: Hutchinson, 1966. Contains references to Manila and the Philippines, links it to the major theme of Spanish America.

1850

Foreman, John. *The Philippine Islands. A Political, Geographical ethnographical, social and commercial history of the Philippine Archipelago embracing the whole period of Spanish rule, with an account of the succeeding American Insular Government*. 3rd ed. Singapore: Kelly & Walsh, 1906. A nearly 700-page book that lives up to its title; a detailed study of the islands, while personal acquaintanceship with the revolutionary leaders makes his final chapters on the late 19th century particularly interesting.

1851

Abella, Domingo. *Bikol Annals*, Vol. 1. *The See of Nueva Caceres*. Manila: Private Printing 1962. A history of a region of Luzon from 1569 to 1950; based on church records in Spain, Rome and elsewhere.

1852

De La Costa, H. *The Jesuits In The Philippines, 1581–1768*. Cambridge: Harvard University Press, 1861. A fascinating and detailed account by a leading historian, covering many aspects of Philippine history and society as well as a scholarly description of the Society of Jesus, during those near 200 years.

1853

Phelan, John Leddy. *The Hispanization of the Philippines: Spanish Aims and Filipino Responses 1565–1700*. Madison: University of Wisconsin Press, 1959. An attempt to show the effects of the impact of Hispanic culture on the Filipino people during the first 135 years of Spanish colonization, in which historical methodology is combined with sociological techniques in appraising the changing pattern of a people's life.

1854

Cushner, Nicholas P. "Legazpi 1564–1672." *Philippine Studies* 13 (1965) 163-206. The difficult first years of Spain's first governor, the transfer to Manila in 1571 and his death the following year.

1855

De La Costa, H. "Church and State in the Philippines during the administration of Bishop Salazar, 1581–1594." *Hispanic American Historical Review* 30, 3 (1950) 314-335. The islands changed during this period from a conquered possession to a colony; in this, the Bishop played an important role.

1856

Boxer, C. R. "Portuguese and Spanish Rivalry in the Far East during the 17th Century." *Journal, Royal Asiatic Society* (1946) 150-164; (1947) 91-105. The quarrelling Iberian partners fought from 1601 to 1603 in the Moluccas, although Manila trade with Macau flourished until 1662; then the two Eastern ports were at war until 1668.

1857

Chang, Tien Tse. "The Spanish-Dutch Naval Battle of 1617 outside Manila Bay." *Journal, Southeast Asian History* 7 (1966) 111-121. Had the Dutch won, they might have captured Manila; they lost.

1858

Almazan, Mario A. "The Manila Galleons," *The Geographical Magazine* 34 (1961) 115-124. Reproduces a number of 17th and 18th Century maps, charts and galleons.

1859

De La Costa, H. "Early French Contacts with the Philippines." *Philippine Studies* 2 (1963) 401-418. Uses French archival material to outline French trading interests in late 17th and 18th century, and to pose some questions for other historians.

1860

Quiason, Serafin D. *English Country Trade With The Philippines 1644–1765*. Manila: University of the Philippines Press 1966. A detailed study based on British and Spanish archival material, of the complex pattern of largely unofficial and illegal but rewarding trade between India, Manila and China.

1861

De La Costa, H. "The Seige and Capture of Manila by the British, September–October 1762." *Philippine Studies* 10 (1962) 607-653). The original and English translations of a series of documents written by the actual participants, together with three maps of Manila at that time, accompanied by a scholarly outline of events.

1862

Thornton, A. P. "British in Manila 1762–1764." *History Today* 7 (1957) 44-53. As part of a world-wide war against Spain, Sepoys from Madras captured Manila.

1863

Cushner, N. P. *The Isles of the West. Early Spanish Voyages to the Philippines 1521–1564*. Manila: Ateneo de Manila, 1966.

1864

Diaz-Trechuelo, Marie Lourdes. "The Economic Development of the Philippines in the Second Half of the Eighteenth Century." *Philippine Studies* 11 (1963) 195-231. A succession of governors gave attention to developing the natural resources of the Islands; as a result, a profit was shown, silver was exported from 1784 onwards, and the Royal Philippine Company was founded in 1785.

1865

Quirino, Carlos and Garcia, Mauro. "The Manners, Customs and Beliefs of the Philippine Inhabitants of Long Ago; being chapters of 'a late 16th century Manila manuscript,' transcribed, translated and annotated." *The Philippine Journal of Science* 87, 4 (1958) 325-452. A description of the Philippines written probably for a newly appointed governor of 1590.

1866

Morga, A. De. *The Philippine Islands, Moluccas, Siam, Cambodia, Japan and China, at the close of the 16th Century, by Antonio de Morga, 1609. Translated, with Notes and a Preface, and a letter from Luis Vaez de Torres, describing his Voyage through the Torres Straits, by Lord Stanley of Alderley*, 1868. repr. 1965. London: Hakluyt Society, Series 1, No. 39, 1965.

1867

Quiason, Serafin D. "The Early Trade of the English East India Company with Manila." *Philippine Historical Review* 1 (1965) 272-297. Trade between India and Manila from 1644 until the 1680's.

1868

Diaz-Trechuelo, Marie Lourdes. "Philippine Economic Development Plans, 1746–1779." *Philippine Studies* 12 (1964) 203-231. Outlines a number of plans drawn up in Manila, mainly with the idea of forming a chartered company in the hope of removing the annual subsidy from Mexico.

1869

————. "Eighteenth Century Philippine Economy: Mining." *Philippine Studies* 13 (1965) 763-800. Iron mines, as well as copper deposits, gold and other minerals are considered.

1870

Le Gentil, Guillaume Joseph Hyacinthe Jean Baptist, De La Galaisiere. *A Voyage To The Indian Seas.* Manila: Filipiniana Book Guild, 1964. First published in 1779, an account of Manila, its environs and other parts of the Philippines as seen in 1776.

1871

Lach, Donald F. *Asia In The Making Of Europe.* Vol. 1. Book 2. The Century of Discovery. Chicago: University of Chicago Press, 1965. The Philippines at, and immediately after, the time of Magellan is dealt with on pp. 623-50.

BEFORE THE REVOLUTION

1872

Cheong, Wang Eang. "Anglo-Spanish-Portuguese Clandestine Trade between the ports of British India and Manila, 1785–1790." *Philippine Historical Review* 1 (1965) 80-94. Complicated unofficial actions taken to overcome state controls and company monopolies; the Royal Philippine Company figures throughout.

1873

McHale, Thomas R. and McHale, Mary C. *Early American-Philippine Trade: The Journal of Nathaniel Bowditch in Manila, 1796.* New Haven: Southeast Asia Studies, Yale University, 1962. A valuable introduction and notes accompanying the vivid and varying impression of 18th century Manila.

1874

Gray, William H. "First Constitution of the Philippines." *Pacific Historical Review* 26 (1957) 341-351. An account of the Philippine experience with the Spanish liberal constitution of 1812, and in 1820, and the Navales and Dagohoy rebellions.

1875

Furber, Holden. "An Abortive Attempt at Anglo-Spanish Commercial Co-operation in the Far East in 1793." *Hispanic American Historical Review* 15 (1935) 448-463. The eminent American authority on the British East India Company contributes an account of negotiations which failed between it and Spain in 1793 over trade with Manila.

1876

De La Gironiere, Paul P. *Twenty Years In The Philippines.* Manila: Filipiana Book Guild, 1962. First published in 1853, an interesting account of life in Manila at that time.

1877

Bowring, Sir John. *A Visit To The Philippine Islands.* Manila: Filipiana Book Guild, 1963. The Spanish-speaking governor of Hong Kong visited Manila, Zamboanga and other parts of the archipelago, newly opened to the world, and wrote a detailed account, first published in 1859, of all that he saw, heard and read.

1878

Tarling, Nicholas. "Consul Farren and The Philippines." *Journal, Malaysian Branch, Royal Asiatic Society* 38, 2 (1965) 258-173. Britain's first consul to Manila, appointed in 1844, was a witness to Spanish penetration of the Sulu Archipelago.

1879

Saniel, J. M. *Japan and the Philippines: 1868–1898.* Manila: University of the Philippines, 1963. Tenuous contacts and expansionist ideas by a few Japanese; the beginnings of an interest that became more serious later.

1880

Abella, Domingo. "State of Higher Education in the Philippines to 1863 — An historical re-appraisal." *Philippine Historical Review* 1 (1965) 1-46. Outlines the establishment of colleges in the Philippines, and doubts whether they were for Filipinos; points to the late flowering of an intelligentsia only after 1863.

1881

Fox, Frederick and Mercader, Juan. Some Notes on Education in Cebu Province, 1820–1898." *Philippine Studies* 9 (1961) 20-46. A study of the half-million Visayans on Cebu Island; their way of life, exports and education; with eight illustrations of old school, and two maps.

1882

Hoskyn, Margaret (ed.). *A Britisher In The Philippines, or The Letters of Nicholas Loney.* Manila: The Bureau of Printing, 1964. Loney was a vice-consul in Iloilo in 1856, and his letters describe Filipino life at that time.

THE CHINESE

1883

Wickberg, Edgar. *The Chinese In Philippine Life 1850–1898.* New Haven: Yale University Press, 1965. Superior perhaps to anything in the literature on the overseas Chinese of any country, this is a detailed study of the economic and social position of a dramatically increasing Chinese population, and its relations both with the Spanish and the Filipinos, and with China.

1884

Felix, Alfonso (ed.). *The Chinese In The Philippines 1570–1770.* Vol. 1. Manila: Solidaridad Publishing House, 1966. A collection of original papers, of uneven quality, some excellent, on various aspects of the Chinese during these 200 years.

1885

Janse, Olov R. T. "Notes on Chinese Influences in the Philippines in Pre-Spanish Times." *Harvard Journal of Asiatic Studies* 8, 1 (1944).

1886

Wickberg, E. "The Chinese Mestizo in Philippine History." *Journal, Southeast Asian History* 5, 1 (1964) 62-100. The development of a locally-born Chinese community of mixed descent is traced, with particular reference to the period from 1741 to 1898.

1887

―――――. "Early Chinese Economic Influence in the Philippines 1850–1898." *Pacific Affairs* 35, 3 (1962) 275-285. Before 1850 the Chinese were considered a "problem" only by the Spanish; after 1850 they were so considered by the Filipinos too. The author explains why.

1888

Chen, Ching-Ho. *The Overseas Chinese In The Philippines During The Sixteenth Century.* Hong Kong: Monograph 2, New Asia Research Institute, Hong Kong, 1963. A collection of Chinese and Western sources.

1889

Wu, Ching-Hong. "A Study of References to the Philippines in Chinese Sources from Earliest Times to the Ming Dynasty." *Philippine Social Sciences and Humanities Review* 24 (1959) 1-181. Several hundred scattered references to the Chinese, or by the Chinese, from 982 A.D.; bibliography.

1890

Purcell, Victor. *The Chinese in Southeast Asia.* 2nd ed. London: Oxford University Press, 1965. The Chinese in the Philippines, mainly in the Spanish period, are treated on pp. 493-568.

The Revolution

The revolt against Spain was the epic period in Philippine history. It can be seen in two stages. At the beginning, the more moderate, who took their inspiration from Dr. Jose Rizal, were grouped together in a propagandist movement. Reforms would be secured, they hoped, by the pen. On the execution of Rizal in 1896, leaders of a more revolutionary calibre such as Bonifacio appeared, until Aguinaldo was leading a guerrilla army. With Spain's defeat by America, this resistance was redirected against the new owners of the Islands; until early in the 20th century fighting died away.

MAJOR WORKS

1891

Zaide, Gregorio F. *The Philippine Revolution.* Manila: The Modern Book Company, 1954. A reliable one-volume work covering the entire period.

1892

Palma, Rafael. *The Pride of the Malay Race: A Biography of José Rizal.* New York: Prentice-Hall, 4th printing 1950. This popular biography of the Filipino nationalist-martyr brings out clearly his opposition to the church as well as his hatred of the abuses of Spanish colonialism.

1893

De La Costa, H. *The Trial of Rizal.* Manila: Ateneo de Manila, 1961.

1894

Rizal y Alfonso, José. *The Lost Eden (Noli Me Tangere).* trs. by Leon Ma Guerrero. Foreword by James A. Michener. Bloomington: Indiana University Press, 1961. A famous and politically significant novel by the Filipino nationalist, which gives a picture of the ignorance and poverty of the Filipinos, and the abuses of church and government. Bloomington has under preparation other novels of significance by Rizal.

1895

Craig, Austin. *Lineage, Life and Labors of José Rizal, Philippine Patriot.* Manila: Philippine Education Company, 1913. A biography of the national hero that includes many contemporary photos and illustrations.

1896

Agoncillo, Teodoro A. *The Revolt of the Masses: The Story of Bonifacio and the Katipunan.* Manila: University of the Philippines, 1956. Bonifacio was the leader of the 1896 revolt against the Spaniards. In this scholarly study, the author, a leading historian, challenges the hitherto unrivaled Rizal as a national hero, by debating whether in fact Bonifacio, the man who actually fought for independence, is not more deserving of that honor.

1897

Agoncillo, Teodoro A. *Malolos: The Crisis of the Republic.* Manila: University of the Philippines, 1960. A major work, a comprehensive study by a fiercely nationalist historian of the 1898 Malolos Conference of revolutionaries, and its constitution; a great moment in the Revolution.

1898

Majul, Cesar Adib. *Apolinario Mabini Revolutionary.* Manila: National Heroes Commission, 1964. A prize winning biography by a leading contemporary scholar of a leader who played a prominent role in the anti-Spanish revolutionary struggle of the period around 1895.

1899

Pilapil, Vicente R. "Nineteenth Century Philippines and the Friar Problem." *The Americas* 18 (Oct. 1961) 127-148. Stresses the complex nature of the anti-clerical movement which formed so large a part of the Propaganda campaign.

1900

Majul, Cesar Adib. *The Political and Constitutional Ideas of the Philippine Revolution.* Manila: University of the Philippines, 1957. Brings out clearly amongst other elements, the anti-clerical element in Filipino nationalist thinking; a penetrating analysis.

THE AMERICAN INTERVENTION

1901

Wolff, Leon. *Little Brown Brother. How the United States Purchased and Pacified the Philippine Islands at the Century's Turn.* New York: Doubleday, 1961. A study of American hostilities in the Philippines, first against the Spaniards and then against Filipino insurgents, from 1898 to 1902, which cost 250,000 lives; contemporary illustrations.

1902

Quirino, Carlos. *Aguinaldo's Odyssey, as told in the diaries of Col. Simeon Villa and Dr. Santiago Barcelona.* Manila: Bureau of Public Libraries, 1963. The defeated but indomitable stand of the young general-president, in the Luzon mountains between 1899 and 1901, and his final capture.

1903

McCormick, Thomas. "Insular Imperialism and the Open Door: The China Market and the Spanish-American War." *Pacific Historical Review* 32 (1963) 155-169. Sees the action of various European powers in China in 1897-98 as influencing McKinley to occupy the Philippines so as to safeguard the Open Door in China.

1904

McHale, Thomas R. "American Colonial Policy Towards The Philippines." *Journal, Southeast Asian History* 3 (1962) 24-43. Various reasons for the surge of imperialism, and, in less detail, an account of the policy of political disengagement which followed.

1905

Colette, P. E. "Bryan, McKinley, and the Treaty of Paris." *Pacific Historical Review* 26 (1957) 131-146. The political pressures, translated into diplomacy, which played a part in the treaty whereby America secured the Philippines.

1906

Laing, E. A. M. "Admiral Dewey and the Foreign Warships at Manila, 1898." *The Mariners Mirror.* 52, 2 (1966) 167-171. A number of minor incidents involving German warships.

1907

Guerrero, Leon Ma. "The Kaiser and the Philippines." *Philippine Studies* 9 (1961) 584-600. Translates 13 German documents pertaining to this period.

1908

Eyre, James K. "Russia, and the American Acquisition of the Philippines." *Mississippi Valley Historical Review* 28 (1942) 539-562. The ripples created by America's giant hop across the Pacific spread far. Russia's reaction is treated here.

1909

————. "Japan and the American Annexation of the Philippines." *Pacific Historical Review* 11 (1942) 55-71.

1910

Shippee, Lester B. "Germany and the Spanish-American War." *American Historical Review* 30 (1925) 754-777.

SULU

1911

Saleeby, Najeeb M. *The History of Sulu.* Manila: Filipiana Book Guild, 1963. First published in 1908, and here republished with a valuable introduction by a distinguished Filipino Moslem scholar Cesar A. Majul: a geographical and historical narrative of the Muslim Sultanate of Sulu up to the eve of its decline during the Spanish regime.

1912

Majul, Cesar Adib. "Islamic and Arab Cultural Influences in the South of the Philippines." *Journal, Southeast Asian History* 8, 2 (1966) 61-73. A Moslem scholar on the impact of Islam in the Sulu Archipelago.

1913

————. "Succession in the Old Sulu Sultanate." *Philippine Historical Review* 1 (1965) 252-271. Outlines the basic principles dictating government succession in the Sulu Sultanate from the middle of the 17th century; and then narrates the successive Sultans from 1648 to 1937.

1914

De La Costa, H. "Muhammad Alimuddin I, Sultan of Sulu 1735-1773." *Journal, Malaysian Branch, Royal Asiatic Society,* 38 (1965) 43-76. A scholarly study of a strong ruler who had to contend with both Spaniards and English.

1915

Hunt, Chester L. "Moslem and Christian in the Philippines." *Pacific Affairs* 28 (1955) 331-349. Discusses the relationship between Christians and Moslems on Mindanao, particularly in the province of Cotabato, a relationship which is tending to revitalize Islam.

1916

Smythe, Donald. "Pershing and the Disarmament of the Moros." *Pacific Historical Review* 31 (1962) 241-256. Through the tact and patience of the non-belligerent commander, later of World War I fame, together with a judicious show of force, many of the Moslems in Jolo were disarmed in 1911.

1917

_____. "Pershing and the Mount Magsak Campaign of 1913." *Philippine Studies* 12 (1964) 3-31. Some 5 to 10,000 Sulu warriors near Jolo and an American anxious to conquer but reluctant to kill.

1918

Glazer, Sidney. "The Moros as a Political Factor in Philippine Independence." *Pacific Affairs* 14 (1941) 78-90. A brief outline of the political role of the rebellious Moslem community in the south.

The American Period

1919

Bernstein, David. *The Philippine Story*. New York: Farrer, Strauss, 1947. A good compact account of the land, the people, together with the political, economic, social and other developments of the 20th century that led to independence; author was political advisor to Quezon and Osmena.

1920

Friend, Theodore. *Between Two Empires; the Ordeal of the Philippines 1929–1946*. New Haven: Yale University Press, 1965. A sophisticated and provocative study, based on detailed scholarship, of Philippine nationalism, and the impact of American and Japanese occupation; with such leaders as Manuel Quezon, Sergio Osmena and Manuel Roxas treated in detail. A useful bibliographical essay is included.

1921

Forbes, William Cameron. *The Philippine Islands*. 2 Vols. Cambridge: rev. ed. Harvard University Press, 1945. A comprehensive account of the government, finances, economic development and other aspects of the Philippines in the first 40 years of the 20th century.

1922

Hayden, Joseph Ralston. *The Philippines, a Study in National Development*. New York: MacMillan, 1947. A detailed and perceptive study of the development of Philippine self government and its modern civil service educational system; the effects of U. S. policy and administration are considered throughout.

1923

Grunder, Garel A. and Livezey, William E. *The Philippines and the United States*. Norman: University of Oklahoma Press, 1951. A concise yet thorough study of the origins and evolution of U. S. political and economic policy in the Philippines from 1898 to 1946 based on U. S. government documents; useful 20-page bibliography.

1924

Achutegui, Pedro S. de and Bernad, Miguel A. *Religious Revolution in the Philippines: The Life and Church of Gregorio Aglipay, 1860–1960*. Vol. 1. *From Aglipy's Birth to his Death. 1860–1940*. Manila: Ateneo de Manila, 1960. A detailed study of the founder of the Philippine Independent Church; the changing background is brought out clearly.

1925

Malcolm, George A. *First Malayan Republic. The Story of the Philippines*. Boston: Christopher Publishing House, 1951. An over-all outline of the country's 20th century political, administrative, judicial, educational, economic and social and other features by an American lawyer who served in Manila from 1906 to 1942.

1926

_____. *American Colonial Careerist. Half a Century of Official Life and Personal Experience in the Philippines and Puerto Rico*. Boston: Christopher Publishing House, 1957.

1927

Kirk, Grayson L. *Philippine Independence: Motives, Problems and Prospects*. New York: Farrer and Rinehart, 1936. The nationalist movement from American military occupation to the establishment of the 1935 Commonwealth a full internal home rule.

1928

Quezon, Manuel Luis. *The Good Fight* . . . New York: Appleton-Century, 1946. The autobiography of a brilliant Filipino who fought the Spaniards and the Americans, rose to become political leader and then president of his country, escaped from Manila in 1942 with MacArthur and died in 1944.

1929

Friend, Theodore. "Manuel Quezon: Charismatic Conservative." *Philippine Historical Review* 1 (1965) 153-169. To be conservative and yet be charismatic is difficult; this throws new light on the nationalist leader of the 1920's and 1930's who secured independence but little else.

1930

Zinkin, Maurice. *Asia and the West*. London: Chatto and Windus, 1951. Philippine socio-economic problems of the 20th century are briefly examined on 161-168.

1931

Spector, Robert M. "W. Cameron Forbes in the Philippines. A Study in Proconsular Power." *Journal, Southeast Asian History* 7, 2 (1966) 74-92. An outline of the work of the American governor-general of 1900–1913.

1932

Friend, Theodore. "The Philippine Sugar Industry and Politics of Independence, 1929–1935." *Journal of Asian Studies* 22 (1963) 179-192.

1933

_____. "Philippine Interests and the Missions for Independence 1929–1932." *Philippine Studies* 12 (1964) 63-82. The political and economic background to the Osmena-Roxas independence mission to Washington of 1931–33.

1934

Goodman, Grant K. "General Artemio Ricarte and Japan." *Journal, Southeast Asian History* 7, 2 (1966) 48-60. A shadowy Filipino nationalist who never accepted America, and who lived in Japan from 1914 to 1942.

1935

Hester, E. D. "Outline of Our Recent Political and Trade Relations with the Philippine Commonwealth." *Annals of the American Academy of Political and Social Science* 226 (1943) 73-85. Outlines constitutional and economic developments to 1940, with particular emphasis on the Tydings-McDuffie Act and the Constitution of the Commonwealth.

1936

Marquardt, W. W. "An Unparalleled Venture in Education." *Far Eastern Quarterly* 4, 2 (1945) 135-139. The introduction of English language education from 1901 and some of its aspects are described. This issue of the Journal is devoted to the Philippines and contains a number of useful articles of this period.

1937

Houston, Charles O. "The Philippine Commonwealth 1934–1946." *Journal of East Asiatic Studies* (Manila). 2 (1953) 29-38. A brief assessment, documented, of the Commonwealth with its two widely separate periods of peace and war.

1938

Hagedorn, Herman. *Leonard Wood*. 2 Vols. New York: Harper & Brothers, 1931. Based on his diaries and correspondence, vol. 2 deals with his governorship of the Moro Province, General of the U. S. Army in the Philippines and finally as governor-general.

1939

Harrison, Francis Burton. *The Cornerstone of Philippine Independence*. New York: Century, 1922. Relates the sequence of events during his outstanding tour between 1913 and 1921 as governor-general.

1941 to 1945

1940

Agoncillo, Teodoro A. *The Fateful Years; Japan's Adventure in the Philippines 1941–1945*. 2 vols. Manila: R. P. Garcia Publishing, 1965. A forceful and thorough account by a distinguished historian of the Japanese invasion and occupation and the varied Filipino reaction.

1941

Falk, Stanley L. *Bataan: The March of Death*. New York: Norton, 1962 An account of the fate of the U. S. and Philippine forces captured after their surrender in early 1942.

1942

Hartendorp, A. V. H. *The Santo Tomas Story*. New York: McGraw-Hill, 1964. One of the thousands of Americans and others who were interned during the Pacific War at the Santo Tomas University in Manila tells of those years.

1943

Morton, Louis. *The History of The War In the Pacific*. Vol. 4 *The Fall Of The Philippines*. Washington: Office of the Chief of Military History, Department of the Army, 1953. One of the volumes of the official history of the U. S. Army in World War II; detailed and accurate.

1944

Lear, Elmer. *The Japanese Occupation of the Philippines, Leyte, 1941–1945*. Ithaca: Data Paper 42, Southeast Asia Program, Cornell University, 1961. An account of the disintegration of the framework of public administration and economic organization that existed, and the painful adaptation of society to the insecurity, violence and privations of war and occupation; a social history of an extraordinary period which became normal.

1945

Hart, Donn V. "Guerrilla Warfare And The Filipino Resistance on Negro Island in the Bisayas 1942–1945." *Journal, Southeast Asian History* 5, 1 (1964) 101-125. A bibliographical essay, referring to seven major sources.

1946

Baclagon, Uldarico S. *Philippine Campaigns*. Manila: Graphic House, 1952. A Filipino Colonel describes from primary sources his people's military history; battles against the Spanish, the Americans, and, by Resistance forces and returning liberators, against the Japanese.

1947

Abaya, Hernando J. *Betrayal In The Philippines*. New York: Wyn, 1946. A bitter account of those who supported the Japanese and were later rewarded by the returning Americans, to the exclusion of those who fought in the jungle.

1948

Recto, Claro M. *Three Years of Enemy Occupation: The Issue of Political Collaboration in the Philippines*. Manila: Peoples Publishers, 1946. The title tells the story; a defense of some Filipinos who were labeled as collaborators.

1949

Vellut, J. L. "Foreign Relations Of the Second Republic Of The Philippines 1943–1945." *Journal, Southeast Asian History* 5, 1 (1964) 126-142. The activities and attitudes of those who worked under the Japanese in 1942 and 1945.

1950

Morison, Samuel Eliot. *History of United States Naval Operations In World War II*. Vol. 3, *The Rising Sun in the Pacific 1931–April 1942*. Boston: Little Brown, 1950. A major study by an eminent historian given all facilities by President Roosevelt; part of an internationally renowned multi-volume survey which deals with far more than the U. S. navy.

1951

_____. *History of United States Naval Operations In World War II*. Vol. 13, *The Liberation of the Philippines, Luzon, Mindanao, the Visayas 1944–1945*. Boston: Little Brown, 1959. A substantial and vigorous work.

1952

Steinberg, David. "The Philippine Collaborators: Survival of an Oligarchy," in Josef Silverstein (ed.) *Southeast Asia in World War II: Four Essays*. New Haven: Monograph Series 7, Southeast Asia Studies, Yale University, 1966, 67-86. Philippine society bore little ill will against those who served in the wartime governments, and they went on to high places after the Japanese had gone.

POLITICAL PATTERNS

The political patterns of the Philippines will be most familiar to Americans. The long colonial tutelage helped create political institutions modeled on the U.S.A. The elected president, the separate chambers, the system of voting and administration were copied from the U.S.A. Yet the patterns discernible in the Philippines are not shadow patterns of U.S.A. realities, they have a Philippine reality as well. These institutions and the forces that make them work and which give them an indigenous life are in no way alien to the Philippines. They have become part and parcel of a vigorous political milieu, and are as much a part of the Philippines as the rice on the hill terraces or the priest in the barrio.

General Works

1953

Wurfel, David. "The Philippines." G. McT. Kahin (ed.). *Governments and Politics of Southeast Asia* 2nd ed. Ithaca: Cornell University Press, 1964. 679-769. A basic reference work. In four major sections, deals with the historical background to modern politics, the contemporary scene, the political process and the major problems facing the nation; gives a useful reading list.

1954

Grossholtz, Jean. *The Philippines*. Boston: Little Brown, 1964. A full-length study of post-war Philippine political patterns, giving a fresh view of the political structure, and the functions of the parties, and presidency.

1955

Lande, Carl H. "The Philippine Political Party System." *Journal, Southeast Asian History* 8, 1 (1967). A detailed critical analysis of high calibre of the main characteristics of the political party system as it has operated since independence in 1946.

Specialized Studies

1956

Wurfel, David. "The Philippine Elections: Support for Democracy." *Asian Survey* 2 (1962) 25-37.

1957

Smith, Robert A. *Philippine Freedom, 1946–1958*. New York: Columbia University Press, 1958. A brief account of some aspects of the post-war political and other developments; useful appendices.

1958

Meadows, Martin. "Philippine Political Parties and the 1961 Election." *Pacific Affairs* 35 (1962) 261-274.

1959

Hartzell, Spence. *For Every Tear A Victory. The Story of Ferdinand E. Marcos*. New York: McGraw-Hill, 1964. A journalistic but useful biography of a man with many adventures, convicted of murder, honored as a war hero; a brilliant lawyer and a youthful senator, who became president of the Republic.

1960

Corpuz, Onofre D. "The Cultural Foundations of Filipino Politics." *Philippine Journal of Public Administration* 4, (1960) 297-310.

1961

Milne, R. S. "The Uniqueness of Philippine Nationalism." *Journal, Southeast Asian History* 4 (1963) 75-87. Its uniqueness is a non-hate relationship with its former colonial master, and a lack of ideology.

1962

Keith, Agnes. *Barefeet In The Palace.* Boston: Little Brown, 1955. An interpretation of events in the Philippines which caused shock in Manila, but which describes the social conditions and the movement that had Magsaysay elected President.

1963

Agpalo, Remigio. "The Politics of Occidental Mindoro." *Philippine Journal of Public Administration* 8 (1964) 83-111. The style of politics resembles a local peasant dance; non-ideological, non-violent, non-doctrinaire; but personal, practical, and pragmatic.

1964

Berreman, Gerald D. *The Philippines: A Survey of Current Social, Economic and Political Conditions.* Ithaca: Data Paper 19, Southeast Asia Program, Cornell University, 1956. Conditions as they were in 1955; a useful summary.

1965

Thomas, M. Ladd. "Historical Origins of Philippine Centralism." *Journal, Southeast Asian History* 4, 2 (1963) 51-64. All real political power is at the national level; this was established by the Spaniards and maintained by the Americans.

1966

Coquia, Jorge. *The Philippine Presidential Election of 1953.* Manila: University Publishing Co., 1955. The parties involved, the interests at stake, the issues seized upon and underlying the choice, and the result; an impartial and comprehensive study.

1967

Elsbree, Willard H. "The Philippines." Rupert Emerson (ed.). *Representative Government in Southeast Asia.* Cambridge: Harvard University Press, 1955. 92-117. A survey and analysis of post-war Philippine government and politics.

1968

Romulo, Carlos P. and Gray, Marvin M. *The Magsaysay Story.* New York: John Day, 1956. A biography of a barefoot boy who rose in a conservative society to become perhaps the outstanding president of the Republic.

1969

Quirino, Carlos. *Magsaysay of the Philippines.* Quezon City: Phoenix Press, 1958. A collection of ancedotes and reminiscences, somewhat disjointed but nevertheless useful and revealing.

1970

Dalton, James. "Ins and Outs in the Philippines." *Far Eastern Survey* 21 (1952) 117-123. A good analysis of the 1951 elections.

1971

Vinacke, H. M. "Postwar Government and Politics of the Philippines." *Journal of Politics* 9 (1947) 717-730. Discusses the constitution of independent Philippines, particularly those aspects of it different from the U.S.A., and its regrettable economic dependence on the U.S.A., not materially helped by the 1946 Trade Act.

1972

Chapman, Abraham. "Note on the Philippine Elections." *Pacific Affairs* 19 (1946) 193-198. A good account of both winner and loser in the 1946 election.

Foreign Relations

1973

Paterno, Roberto. "American Military Bases in the Philippines: the Brownell Opinion." *Philippine Studies* 12 (1964) 391-423. The U. S. military bases became one of the most serious causes of post-war friction between Manila and Washington. This study examines the dispute over ownership and sovereignty.

1974

Taylor, George E. *The Philippines and the United States: Problems of Partnership.* New York: Praeger, 1964. In two parts, surveying the pre-independence political legacy of the U. S., and then U.S.-Philippine relations after 1946.

1975

Meyer, Milton W. *A Diplomatic History of the Philippines.* Honolulu: University of Hawaii Press, 1965. Philippine diplomacy from 1946 is traced here in a thorough and discerning study.

1976

Smith, Roger M. and Somers, Mary F. *Two Papers On Philippine Foreign Policy. The Philippine and the Southeast Asia Treaty Organization; The Record of the Philippines in the United Nations.* Ithaca: Data Paper 38, Southeast Asia Program, Cornell University, 1952. Anti-communism and anti-China are main themes in these two brief studies.

1977

Modelski, George (ed.). *Seato: Six Studies.* Melbourne: F. W. Cheshire, 1962. The part played by the Philippines in this international organization receives ample treatment.

1978

Fifield, Russell H. *The Diplomacy of Southeast Asia: 1945–1958.* New York: Harper and Bros., 1958. Foreign relations of the Philippines are dealt with in chapter four, pp. 60-107.

Administration

1979

Corpuz, Onofre D. *Bureaucracy in the Philippines.* Manila: Institute of Public Administration. University of the Philippines, 1957. A historical treatment of the evolution of the civil service from Spanish times, major themes being its non-political position and its Filipinization.

1980

De Guzman, Raul. *Patterns In Decision Making: Case Studies in Philippine Public Administration.* Honolulu: East-West Center Press, 1965. Fifteen comprehensive case studies, with an analysis of environmental factors and the decision-making process, together with the considerations involved in the actual choices made.

1981

Jacobini, H. B. and associates. *Governmental Services in the Philippines.* Manila: Institute of Public Administration, University of the Philippines, 1956. A sound study by a number of scholars of the branches of the government and their activities.

1982

Stene, Edwin O. and associates. *Public Administration In The Philippines.* Manila: Bureau of Printing, 1955. A collection of 17 articles describing the principal features and characteristics of the theme: a text for Filipino students.

1983

Heady, Ferrel. "The Philippine Administrative System — Fusion of East and West," in William J. Stiffin (ed.) *Toward the Comparative Study of Public Administration.* Bloomington: Indiana University, 1957. 253-277. The influence of Spain, America and the Filipinos on administrative structure and behavior.

1984

Socorro, C. Espiritu and Hunt, Chester I. (eds.). *Social Foundations of Community Development. Readings on the Philippines.* Manila: R. M. Garcia, 1964. Rural social life, community development, rural government, social stratification, communication channels and other aspects of community development are illustrated by extracts from leading writers such as O. D. Corpus, Jose V. Abueva, Frank Lynch and others.

1985

Romani, John H. *The Philippine Presidency.* Manila: Institute of Public Administration, University of the Philippines, 1956.

1986

Romani, John H. and M. Ladd, Thomas. *A Survey of Local Government in the Philippines*. Manila: Institute of Public Administration, University of the Philippines, 1954.

The Huks

The Huks defy tidy bibliographical listing. The problem they represent, the rural poor, is as much a part of Economics as Political Patterns; as much a part of History as of Social Patterns. Little noticed before independence, ignored by all except when they revolted, they constitute a challenge and a blight today. The problem of rural poverty is a world-wide one; here distinctive characteristics permit a grouping of work done on this subject.

1987

Abueva, José C. *Focus on the Barrio: the Story Behind the Birth of the Philippine Community Development Program Under President Ramon Magsaysay*. Manila: Institute of Public Administration, University of the Philippines, 1959. Gives liberal treatment to the major Magsaysay program aimed at rural problems, and portrays the shifting Philippine political background before the President's death in 1957.

1988

Starner, Frances Lucille. *Magsaysay and the Philippine Peasantry: the Agrarian Impact on Philippine Politics, 1953–1956*. Berkeley: University of California Press, 1961; Magsaysay's awareness of rural problems and their political significance; he won agrarian support for his Presidential campaign of 1953, and in return enacted the Land Reform Bill of 1955.

1989

Taruc, Luis. *Born of the People, an Autobiography*. New York: International Publishers, 1953. Taruc, a communist, deals more with the Hukbalahap movement and the social and economic ills which encouraged it, than with his own life, but both strands provide an insight into a long-lasting and contemporary problem.

1990

Sturtevant, David R. "Sakdalism and Philippine Radicalism." *Journal of Asian Studies* 21 (1962) 199-213. A rising of discontented peasants in May 1935 failed; yet the bitterness remained, to be utilized by other radical agrarian movements culminating in the Hukbalahap.

1991

Scaff, Alvin H. *The Philippine Answer to Communism*. Stanford: Stanford University Press, 1955. The Huk rebellion of 1946-54 and its defeat by Magsaysay, then Secretary of National Defense, who used social and economic measures along with military force.

1992

Cater, Sonya Diane. *The Philippine Federation Of Free Farmers. A Case Study in Mass Agrarian Organizations*. Ithaca: Data Paper 35, Southeast Asia Program, Cornell University, 1959. Formed in 1953, supported by Magsaysay, aimed at creating a non-revolutionary agrarian reform movement, the Federation's disheartening results are considered here.

1993

Pomeroy, W. J. *The Forest: A Personal Record of the Huk Guerrilla Struggle in the Philippine*. New York: International Publishers, 1963. A fiercely personal account by a communist, naïve and oversimplified, of the Huk rebellion.

1994

Valeriano, Napoleon D. and Bohannan, Charles T. *Counter-Guerrilla Operations: the Philippine Experience*. New York: Praeger, 1962. Endeavors to use as basic for all guerrilla work the military experiences against the Huks to which he constantly refers.

1995

De Young, John C. and Hunt, Chester L. "Communication Channels and Functional Literacy in the Philippines Barrio." *Journal of Asian Studies* 22 (1962) 67-78.

1996

Romani, John H. "The Philippine Barrio." *Far Eastern Quarterly* 15 (1956) 229-238. The primary unit in Philippine local government outlined in geographical, economic and political terms; its bleak prospects are stressed.

1997

Rivera, Generoso, and McMillan, Robert. *The Rural Philippines*. Manila: Mutual Security Agency, 1952. Government neglect of the barrios in a sociological study of Christian rural villages.

1998

Ravenholt, Albert. "The Philippines: Where Did We Fail?" *Foreign Affairs* 29 (April, 1951) 406-416. A survey of the post-war Huk revolt and the economic and social conditions that caused it, in which America has a direct share of the responsibility.

1999

Fifield, Russell H. "The Hukbalahap Today." *Far Eastern Survey* 20 (1951) 13-18.

2000

Stephens, Robert P. "The Prospect for Social Progress in the Philippines." *Pacific Affairs* 23 (1950) 139-152. Considers the possibility of social reform slight.

2001

Bernstein, David. "Lessons from Luzon." *Yale Review* 38 (1949) 509-519. An examination of the failure of the 1948 amnesty campaign and the conditions that had the Huks persisting in their armed opposition.

2002

Entenberg, Barbara. "Agrarian Reform and the Hukbalahap." *Far Eastern Survey* 15 (1946). The formation of the Huk movement and its anti-Japanese resistance, and the facts of its immediate post-war agrarian demands.

2003

Ruiz, Leopoldo T. "Farm Tenancy and Co-operation in the Philippines." *Far Eastern Quarterly* 4 (1945) 163-169. Outlines the wretched life led by a peasant under Spanish and American rule; co-operatives are seen as a faint hope for alleviation in the future.

ECONOMIC PATTERNS

As it is in other parts of Southeast Asia, the economic pattern of the Philippines before the post-Suez-Canal era was largely a self-sufficient one, with few estate exports, and little trade. The 20th century witnessed a great development of primary commodity exports, particularly to America. Indeed, the Philippines became linked economically to the U.S.A. to an extent far surpassing any other colonial-metropolitan link elsewhere; and this at a time when the political pattern of disengagement was proceeding apace.

With independence the new state made efforts in the midst of many problems to diversify its economy, to establish its own economic viability and to weaken its excessive dependence on the U. S. A. These efforts are still necessary and are still continuing.

General Works

2004

Golay, Frank. *The Philippines: Public Policy And Economic Development.* Ithaca: Cornell University Press, 1961. A survey of the Philippine economy before and after the war, analyzing fiscal and monetary policies, agriculture, foreign aid and economic planning, with critical comments on the low priority of welfare goals, and the narrow concentration of wealth. An indispensible book on Filipino economic pattern.

2005

Hartendorp, A. V. H. *History of Industry and Trade of the Philippines.* 2 vols. Manila: Philippine Education Co. 1958–1961. Vol. 1 is a general coverage of the Philippine economic and social scene after the Pacific War, Vol. 2 is devoted to the industrialization initiated or under way during the Magsaysay period of the 1950's.

2006

Golay, Frank. "Economic Consequences of the Philippine Trade Act." *Pacific Affairs* 28 (1953) 52-70. The 1946 *Act,* an unfortunate compromise, is seen as a blemish on U. S. relations with a proven ally, and a hapless excursion into economic imperialism.

2007

_____. *The Revised United States-Philippine Trade Agreement of 1955.* Ithaca: Data Paper 23, Southeast Asia Program, Cornell University, 1956. The revised Agreement eliminated all the provisions of the 1946 Bell Act which had irritated the Philippines.

2008

Carroll, John J. *The Filipino Manufacturing Entrepreneur: Agent and Product of Change.* Ithaca: Cornell University Press, 1965. A careful study of Filipino businessmen in new industrial enterprises; family background, war and foreign, particularly American, experience, and personal attributes are evaluated and summarized, as are the problems they face with government and family enterprises.

2009

_____. "Filipino Entrepreneurship in Manufacturing." *Philippine Studies* 10 (1962) 100-126. Considers the geographical and socio-economic origins of Filipinos in manufacturing, and what factors favor their success.

2010

Golay, Frank. "Entrepreneurship and Economic Development in the Philippines." *Far Eastern Survey* 29 (1960) 81-86. Private enterprise being the basic factor in Philippine economic development, much depends on the quality of its entrepreneurs; here the post-war record of the manufacturing sector is examined.

Specialized Studies

2011

Goodstein, Marvin E. *The Pace and Pattern Of Philippine Economic Growth: 1938, 1948 and 1956.* Ithaca: Data Paper 48, Southeast Asia Program, Cornell University, 1962. A meticulous construction of indices of Philippine real product for 1938, 1948 and 1956; confirms from this that post-war growth per capita real product has been great. Establishes divergences from official reports. A wealth of information on Philippine economic statistics.

2012

Jenkins, Shirley. *American Economic Policy Toward The Philippines.* Stanford: Stanford University Press, 1954. Devoted in the main to the immediate post-war period, when the Bell Act was passed in the U.S.A. The economic and political implications of this and the failure in many respects of the Philippine economy are studied in detail.

2013

Milne, R. S. "The New Administration and the New Economic Program in the Philippines." *Asian Survey* 2 (1962) 36-42. Decontrol as a new feature of a five-year program introduced in 1962.

2014

Stifel, Lawrence Davis. *The Textile Industry — A Case Study of Industrial Development In The Philippines.* Ithaca: Data Paper 49, Southeast Asia Program, Cornell University, 1963. Outlines the forced and rapid growth of the textile industry from the 1950's, with the role of the government, the central bank, entrepreneurship, management and labor all studied.

2015

Wernstedt, Frederick L. *The Role And Importance Of Philippine Inter Island Shipping And Trade.* Ithaca: Data Paper 26, Southeast Asia Program, Cornell University, 1957. Considers Manila port and other foci coastal shipping, illustrates the radius of interest of each, surveys the cargoes and laments on the post-war condition of the ships.

2016

_____ and Simkins, Paul D. "Migrations and the settlement of Mindanao." *Journal of Asian Studies* 25 (1965) 83-103. Emigration has encouraged agriculture, particularly since World War II; a study of aspects of this movement.

2017

Villaluz, Domiciano K. *Fish Farming in the Philippines.* Manila: Bookman, 1953.

2018

Herre, Albert W. "Philippine Fisheries and their Possibilities." *Far Eastern Quarterly* 4 (1945) 158-162. A nostalgic outline of where the big ones were biting in 1941 and how they could be caught.

2019

Araneta, Salvador. "Basic Problems of Philippine Economic Development." *Pacific Affairs* 21 (1948) 280-285. Colonial style economy geared only to produce primary materials, and a free trade tunnel to the U. S., were two basic problems.

2020

Golay, Frank H. "The Philippine Monetary Policy Debate." *Pacific Affairs* 29, (1956) 253-264.

2021

Cuaderno, Miguel. *Problems Of Economic Development. The Philippines — A Case Study.* Manila: Private Printing, 1960. The first head of the central bank gives a personal account of the post-war banking and monetary problems, internal and external, as well as other economic aspects of his country.

2022

Araneta, Salvador. *Economic Re-Examination Of The Philippines.* Manila: Areneta Institute of Agriculture, 1953. A collection of 1947-1953 articles and speeches on trade. U. S. - Philippine economic relations and other aspects of post-war economics.

Labor

2023

Kurihara, Kenneth K. *Labor in the Philippine Economy.* Stanford: Stanford University Press, 1945. A slim study of the history and problems of the organized labor movement in the Philippines attempting to improve labor conditions in the face of a conservative social milieu.

2024

Jacoby, Erich H. *Agrarian Unrest in Southeast Asia.* New York: Columbia University Press, 1949. The Philippines is studied on 167-222; agricultural labor in a peasant-landlord relationship, and peasant labor problems, particularly in the sugar industry, outlined.

2025

Carroll, John J. "Philippine Labor Unions." *Philippine Studies* 9 (1961) 220-254. The historical background to organized labor from 1899 onwards, factors that have limited or enhanced its freedom, together with an examination of its role in contemporary economic development.

2026

Salazar, Meliton. "Philippine Labor Unions: An Appraisal." *Pacific Affairs* 26 (1953) 146-155.

2027

Stine, Leo C. "Philippine Labor Problems and Policies." *Far Eastern Survey* 18 (1949) 162-167. An independent state inherited problems from a U. S. policy of cheap labor; initial steps to protect the worker outlined.

2028

Lasker, Bruno. "The Shadow of Unfreedom." *Far Eastern Quarterly* 4 (1945) 127-134. Slavery, peonage and bondage as debt payment survived throughout the American regime, although compulsory labor services ceased to exist; see also his *Human Bondage In Southeast Asia.* Chapel Hill: University of North Carolina, 1950.

2029

Polson, Robert A. and Pal, Agaton P. *The Status of Rural Life in the Dumaguete City Trade Area. Philippines 1952.* Ithaca: Data Paper 21, Southeast Asia Program, Cornell University, 1956.

SOCIAL AND CULTURAL PATTERNS

The contemporary social patterns of the Philippines deserve far closer study than is indicated here. Valuable work has been done on the non-urban peoples of the highlands, and the Chinese minority, but little work of the calibre of Geertz in Indonesia has been done on the major groups, and the urban people of Manila. The basic social pattern of the Philippines is one dominated by a conservative Catholic clergy, yet the attitude and role of the Church have been little explored. In other ways too the sociology of the Philippines presents yet another of the many gaps in our knowledge of Southeast Asia, despite the scholarly papers presented here.

Patterns of Specific Culture Groups

2030

Eggan, Fred. "The Sagada Igorots of Northern Luzon," in George P. Murdock (ed.) *Social Structure in Southeast Asia.* Chicago: Quadrangle Books, 1960. 24-50. The social structure and behavior patterns of mountain people who live on irrigated rice grown on hillside terraces.

2031

Frake, Charles O. "The Eastern Subanum of Mindanao," in George P. Murdock (ed.) *Social Structure in Southeast Asia.* Chicago: Quadrangle Books, 1960. 51-64. A pagan hill people, inland from Moslem Zamboanga who live a litigious and alcoholic life in small groups.

2032

Keesing, Felix M. *The Ethnohistory of Northern Luzon.* Stanford: Stanford University Press, 1962. Nine areas of the mountainous area of northern Luzon are studied, to illustrate the cultural conditions that prevailed when Spanish expeditions came in contact with the various groups, and how acculturation then occurred.

2033

Warren, Charles P. *The Batak of Palawan: A Culture in Transition.* Chicago: Research Series 3, Philippine Study Program, Department of Anthropology, University of Chicago, 1964. A six chapter report, based on 1950–51 field work, on various aspects of the life, social organization and beliefs of people living on the island of Palawan.

2034

De Raedt, Louis. *Religious Representation In Northern Luzon.* Chicago: Research Series 4, Philippine Study Program, Department of Anthropology. University of Chicago, 1964. A 100-page study published originally in the *Saint Louis Quarterly* of Baguio City, of eight ethnic groups of northern Luzon, in particular of the correlation between their socio-economic system and their religious systems.

2035

Dozier, Edward P. *Mountain Arbiters: The Changing Life of a Philippine Hill People.* Tucson: The University of Arizona Press, 1966. Detailed firsthand study of the Northern and Southern Kalinga who, under Western influence and a changing agriculture, have shifted from a headhunting society to one preoccupied with custom law.

2036

Barton, Roy Franklin. *The Mythology of the Ifugaos.* Philadelphia: American Folklore Society, 1955. A collection of 30 myths from northern Luzon, with an introduction and analysis of the qualities of Ifugao mythology.

2037

_____. *The Kalingas: their Institutions and Custom Law.* Chicago: University of Chicago Press, 1949. A socio-anthropological study of a northern Luzon group.

2038

_____. *Philippine Pagans. The Autobiographies of Three Ifugaos.* London: Routledge, 1938. Revealing accounts by three Ifugaos, with explanatory notes, commentary and introduction by the author.

2039

Keesing, Felix M. and Keesing, Marie. *Taming Philippine Head-hunters. A Study of Government and of Cultural Change in Northern Luzon.* London: Allen & Unwin, 1934. A careful study of the non-Christian people of the highlands, their beliefs and changing way of life.

2040

Kroeber, A. L. *Peoples of the Philippines.* New York: Handbook Series 8, American Museum of Natural History, 2nd and revised ed., 1943. A detailed coverage of aboriginal, pagan, and other minority groups, their conditions and cultures.

2041

Hunt, Chester L. and others. *Sociology In The Philippine Setting.* Manila: Alemars, 1954. The basic social institutions, collective behavior, community life, institutional change and social welfare in the contemporary Filipino environment.

2042

Kreiger, Herbert W. "Races and Peoples in the Philippines." *Far Eastern Quarterly* 4 (1945) 95-101. Negrito, Igorot, Malay, Indonesian and other peoples; with a language map.

2043

Gowing, P. C. *Mosque and Moro: A Study of Muslims in the Philippines.* Manila: Philippine Federation of Christian Churches, 1964. A slim account of the social patterns, culture and history of the Sulu Archipelago; useful notes and bibliography.

2044

Aree, Wilfredo F. "Social Organization of the Muslim Peoples of Sulu." *Philippine Studies* 11 (1963) 242-266. Social patterns of the southern islanders.

2045

Kuder, Edward M. "The Moros in the Philippines." *Far Eastern Quarterly* 4, 2 (1945) 119-126. The location and distribution of eight main groups of Moslem Filipinos, and something of their way of life.

2046

Zabilka, Gladys. *Customs and Culture of the Philippines.* Tokyo: Charles E. Tuttle, 1963. A gentle book for the non-specialist.

2047

Hart, Donn V. *The Philippine Plaza Complex: A Focal Point in Culture Change,* New Haven: Cultural Report Series 3, Southeast Asia Studies, Yale University, 1955.

2048

_____. *The Cebuan Filipino Dwelling in Caticugan, its construction and cultural aspects.* New Haven: Cultural Report Series 7, Southeast Asia Studies, Yale University, 1959.

2049

Polson, Robert A. and Pal, Agaton P. *The Status of Rural Life in the Dumaguette City Trade Area, Philippines, 1952.* Ithaca: Data Paper 21, Southeast Asia Program, Cornell University, 1956.

Literature and Art

2050

Cordero-Fernando, Gilda (ed.). "Fiction and Poetry." *Philippine Studies* 13, 1 (1965). A selection of poetry and prose pieces by contemporary Filipinos, including seven of the best known modern short story writers.

2051

Agcaoili, T. D. (ed.). *Philippine Writing: an Anthology.* Manila: Archipelago Publishing House, 1953. A collection of modern Filipino poems and prose, with a critical introductory survey by Edith L. and E. K. Tiempo.

2052

Yabes, Leopoldo Y. *In Larger Freedom: Studies in Philippine Life, Thought and Institutions.* Manila: University of the Philippines, 1961. A collection of essays by one of the leading literary figures in the Philippines.

2053

Castaneda, Dominador. *Art in The Philippines.* Manila: University of the Philippines, 1964. A survey of art from the Spanish conquest to the present: architecture, painting, sculpture; by the professor of fine art at the University of the Philippines.

2054

Szanton, David. "Art In Sulu." *Philippine Studies* 11 (1963) 463-502. With two maps and 86 illustrations. Moslem art in the south Philippines; architecture, wood carvings, mat-making and minor arts.

Modern Chinese

2055

Liao, Shubert S. C. (ed.). *Chinese Participation in Philippine Culture and Economy.* Manila: Bookmark, 1964. A defensive series of articles by a number of writers, on Chinese in the history, economics, and politics of the Philippines, and the various possibilities posed by their presence.

2056

Blaker, James Roland. "The Chinese Newspaper in the Philippine: Towards the Definition of a Tool." *Asian Studies* (Manila) 111, 2 (1965) 243-261. An examination of 33 Chinese newspapers, separated into four types, providing an insight into Chinese thinking and changing attitudes.

2057

Amyot, Jacques. *The Chinese Community of Manila: A Study of Adaptation of Chinese Familism to the Philippine Environment.* Chicago: Philippine Study Program, Department of Anthropology, University of Chicago, 1960. A survey of Chinese in contemporary Manila: where they came from, their pattern of emigration, the ecology of the Chinese community, the problem of adaptation in Manila and the clan and social organization prevailing.

2058

Appleton, Sheldon. "Overseas Chinese and Economic Nationalization in the Philippines." *Journal of Asian Studies,* 19 (1960) 151-161. An outline of the background and current economic and political role of the immigrant Chinese.

INDEX

*Entries cited in more than one place in the text are indicated by
the use of parentheses after their initial citation in the index.*

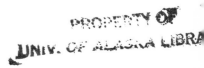